NIKE CULTURE

Core Cultural Icons

SERIES EDITOR: George Ritzer, Professor of Sociology, University of Maryland – College Park

Core Cultural Icons aims to combine theoretical and practical analysis. The series, edited by the author of *The McDonaldization of Society*, George Ritzer, focuses on key icons in contemporary consumer culture and analyzes them using the latest cultural theories. In this way, the series seeks to further our understanding of contemporary culture and to make theoretical issues more accessible to students who complain that theory is often too forbidding or daunting. Core Cultural Icons offers a route map for understanding contemporary culture and the leading cultural theories of today.

NIKE CULTURE

THE SIGN OF THE SWOOSH

ROBERT GOLDMAN
AND
STEPHEN PAPSON

SAGE Publications
London • Thousand Oaks • New Delhi

First published 1998
Reprinted 2000

SAGE Publications Ltd
6 Bonhill Street
London EC2A 4PU

SAGE Publications Inc
2455 Teller Road
Thousand Oaks, California 91320

SAGE Publications India Pvt Ltd
32 M-Block Market
Greater Kailash - I
New Delhi 110 048

British Library Cataloguing in Publication Data

A catalogue record for this book is
available from the British Library

ISBN 0-7619-6148-8
ISBN 0-7619-6149-6 (pb)

Library of Congress catalog record available

Typeset by The Bardwell Press, Oxford
Printed in Great Britain by The Cromwell Press, Trowbridge, Wiltshire

CONTENTS

PREFACE

This is a book about the aesthetic power of television images. More properly it is about the power of television advertising images presented by one company, *Nike*.* *Nike*'s ads – as cultural documents – are our primary source of data. We begin with this evidence because we regard advertising as a rich cultural form, not simply as trivia wedged in between shows. The deep analysis of ads can provide insight into the workings of contemporary culture. Television images and cultural power go together like hand and glove, and there was no hotter commercial property in the mid 1990s than *Nike*. The subject of *Nike* ads interests us because their study permits us to pose questions about relationships between an unfolding global economy and the importance of what may be seen as an economy of imagery.

Our focus is on advertising texts themselves. Although intended to illuminate much broader matters, this approach none the less risks leaving other aspects of the story in the background. Matters central to the operation of *Nike,* such as sports marketing and shoe design, remain out of sight. And, though we give considerable attention to *Nike*'s Asian labor problem, we have not provided much detail about the actual relations of production from the Asian end. Although our story of *Nike* advertising lacks an ethnography of audiences, our narrative is informed by our daily attention to how people make sense of ads. Just as significant, we have elected to tell our story without drawing attention to the personalities who make these ads, or to the organizational constraints that drive their work. In the course of our research, we have conducted some interviews with *Wieden & Kennedy* writers (*Nike*'s advertising agency) and *Nike* personnel charged with managing the advertising. We have attempted to weave what we learned from those interviews into our analysis rather than drawing attention to the drama of producing commercial art under pressure-filled conditions.

It is not so easy to write about television ads without being able to see them, hear them, or engage them directly. This project would work much better as a multimedia project, but that is not a luxury we have at present,

* *Nike* is a trademark of the Nike Corporation.

given the current state of copyright law. Our wish that this text would be accompanied by a CD-ROM of *Nike* commercials remains a fantasy. Consequently, we wrote this book with the assumption that the reader has some familiarity with *Nike* advertising. On numerous occasions we provide thick description of advertising texts. Still, it is an uneasy line that we walk between too much detail about the texts or too little.

In the 1980s, one of *Nike*'s most memorable TV commercials aimed at athletes ended with the tagline that there is no finish line. The double meaning of the tagline encompassed what the folks at *Wieden & Kennedy* believed summed up the *Nike* philosophy of sports. The line spoke to athletes: it conveyed a non-instrumental attitude about athletics that translated into a philosophy of life. As we have tried to finish this study of *Nike*'s cultural imagery, this tagline has taken on new meaning for us. Every time we have approached the completion of this book, history has continued to unfold in significant ways that altered the stories we seek to tell. *Nike* was in the news almost every week, on the front page, the sports page, and the lifestyle sections. *Nike* continued to spill out new ads, prompting us to jokingly ask them if they would please put just a brief moratorium on the ads. Of course, they did not. While this sense of perpetually running to catch up to our object of study has been frustrating, it also serves as a useful reminder. History is never done, and its complete retelling, if ever there was such a thing, is an elusive desire. Even if the *Nike* folks had acceded to our wish and stopped the ads, this would remain an incomplete and partial analysis of *Nike*'s public discourse. We cannot claim to know all the meanings that *Nike* ads elicit among athletes, non-athletes, women, men, gays, straights, the elderly, children, African Americans, Euro Americans, third world workers, and so on. What we offer here is our interpretation of a phenomenon that by its very nature is constituted by a range of interpretations. Our goal remains to stimulate critical public conversations about the place of advertising and commodity culture in our social cosmos, because in the world of cultural studies as well as in ideologies of sport, there is no finish line …

Just after we completed writing this book, *Nike* even replaced its "Just do it" tagline, a saying etched into global consciousness, with the new tag of "I can." While *Nike* changed its slogan, the underlying themes of empowerment and transcendence remain the same. *Nike* justified the surprising announcement as extending the spirit of its basic philosophy with a more enabling dimension. It should be added, however, that *Nike*'s revenue peaked in 1997 and has been followed by a pronounced growth slow-down, and with a flattening of revenues came a tumble in the stock price. One response was to change slogans. There may have been multiple motivations behind this change, but we believe that each can be explained by a theory of advertising that sees it as a tool for engineering ties between commodities and images. Jettisoning what was arguably one of the preeminent taglines in advertising history tells us possibly two things. First, it testifies to the extraordinary reliance of corporations like *Nike* on the power of advertising to revitalize the currency of its commodities. We are more convinced than ever that this is an industry dependent on sign values. Second, it is a reminder that in an economy of signs, slogans and image styles are ephemeral and unstable. The apparent solidity of *Nike*'s powerful slogan "Just do it" evaporated in a heartbeat subject to the inexorable calculus of Capital.

ACKNOWLEDGMENTS

We are appreciative of the students and former students who performed library research and who have read drafts of various chapters and given valuable feedback. Thanks to Heather Thompson, Lynn Kaplan, Jen Hambleton, Kerry Schniewind, Dawn Stanley, Anna Ryan, and Myka Hunter. Thanks also to Steve Gardiner, Alicia Rebensdorf, and Jessica Kreutter, as well as ex-ad avengers Arjan Schütte and Anne Wehr for their lively interaction around the matters discussed in this book. Thanks to Gary Gereffi for his suggestions on earlier drafts of the commodity chain map. We also gratefully thank those professionals at *Nike* and *Wieden & Kennedy* who gave generously of their time and patience to answer our questions. Finally thanks to family, friends, and colleagues for their good humor, patience, and support.

1.

SUDDENLY THE *SWOOSH* IS EVERYWHERE

The credo in today's arenas: no swoosh, *no swagger.*[1]

We live in a cultural economy of signs and *Nike*'s *swoosh* is currently the most recognizable brand icon in that economy.* *Nike*'s *swoosh* is a commercial symbol that has come to stand for athletic excellence, a spirit of determination, hip authenticity, and playful self-awareness. While the logo carries the weight of currency, *Nike*'s "Just do it" slogan has become part of the language of everyday life. Indeed, the *Nike swoosh* is so firmly lodged in the public consciousness that *Nike* no longer necessarily includes its name in its ads or on billboards. The shoe vanished from *Nike* TV ads some time ago. Then in the mid 1990s the *Nike* name has also quietly disappeared, leaving only the *swoosh* logo to mark the ads. *Nike* signs its ads with only its icon, so confident are they that the *swoosh* can be interpreted minus any accompanying text. *Nike*'s 1997 annual report makes just this point: the "company has come to be known by a symbol — the *swoosh*."

The *swoosh* achieved visual omnipresence. And yet this, precisely, has been *Nike*'s achilles heel. The visual embedding of the *swoosh* onto all environments – the clothing products we use, the social spaces we occupy and the media we watch – gave rise to *overswooshification* (when every surface has a *swoosh* across it like the Air Max running shoes with seven *swoosh* exposures on each shoe). Overexposure, for *Nike*, *overswooshification*, presents the peril of sign inflation – the more common the *swoosh* becomes the less value it has. *Nike* sought to combat this in December 1997 by moving away from its *swoosh* signature to signing its commercials as *Nike*, in a small, tight cursive font.

Nike and its advertising agency, *Wieden & Kennedy*, currently stand out as leaders in what may be described as a cultural economy of images. The *Nike swoosh* sign has rapidly gained an identification level that rivals the *Coca-Cola* icon, while its brand value is currently unparalleled. The preeminence of the *Nike* logo has translated into record corporate earnings fiscal

The swoosh *tattooed on this athelete's chest expresses identification with* Nike's *philosophy to "just do it" by reminding him to stay committed to working out.*

---

* *Nike* and the *swoosh* are trademarks of the Nike Corporation.

This cartoon by Lalo appeared in
La Jornado, *a Mexico City news-*
paper. Reproduced by permission
of Lalo Alcaraz.

quarter after fiscal quarter, making *Nike* a blue chip stock. Instantly recognized throughout the world, the *Nike swoosh* sometimes seems to be everywhere – on shirts and caps and pants. The icon is no longer confined to shoes
as sponsorship deals have plastered the *swoosh* across jerseys and sporting
arenas of all manner, from basketball to football to volleyball to track to soccer to tennis to hockey. *Nike*'s growth strategy is based on penetrating new
markets in apparel while making acquisitions in sporting goods. The value
of the *swoosh* now runs so deep that visitors to remote, rural, and impoverished regions of the Third World report finding peasants sewing crude *swoosh*
imitations on to shirts and caps, not for the world market but for local consumption. Even in the hinterlands of places like Jamaica and Guatemala,
the *swoosh* symbol carries recognition and status. As the *Nike* symbol has
grown ascendant in the marketplace of images, *Nike* has become the sign
some people love to love and the sign others love to hate.

  It is now a commonplace to observe that *Nike* advertising is no longer
about selling shoes but about keeping the *swoosh* highly visible and highly
valued. This does not surprise us because we view advertising as a cultural
space in which competitors try to maximize the value of their visual logo
in an always-fluctuating economy of signs. We view advertising as a vehicle
for articulating a brand's sign value. This means that an ad campaign gives
visibility and meaning to a brand image, and that it **joins together** meanings of the product with meanings evoked by the imagery. Virtually every ad
these days is an investment in this kind of brand identity. In *Nike*'s case this
involved joining images of Michael Jordan with the meaning of *Nike* shoes –
Michael Jordan joined to *Nike* shoes lends value to the meaning of the *swoosh*.
Since he provided the initial source of value in this exchange, it is no surprise that Michael Jordan himself has long since been transformed into a
global iconic presence in the media, so much so that in 1996 *Nike* introduced
a "Brand Jordan" line of shoes and apparel.

  Consumer ads usually invite viewers into fantasies of individualism,
although the promise of individualism is likely premised on conformity of
consumption preferences. Since the 1960s advertising has grown reliant on
formulas for branding goods with the imagery of individual identity and
well being. But as the number of consumer products has steadily increased,
so has advertising clutter. Ads became predictable and boring, and what is
worse, too many of them looked the same. Hence, though every advertiser
seeks to differentiate their product name and symbol from competitors,
when they use the same formulas and clichés everyone else uses, they thwart
their own purpose. Every once in a while, someone will break away from
the pack, but competitors usually respond by imitating the innovative look
or style until it is no longer distinctive. By the early 1980s, widespread consumer discontent with the recipes of advertising had developed. By the late
1980s, a few leading edge advertising agencies recognized that media-literate baby boomers and post-baby boomers had grown alienated from slick

ads built around appeals to consuming individualism and status through commodities.

Nike and its advertising agency, *Wieden & Kennedy*, have built their reputation on advertising that is both distinctive and avoids claims of packaged individualism. Their ads have garnered public admiration because they seem to speak in a voice of honesty and authenticity. Paradoxically, their aura of authenticity has been a product of their willingness to address alienated spectators about feeling alienated from media-contrived images. *Wieden & Kennedy* has cobbled together a style that sometimes ventures into the waters of political provocation; a style situated at the intersection between public and private discourses where themes of authenticity and personal morality converge with the cynical and nihilistic sensibility that colors contemporary public exchanges. Ranging from moral indictment to showers of praise, *Nike* ad campaigns have sometimes provoked intense public interest. Within the realm of popular culture, *Nike* ads constantly surprise and excite, because they are unafraid of being controversial. This willingness to take chances in its ads has translated into *Nike*'s dominance in the sign economy.

Looking at *Nike*'s advertising from the late 1980s through the mid 1990s, we find *Nike* ads come in two basic flavors. One flavor is of an irreverent, winking attitude toward everything that smacks of commodity culture. *Nike* adopts a self-reflexive posture about the formulas of consumer-goods advertising as well as a self-aware attitude about its own position as a wealthy and powerful corporation in an industry based on influencing desires and tastes. These ads speak to savvy and jaded viewers about the glossy, staged exultations of one brand or another that daily assault us. In these ads, *Nike* hails viewers wary of the continuous incursion of commodified discourses into all life spheres. In the second flavor, however, *Nike* constructs itself as the vehicle of an ethos that integrates themes of personal transcendence, achievement, and authenticity. We call this *Nike*'s motivational ethos. By mixing these two flavors of advertising, *Nike* has created an advertising discourse that is able to present itself as a legitimate public discourse. *Nike* advertising has ventured beyond the typical advertising agenda of merely building up its own sign to construct what appears to be a personal philosophy of daily life.

Nike's advertising has invested the *swoosh* with a sensibility that resists the profane and cheesy tendencies that consumers associate with commercial culture. *Nike* advertising does more than simply sell shoes as commodities, it gives voice to important cultural contradictions that define our era. In this regard, we see *Nike* advertising as representative of a newly unfolding stage of commodity culture mixed with cultural politics. This is evident where *Nike* has pursued a calculated approach to provoking public debate and controversy, something that previous rounds of consumer advertising sought to avoid at all costs. In this vein, *Nike*'s method of advertising as storytelling interests us because of the way it draws on the rhetorical legacy of middle

The two sides of Nike: (top) *the cynical side, Dennis Hopper parodying Patton's speech; and* (bottom) *the inspirational sides. Eighty-year-old Walt Stack running 17 miles a day.*

class morality to raise questions that are not immediately resolvable through recourse to commodities. We believe that *Nike*'s advertising is popular because of the way it speaks to, and embraces, the contradictions of both middle-class morality and the language of commodities.

NIKE'S GLOBAL LANDSCAPE

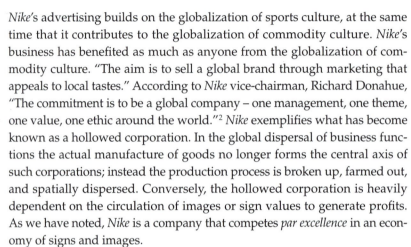

Above, a Nike *billboard graces St. Petersburg, Russia.*

Below, cheerleaders open a Nike *store in St. Petersburg. Is Nike appealing to local tastes or fashioning a global monoculture?*

Nike's advertising builds on the globalization of sports culture, at the same time that it contributes to the globalization of commodity culture. *Nike*'s business has benefited as much as anyone from the globalization of commodity culture. "The aim is to sell a global brand through marketing that appeals to local tastes." According to *Nike* vice-chairman, Richard Donahue, "The commitment is to be a global company – one management, one theme, one value, one ethic around the world."[2] *Nike* exemplifies what has become known as a hollowed corporation. In the global dispersal of business functions the actual manufacture of goods no longer forms the central axis of such corporations; instead the production process is broken up, farmed out, and spatially dispersed. Conversely, the hollowed corporation is heavily dependent on the circulation of images or sign values to generate profits. As we have noted, *Nike* is a company that competes *par excellence* in an economy of signs and images.

In 1997 *Nike* grossed over $9 billion of sales in its athletic footwear business and its related apparel and sports equipment businesses (e.g., hockey skates, swim goggles, soccer balls). In the US, *Nike*'s share of the branded athletic footwear business expanded to 43.6%, taking further market share away from then second-ranked *Reebok*, which slipped to 15.9% of market share, with *Adidas* and *Fila* emerging from the pack in third and fourth place. Few probably remember any more that just ten years earlier in 1987 *Nike* trailed *Reebok* by a score of 30.1% to 18.2% in the market share battle. Though the top four firms accounted for over 72% of the one billion pair of athletic shoes sold in 1996 in the US, *Nike* dominated the industry. It accounted for nearly 60% of shoes in stock at major retail chains including *Finish Line, Footaction*, and *Foot Locker*.[3] This dominance in the athletic footwear industry has led some retailers to see the "*swoosh* as double-edged sword" – bringing in fat profit margins but also making them overly dependent on *Nike* and reducing retailers' relative bargaining power with the shoewear giant.[4] Phil Knight, *Nike* CEO, summarized the primary reason for the expansive 40% annual growth of the *Nike* brand: "The 99% increase in sales of US athletic apparel is testament to the powerful brand equity we've created."

Analysts see *Nike* evolving from "a shoe giant to marketing behemoth whose trademark "*swoosh*" symbol now graces everything from hockey gear to swimwear."[5] A review of *Nike*'s annual reports shows that *Nike*'s revenue machine has been propelled in recent years by the expansion of its branded apparel business, by its entry into the sports equipment business, by the surging popularity of women's athletic shoes, and by the continuing growth of its international markets. As a proportion of total revenues, *Nike*'s international sales of footwear and apparel grew from approximately 27% in 1987 to more than 37% in 1997. And *Nike* expects that the fastest growth to come will be in the emerging markets of Latin America and the Asian-Pacific region. Driven by Japanese consumers' panic-buying of *Nike* shoes at wildly inflated prices, *Nike*'s Asia-Pacific shoe sales increased by 70% in 1997.[6] In 1996 *Nike* signed a celebrity endorsement deal with the Brazilian national soccer team, perennially one of the top soccer teams in the world, in an effort to build brand recognition in soccer-crazy South America.[7] Though *Nike*'s market share in the international footwear arena does not yet compare with its domestic dominance, *Nike* President Tom Clarke predicts that *Nike*'s international sales will surpass domestic sales by the close of the 1990s.[8]

Before we discuss the cultural politics of *Nike* advertising, the development of *Nike*'s brandpower, and the cultural significance of the *Nike* icon, we need to consider the significance of the *Nike swoosh* in the context of changes that have reshaped a global capitalist system of producing, distributing, and selling goods. In the reshaping of the global business system one watchword has been **flexibility** – the flexibility of production facilities, of location, of communications, and of course, jobs, as manifested in what is now known as outsourcing.[9] Producers as diverse as *Nike*, *Intel* (computer semiconductors), and *Seiko* (watches) all operate global production processes "organized through dispersal, geographical mobility, and flexible responses in labor markets, labor processes, and consumer markets."[10] Going hand in hand with outsourcing and flexible production practices is a general process of "sneakerization" which refers to the proliferation of niche, and sub-niche, markets. While *Nike* produced over 300 models and 900 styles of shoes in 24 different footwear categories in 1989,[11] by 1996 *Nike* technology had evolved into the design of approximately 1,200 shoe models, which translates into approximately 3,000 styles and colors of shoes. As *Nike*'s general manager for China observed, "In the old days we'd make one model and it would run for 9–12 months. But no more. Now we are changing models every week."[12]

Though "sneakerization" was obviously coined in reference to the shoe industry and the creation of specialty shoes, the same tendency manifests itself just as readily in automobiles, watches, fashion, and semiconductors.[13] So it is not surprising that *Intel* is investing in its logo just as *Nike* has.

> Even from the window of a jet soaring over Silicon Valley, the "*Intel* Inside" swirl logo is part of the landscape, splashed across the roof of the giant chip-maker's headquarters. The symbol is everywhere today, notably plastered to the front of most brands of personal computers.[14]

This is exactly what we would expect in an industry where proprietary products rapidly turn into commodities after their introduction, product life-cycles shrink more and more rapidly, and producers who wish to stay competitive must be prepared to specialize for niche markets. We could repeat this mantra a thousand times to stress the underlying point here: in a commodity world, you've got to have a logo to make your product stand out.

Nike is a transnational corporation that links national economies into a complex web of global production arrangements. In its 1996 Securities & Exchange Form 10-K Filing, *Nike* describes its business as follows:

> The Company's principal business activity involves the design, development and worldwide marketing of high quality footwear, apparel, and accessory products. The Company sells its products to approximately 18,000 retail accounts in the United States and through a mix of independent distributors, licensees and subsidiaries in approximately 110 countries around the world. Virtually, all of the Company's products are manufactured by independent contractors. Most footwear products are produced outside the United States, while apparel products are produced both in the United States and abroad.

Notably absent from this description, *Nike* makes no mention of producing shoes or apparel. This is because *Nike* is not a production company. Almost all production of shoes, apparel, and accessories is outsourced to contract suppliers in developing nations while the home office in Beaverton, Oregon designs, develops, and markets the branded goods. In the global athletic footwear industry, shoe design, distribution, advertising, marketing and promotion "constitute the epicenter of innovative strategies that allows enterprises to capture greater shares of wealth within a global commodity chain."[16] *Nike* coordinates and organizes a complex logistical enterprise that weaves together material and non-material inputs across national boundaries. While the most complicated of *Nike*'s shoes contain over 200 component pieces, a quick glance at a more modest shoe reveals the direction of globalized production. The *Nike* Air Max Penny basketball shoe consists of 52 material components produced in five different nations. Assembly of these components which include items such as a midsole, an outsole, a carbon fiber composite plate, along with proprietary technology components such as the Forefoot Zoom Air Unit, requires that a pair of *Nike* shoes will have been "touched by more than 120 pairs of hands during production."[17]

Nike's Annual 10-K reports document the diversified manufacturing of "virtually all of the Company's footwear" by contract suppliers operating throughout Asia. The development of the athletic footwear industry has driven the movement of production from Japan to South Korea and Taiwan, and then to lower wage regions in Indonesia, the People's Republic of China, and Vietnam. Whereas South Korea and Taiwan accounted for a combined 76% of *Nike* shoewear production in 1987, by 1997 78% of *Nike*'s shoes came

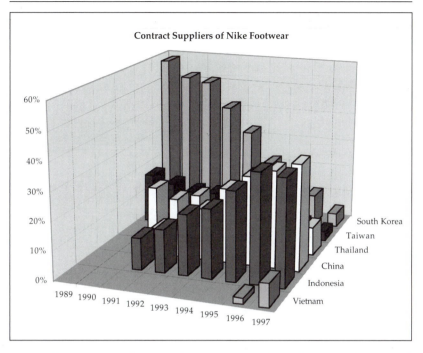

Contract Suppliers of Nike Footwear

from Indonesia and China while the share produced by South Korea and Taiwan had shrunk to 7%. *Nike*'s strategy of overseas sourcing is premised on treating its product as a "global commodity chain" which can be dissected into component processes. This permits the shoe company to seek maximum flexibility over each part of the chain. *Nike*'s strategy (and its competitors do the same thing) is "to retain control over highly profitable nodes in the athletic footwear commodity chain, while avoiding the rigidity and pressures that characterize the more competitive [manufacturing] nodes of the chain."[18] In today's athletic shoe industry, no company has been able to gain a significant advantage over their competition from the actual manufacture of the product. So why take on the headaches of building manufacturing sites and organizing and maintaining a labor force when it makes greater fiscal sense to subcontract the manufacturing process? As a *Nike* vice-president for Asia-Pacific operations was quoted in 1992: "We don't know the first thing about manufacturing. We are marketers and designers."[19] There was an additional benefit to this strategy: it allowed *Nike* to distance themselves from questions regarding the treatment of labor in this manufacturing process. When another *Nike* executive was asked about a labor disturbance in a *Nike* contract factory, he could in fact reply that he didn't know, while adding that "I don't know that I need to know."[20]

It is very difficult to compete in today's athletic footwear industry without engaging in the outsourcing of labor to relatively unskilled laborers in impoverished nations.[21] Companies in the athletic footwear industry depend on the existence of poor Asian nations where there is a ready surplus

Flexible accumulation is synonymous with the flow of capital investment across borders. This factory in Vietnam is a newer site of production of Nike *shoes. Which country will be the next source of cheap labor?*

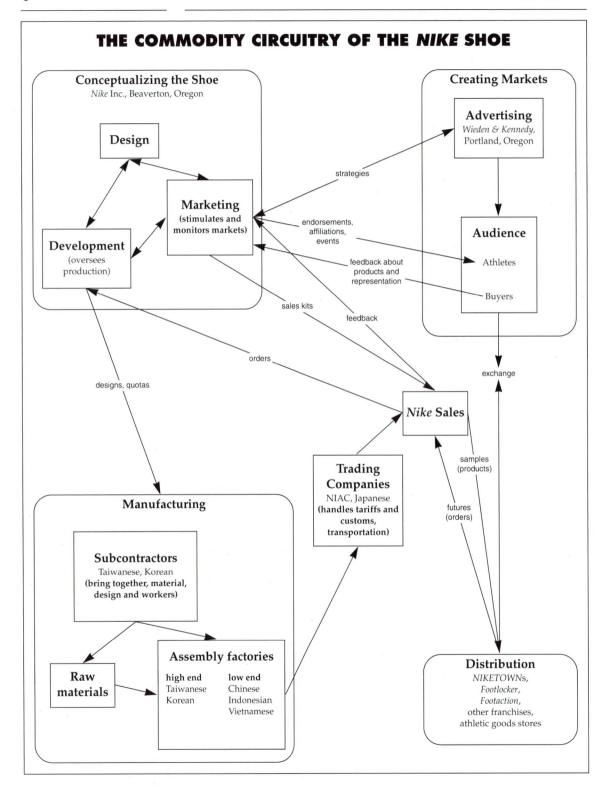

THE COMMODITY CIRCUITRY OF THE *NIKE* SHOE

Conceptualizing the Shoe
Nike Inc., Beaverton, Oregon

Design

Marketing
(stimulates and monitors markets)

Development
(oversees production)

strategies

endorsements, affiliations, events

feedback about products and representation

sales kits

feedback

orders

designs, quotas

Creating Markets

Advertising
Wieden & Kennedy, Portland, Oregon

Audience

Athletes

Buyers

exchange

Manufacturing

Subcontractors
Taiwanese, Korean
(bring together, material, design and workers)

Raw materials

Assembly factories

high end   low end
Taiwanese   Chinese
Korean   Indonesian
                      Vietnamese

Trading Companies
NIAC, Japanese
(handles tariffs and customs, transportation)

Nike Sales

samples (products)

futures (orders)

Distribution
NIKETOWNs,
Footlocker,
Footaction,
other franchises,
athletic goods stores

labor force in need of work and wages, even if those wages are below the poverty line. In fact, researchers point out that the same factories and the same subcontractors often provide shoes for *Reebok, Adidas, Puma, LA Gear, New Balance, Nike,* and others. "While there is fierce competition for market share in developed countries, subcontractors are often shared by sports shoe companies. Visit an Asian factory producing these shoes and you will see the major brands rolling side by side off the same production lines."[22]

During the Summer of 1996, *Nike* became the focus of media scrutiny because of questions about the treatment of the laborers who manufacture *Nike* shoes. Since then, *Nike* has taken considerable public heat along with a large helping of moral condemnation. We believe this dispute can be made to shed light on *Nike*'s role in the emerging global economy of signs. The photographic "discovery" of Pakistani children making *Nike* soccer balls at 6¢ an hour precipitated nothing less than a moral hailstorm, stirring up dormant feelings about justice and questions of right and wrong in a global economy.[23] The global economy refers to a world unified by market forces that have pushed into any and all fresh new areas "worth" exploiting. Since the Reagan–Bush Presidencies, "deregulation" and "free trade" policies prevailed, and capital and people (mostly people looking for work) flooded across national borders.

Opposite: *Unraveling Commodity Circuits*

This map of Nike*'s commodity chain is an analytic fiction, though a useful fiction.[24] It simplifies the relationships that go into getting a shoe to market. In the real world, the relationships are less clean, with more feedback loops. Indeed, the concept of "chain" may be slightly misleading, implying a linearity of relations, like a chain of causality. Perhaps we should call it instead, an intersection of circuits, even though the concept of "circuit" may conceal the asymmetrical dimension to these relationships. Nevertheless, this kind of display helps conceptualize the* Nike *commodity chain as consisting of interrelated circuits – financial; manufacturing; marketing; design; distribution. Please keep in mind the following caveats in viewing this map.*

The most difficult circuit to place within our map is finance and money. The movement of money is implicit in our map, but only barely visible.

An underaccentuated institutional driver in this diagram is the "futures program" that Nike *uses to control and discipline its production, distribution, and reselling partners. This is the mechanism that* Nike *uses to guide what has come to be known as just-in-time production.*

A map such as this implies a set of constant relations. In fact, the chain is more properly conceptualized as a set of pulsing power relations, with power inequalities along the chain defining its character and its outcomes.

We have distinguished the hierarchy of subcontractor plants in terms of technological sophistication and requisite skills, but not in terms of ownership. Though Taiwan has nearly disappeared from Nike*'s production statistics, the Taiwan factories have shifted toward producing higher quality shoes and more technologically advanced shoes, including the new Air Penny made out of foamposite (molded plastic).*

A Nike *criticism of our map is that it fails to place the athlete at the center. Ideologically,* Nike *really does think of the athlete this way. Looking at the* Nike *commodity chain from this perspective can, indeed, illuminate our understanding of it. At the root,* Nike *is about commodifying sport. By* Nike*'s own account it exists to serve the athlete, to provide the athlete with the tools to permit peak performance. If one believes in the immanence of the individual – in the possibility of achieving a self capable, metaphorically, of conquering the world, then one can very easily see how the need that* Nike *serves quickly turns into a Desire. And, generally, the deepest desires make the best commodities. This is the subjective root of the commodity chain.*

The globalization of corporate production has rendered production processes relatively invisible – out of sight and out of mind – to most consumers. At the same time there has been an almost daily bemoaning of the loss of moral fiber in American life. Capitalism may have prevailed in all its glory as the engine of commerce, but it has also plunged us into the scary twilight of social and cultural crisis. For all of the public browbeating about the loss of civility and the erosion of family values, politicians opportunistically try to exploit the symptoms of crisis by romantically calling for a return to the values of yesteryear, while evading the deeper questions of why those values are in crisis. The corporate news media do little better, preferring to spectacularize the symptoms of crisis and commentary, rather than risk the possibility of indicting themselves as contributing culprits. As sociologists, we perceive the source of such problems precisely in the extension of markets as ways of structuring our lives, when most relations must pass through these market forces. Over the time span of the last century, market institutions have inexorably gained ground at the expense of church-organized religions. Markets favor the forces of individualism, particularly the freedom of economic, social, and psychological movement. To achieve well in today's extra-competitive marketplace, individuals find it is to their advantage to be mobile and to pursue their own self-interests. Such practices run counter to common desires for community and a shared spiritual life. It is precisely this kind of vaguely anomic cultural politics that has opened a space for *Nike* to prosper in, as it has constructed for itself an umbrella image of an entity that stands for a moral recentring of relationships.

Hence, the discovery that *Nike* might be associated with slavery and child labor seemed particularly disturbing because it so diverged from the image that most people have of *Nike* through its advertising. We will argue in this book that *Nike* ads construct an impression that *Nike* has a sturdy and durable moral center. Indeed, *Nike* ads allow viewers to project their own need for a moral center on to the *Nike swoosh*. Strange as it may sound, we believe that many people today may find themselves drifting toward preferred advertising images to provide them with a sense of a shared moral ethic. *Nike* has inspired a particularly ardent form of loyalty based on investing some part of one's own identity in the *Nike* name and logo. Could the *Nike* we associate with the *swoosh* and its meanings of empowerment and the freedom to achieve, really be up to its ears in the sordid injustices it is accused of?

In the current media debate about *Nike* contract factories' treatment of women workers in Indonesia, Vietnam, and China, *Nike*'s defenders maintain that relative to other workers in Indonesia the *Nike* jobs are prized for the opportunities they provide.[25] Whether empirically true or not, this view neatly avoids the fundamental structural conditions that explain why shoe factories locate in this region. *Reebok, Adidas, Fila, Asics, LA Gear, Puma, Converse, Keds, K-Swiss,* and *Nike* (in other words most of the industry) seek the best deals they can find among competing contract manufacturers. The subcontractors, in turn, depend on the overall immiseration of places like Indonesia as a means of securing cheap labor and disciplining workers. Given this set of circumstances, it comes as no surprise that in the brutally competitive athletic footwear and apparel industry, companies would have an interest in pitting subcontractors against one another in their contract bids. When this occurs, strict capitalist arithmetic tells us that South Korean and Taiwanese contract suppliers will seek to pass along their costs to their workforce by squeezing out longer hours and lower wages.

Nike's human rights critics, led by *Press for Change* and *Global Exchange,* point to the exploitation of labor in the global shift to "flexible" systems of production where semi-skilled and unskilled manufacturing labor is displaced and outsourced to low-wage regions. On its face, it looks like the same old process of capitalist industrialization that immiserated English workers in order to generate capital for growth. But in the early stages of capitalist industrialization, when Marx was writing, the locus of value production was pretty much in one place. With the global commodity chain, the question of where, and how much, value is added along the many entry points to the commodity chain becomes a critical issue in figuring out who are the winners and who are the losers in these global value-construction chains. There are some who still believe that the primary source of value comes from those who work with their hands on assembly lines. We believe this is an outdated and erroneous premise. In today's athletic footwear commodity chain, the symbolic workers (e.g., advertisers, marketers, and designers) contribute the greater share of value to the product.

Reliable data on worker pay in Indonesia and China is difficult to obtain because all sides in the dispute have vested interests in presenting themselves in the best light. Let's use the Indonesian example. In March 1996, *Press for Change*, a group critical of *Nike*'s labor practices, claimed "that 45 workers shared just over $1.60 for making [a $70 pair of *Nike* Air Pegasus] shoes." Meanwhile, a *Nike* spokeswoman stated that an $80 pair of shoes contains $2.60 in labor costs. In 1996, the daily minimum wage in Indonesia was 5,200 rupiah or roughly $2.35. This contest over wages was accentuated by "the problem that the minimum wage does not provide for minimum subsistence … And beyond that, the companies don't always pay what is required by law."[26]

Despite the obvious discrepancy between the costs of labor and the retail price of the product, the preponderance of the shoe's value does not get produced in the Indonesian factories where the shoe is assembled and stitched. True, the factory is where the actual assembly of materials takes place, where a real material product that we consume is glued and sewed together. But our consumer-based society has reached

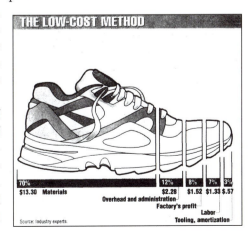

THE LOW-COST METHOD

70%
$13.30 Materials

12%
$2.28
Overhead and administration

8%
$1.52
Factory's profit

7%
$1.33
Labor

3%
$.57
Tooling, amortization

Source: industry experts.

the point where a blank shoe is meaningless. That's right, meaningless – the white shoe is a blank if it is not marked by a sign. Can the same blank shoe inspire desire anymore? No, or at least not often enough to drive market share. In fact, the market value of these products is produced by *Nike*'s design and marketing specialists.

When Indonesian, Vietnamese, and Chinese women are poorly compensated for their labor, are subject to health and safety hazards, and are physically harassed by authoritarian shopfloor managers, old measures of industrial exploitation still define a commonsense index of injustice. The Indonesian case also makes clear that global capitalism means a geographical shift of the locus of harsh treatment in the labor process. As we observed above, unequal power relations govern commodity chains. *Nike* exercises more power along this particular chain than any other player today, from Indonesia to the retail merchant at the shopping mall. Still, *Nike* remains far from able to fully discipline its partners and encounters resistance from its partners. *Nike*'s system of production in Asia is a delicate behemoth that requires careful management to keep all the pieces in balance between *Nike*, its South Korean or Taiwanese contract manufacturers, and the host nation-state that supplies a reserve army of labor. From 1996 to the present, the efforts of watchdog human rights groups to publicize questions regarding the labor relations in *Nike* affiliated factories has made it more difficult for *Nike* to contain contradictions along the chain. During the Spring of 1997 *Nike* arranged to have Andrew Young, the prominent civil rights leader and former Ambassador to the UN, tour the Asian manufacturing facilities and assess the quality of work conditions. Young's report generally gave these factories decent marks, although it called attention to two critical problems. First, the Korean and Taiwanese managers were linguistically and culturally estranged from the Vietnamese, Chinese and Indonesian workers they supervised. Second, Young found that though *Nike* had trumpeted its *Nike Code of Conduct*, few managers or workers seemed to know of it.[27] *Nike* took advantage of the Young report to announce a series of initiatives designed to remedy the situation. But *Nike*'s critics persisted, and in September 1997, *Nike* acceded to the demands of public relations, and severed ties with four factories because "the factories either were not paying the legal minimum wage or were violating other tenets of *Nike*'s *Code* [*of Conduct*]. Workers at one of the factories, for instance, were averaging 70 to 80-hour workweeks, said Dusty Kidd, a *Nike* spokesman."[28]

The industry offers a classic example of the deskilling of production. The migration of shoe assembly jobs from one Asian nation to the next is only possible if the work of making shoes is deskilled. Shoe assembly has been broken down into highly specialized gluing and stitching tasks. Seemingly contradictory forces structure the footwear industry. Though shoes are assembled by a labor-intensive manufacturing sector dependent on the availability of low wage workers to maintain competitiveness, cheap labor as such does not appear to be the determining factor in calculating profitability. Still, since *Nike*'s indirect labor costs cover approximately 500,000 workers scattered throughout Asia's contract factories, wage increases, however modest, will either impact earnings or be passed along to consumers. Despite these constraints, we believe the more significant factors influencing profits for firms like *Nike* are found in the "combinations of high-value research, design, sales, marketing, and financial services that allow the buyers and branded merchandisers to act as strategic brokers in linking overseas factories and traders with evolving product niches in their main consumer markets." As a buyer-driven commodity chain that is "design and marketing intensive," *Nike* has concentrated its strategic efforts at exercising control over the "point of consumption."[29] *Nike* innovated the strategy of futures orders in the athletic shoewear industry to gain greater control over its retail channels while also reducing expenses associated with maintaining inventories. Instead of growing revenues by investing in capital equipment related to production, *Nike*'s key investments have been in advertising and promotion. Whereas *Nike* has historically spent around 3% of its annual revenues on capital expenditures, spending on advertising and promotions consistently runs in the neighborhood of 10% of annual revenues. When we look carefully at these expenditures we see again why *Nike* is thought of as a hollowed corporation. Three per cent per year on capital expenditures is very low compared to traditional manufacturing. Further, even when we take note of *Nike*'s increase in capital spending during 1997 (up from 3% to 5%), we find that capital spending was spent **not on production**, but on distribution infrastructure (warehouse locations), computerized management information systems, administrative infrastructure (world headquarters expansion at the Beaverton campus), and display infrastructure (development of *NIKETOWN* retail locations).[30]

Nike behaves as if its advertising and marketing spending is a key investment driving future earnings growth. A comparison of the annualized growth curves of total revenue and advertising reveals a remarkable correspondence. Which direction the causal arrow is pointing we cannot say, but the correspondence does suggest the possibility that advertising (symbolic

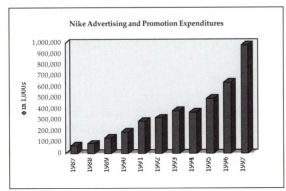

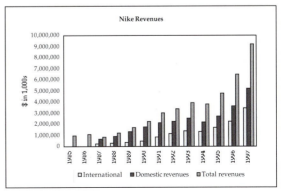

production) is among the more significant "value-added processes" along the *Nike* commodity chain. *Nike*'s critics often adopt the rhetorical strategy of juxtaposing the remarkable size of *Nike*'s annual advertising budget spending against the total of wages paid to the – say Indonesian women – workers who assemble the shoes. One such critic begins by posing the question, "why not pay double the minimum wage?" David Moberg pursues his query by drawing on 1996 data to assert that "analysts say *Nike* annually spends $650 million on marketing, nearly 10 times what it would cost the company to double the wages of all its Indonesian workers."[31] For Moberg, the size of *Nike*'s advertising budget turns into an indicator of *Nike*'s indifference to the factory workers who labor in *Nike*'s behalf in Indonesia. Comparing ad spending with wages in this way suggests misplaced moral priorities on the part of *Nike*. However, this sort of glib moral assumption fails to acknowledge the current political-economic fact that additional dollars spent on advertising and marketing boost profit margins proportionately, while wages are simply a cost of doing business. There is, indeed, a relationship between advertising and exploitation, but only if we shift the focus of moral attack from *Nike* to the contemporary capitalist world economy to examine the relationship between sign production and the global production system.

Phil Knight addresses stockholders.

In 1996, Phil Knight, the founder and CEO of *Nike*, doubled his fortune to over $5.5 billion, because *Nike*'s stock value more than doubled in price, vaulting him from 138th to 7th on *Forbes'* annual list of wealthiest persons. Some injustice, some imbalance, seems obvious here. While *Nike* revenues have grown by around 40% per year, women and children laborers from Indonesia to Vietnam to Pakistan have received bare-subsistence wages and, in some cases, have been subject to corporal punishment in the labor-intensive factories.[32] Cartoonists and columnists teed off on the flagrant inequalities. A *Christian Science Monitor* cartoon by Jeff Danziger titled "The World According to *Nike*" cast *Nike*'s relationships with American youth and third world workers in stark ironic relief. On the side of the cartoon labeled "USA," a young male slouches against a brick wall, with the caption above reading "No work" while the caption below reads "$150 shoes." By contrast, the frame to the right labeled "Indonesia" pictures a shoeless Indonesian woman who labors hunched over a sewing machine, while the caption reads, "Lots of work. No shoes."[33] This seems to confirm Karl Marx's account of the operation of Capital built on the exploitation of labor. And yet, moral indignation aside, *Nike*'s stock value has soared in direct proportion to its dominance in the field of imagery – the dominance of its signifier, the *swoosh*.

The primary source of value is now located in the cultural production and appropriation side of the coin. This means that while Asian firms "are producing the actual shoe, US-based *Nike* promotes the symbolic nature of the shoe and appropriates the greater share of value resulting from its sales."[34] *Nike*'s advertising sifts through the cultural politics of consumption and distills from it the appropriate visual and moral aesthetic to attach to its logo. Though the *Nike swoosh* represents a unified, or global, symbol in the sense that it points universally to *Nike*, the *swoosh* can also accept a multiplicity of localized and specific meanings. If we were to judge the new system of flexible accumulation by *Nike*'s operations, the manipulation of cultural meanings has become the key to value production, and not just an addendum. This claim bears repeating. In this newly emerging era of global production, advertising as a system of producing sign values has made culture a central component of the economy.

Even though *Nike* officials pride themselves in both public and private on making the "best athletic shoe technology" to advance athlete's performance, overall the athletic shoe industry tends to deliver parity products produced under similar conditions using relatively standardized production practices. Once competitors mimic or adapt *Nike*'s leading technology, and its system of futures' orders, and its methodology of outsourcing, what is left? The key to making a profit in a parity industry is finding a way to differentiate your product from every other product. In the intensely competitive athletic footwear industry, products can be differentiated by function, appearance or style, price, and logo. While rapid changes in technology and consumer preference drive competition, there is considerable evidence to support the view that product value has less to do with the material properties of the product than with its symbolic properties. The real value of the *Nike* shoe is the *swoosh* it carries on its side. The *swoosh* has become a form of social and cultural currency that draws its value from factors such as the style of shoe design and the power of celebrity endorsers. *Nike* competitiveness depends primarily on its logo or "trademark."

> *NIKE* utilizes trademarks on nearly all of its products and believes that having distinctive marks that are readily identifiable is an important factor in creating a market for its goods, in identifying the Company and in distinguishing its goods from the goods of others. The Company considers its *NIKE®* and *Swoosh®* design trademarks to be among its most valuable assets and has registered these trademarks in over 100 countries. In addition, the Company owns other trademarks which it utilizes in marketing its products. *NIKE* continues to vigorously protect its trademarks against infringement.[35]

The *swoosh* is Nike's core value, and it becomes more crucial as product differentiation increases. The power of the *swoosh* unites a product line governed by the rule of sneakerization. And as *Nike* expands from athletic footware to sporting goods equipment and apparel and sunglasses, the economic importance of the *swoosh* logo increases. In recent years, *Nike* has leveraged the power of its logo by making it the unifying centerpiece of its *NIKETOWN* stores. *Nike*'s most visible and grandiose *NIKETOWN* space opened in Manhattan in 1996. It is already, like its precursor sister sites in Portland and Chicago, a significant tourist destination. The *NIKETOWN* spaces have been

NIKETOWN, *Portland, Oregon.*
Expect to see many more.

constructed as atrium spaces to maximize the visual display of *Nike*'s image along with the display of the array of *Nike*'s 1,200 shoe models.[36] In the Portland store, suspended from above is a sculpture of *Nike*'s superstar Michael Jordan. These spaces have been designed with sports-themed pavilions or boutiques arranged around a central "town square." Each space includes its own video backdrops and sound effects. Contributing to the futuristic feel of *NIKETOWN* spaces are acrylic shoe tubes that transport the product from the stockroom to the customer. These "glitzy stores, with climbing walls and basketball courts for trying out the goods, are meant to build the brand rather than just move products," and *Nike* plans to expand the *NIKETOWN* concept to various global cities.[37]

LOGOMANIA

"Brand consciousness" of *Nike*'s "global power brand" now extends "anywhere there is the faint possibility of a growing middle class."[38] To get a sense of how people value and rank their brand preferences, survey researchers routinely ask them to make lists. One recent study by *Teenage Research Unlimited* asked 200 teenagers for their top twenty brands, regardless of product category. The results cast light on how important logos or signs are to the athletic footwear industry. Out of the top 20, the survey reveals that five are in the athletic footwear industry – *Nike*, *Reebok*, *Adidas*, *Fila* and *Converse*. Of all the brands to choose from, including *Coke*, *Nike* led the list with a whopping 38% of teens ranking it number one. *Guess* jeans came in a distant second at 17%.[39]

In 1993, *Nike* spent roughly $250 million on advertising, marketing and promoting the *Nike* brand; by 1997 that total had grown to $978 million. The visibility and power of *Nike*'s *swoosh* sign has been largely a function of *Nike* being the current leader in a competitive advertising system geared to producing and maintaining the highest sign values. We call it sign value to pinpoint the primary product of consumer-goods advertising today. In this following section we will briefly discuss what we mean by sign values, noting how they are constructed and circulated, and how the competition between brands for recognition and dominance has led to what we call sign wars.[40]

The *swoosh* logo was born of business necessity. By 1971 Phil Knight's fledgling shoe distribution company, named *Blue Ribbon Sports*, had grown to the point where its product line consisted of a haphazard combination of Japanese knockoffs of German running shoes (*Adidas*) and a few shoes of *BRS*'s own design. But it had also outgrown its relationship as exclusive distributor of *Onitsuka Tiger*, its Japanese shoe supplier, and Knight engineered "a partnership with *Nissho-Iwai*, a large Japanese *sogo sosha* (trading company). *Nissho* agreed to contract independent manufacturing sources (*Nihon-Koyo* and *Nippon Rubber*) for the *BRS* line of shoes."[41] In 1971, Knight decided

he needed a logo and a change of name as he moved to market his own brand of shoes. Knight asked a Portland State University arts student named Carolyn Davidson to design a "stripe, or logo, for the side of the shoe. Because *Adidas* used stripes as its logo, all athletic shoe logos, no matter what shape, were called stripes."[42] Davidson's fee for the task was $35. Knight asked her to try to make it suggest 'movement' and 'speed,' make it visible from a distance, while also functionally contributing to the shoe support system. At the time, the 'stripes' on other athletic shoes served a structural or functional purpose: the "distinctive three stripes" on *Adidas* shoes held the upper and lower soles together while the *Puma* stripe supported the ball of the foot. By contrast, despite Knight's desire for something comparable to the *Adidas* stripe, the *swoosh* was from the outset strictly a symbolic and aesthetic accouterment.[43] Knight and his associates did not particularly like the design, but half-heartedly accepted it because they had nothing better. Knight reportedly said "I don't love it. But I think it will grow on me."[44] *Nike* insiders would come to call it the *swoosh*, so the story goes, after a customer placed an order for the shoe with the "swooshie fiber" on the side. Shortly thereafter, the story of the *Nike* name change bears a striking similarity to the birth of the *swoosh* logo. Knight had been toying with the name *Dimension Six*, but nobody else liked that name. The pressure for a new name was spurred by a printer's deadline to put a name – any name – on the side of the shoe boxes that were being made. When an employee named Jeff Johnson came up with the name *Nike*, after the winged Greek goddess of victory, it too was met with a lack of either recognition or enthusiasm. "I guess we'll go with the *Nike* thing for now," said Knight. "I really don't like any of them [the names], but I guess that's the best of the bunch."[45]

The point here is that initially, the *swoosh* logo was an empty vessel – a visual marker that lacked any intrinsic meaning. At first, people described it as a fat checkmark. The *swoosh* has acquired meaning and value through repeated association with other culturally meaningful symbols. By placing the *swoosh* in the same frame with Michael Jordan, *Nike* was able to draw upon the value and meaning of Michael Jordan as a star basketball player. The meaning of "Air" Jordan was transferred to the meaning of "Air" *Nike*.

Nike is in their fifth version of its logo. First came the swoosh *with* Nike *written in script across it. Second was the* swoosh *with* NIKE *in caps above it. This was replaced by a box around the second version and, currently, there is the* swoosh *alone. According to Liz Dolan, the* swoosh-*only corporate logo was unplanned. The* swoosh-*only design had been put on a hat for Jim Courier, the tennis player, during the 1992 Wimbledon tournament. But Courier had been eliminated early in the tournament, and gave his hat to fellow* Nike *athlete, Andre Agassi, who proceeded to an upset win of the championship. Afterward,* Nike *was besieged with calls asking where can I get that hat? Suddenly, the* Nike *decision-makers realized that, thanks to the power of television, viewers could readily recognize the significance of just the* swoosh. *Subsequently* Nike *signed all of its correspondence simply* swoosh. *The fifth incarnation was prompted by concern that the* swoosh *had become overused,* Nike *now signs its ads with* 'Nike' *printed in a cursive font.*

Only through a process of abstracting and "emptying out" the meanings of other cultural images did the *Nike* logo become invested with the value and meaning it possesses today. Today, that fat checkmark is not only instantly identifiable, it has also come to inspire devotion. Today, the *Nike swoosh* is so 'rich' in meaning that it is now capable of extending value to other objects and persons. In 1991 *Nike* was inducted into the *American Marketing Association's* Hall of Fame because its ads "have had a dramatic impact on our lifestyle, becoming enshrined as American icons."[46]

These days, concerns about selecting the right logo may seem ho-hum since every company that wants to compete in this arena must be able to compete at the level of logo recognition. Companies like *Nike*, *Reebok*, *Adidas*, *Fila*, *Starter*, and *Champion* all acknowledge that branded sales are essential to their growth, and each competes to try to convince viewers that they want to wear the company name or symbol. David Chandler, vice-president of *Reebok International's* apparel marketing, observes that consumers are "looking for brands that mesh with their personalities."[47] So the name of the game is to invest one's logo with recognizability and culturally desirability. To a certain extent, consumers (wearers) become advertisements themselves for the brand logo they have chosen to display.

Think about it. Everyone knows the name of *Nike*'s icon is the *swoosh*, but do you know what *Reebok* calls its icon? They call it the *vector*. Though historically *Nike*'s chief competitor, *Reebok*'s advertising has not established a similarly viable or coherent sign or logo. However, it is instructive to note that *Reebok* advertising circa 1995 shifted to emulate the *Nike* concentration on the logo. Indeed, *Reebok* advertising has become notable for its attention to what might be called sign-work. *Reebok*'s commercials from the 1996 Summer Olympics each ended by turning the *vector* on its side so that it could double as the symbol for the Olympic torch. We could not invent a better example of a company trying to leverage the value of one meaning system (the Olympics) to add value to its brand symbol.

As the stakes of logo identification and sign value escalate so too does the amount of energy that goes into both promoting these signs and protecting the value of those logos. There is certainly nothing in the following headline that would make us blink twice: "Athletic wear companies are pumping billions into the world's sports tank, fueling a proliferation of logos in places such as high school gyms and Olympic victory stands; draped in logos and letters."[48] And yet it speaks to a fundamental penetration of more and more social spaces by the discourse of signs and logos. At the same time that companies are investing to cover our consciousness in logos that seem genuine, we have also begun to hear a new phrase bandied about – the logo police. They were at the 1996 Summer Olympics to make sure everyone followed the logo rules, and "logo cops prowl the sidelines in the *NFL*, protecting a $3 billion licensing business by making sure everyone is wearing the right cap. A player caught wearing the wrong logo faces a $5,000 fine,

The vector.

Olympic sponsorship transformed into sign value: vector *plus Olympic torch.*

$100,000 if he does it in the Super Bowl."[49] We've heard anecdotal stories of *Nike* going to great lengths to protect the value of its logo, such as squads of enforcers who tour Asian factories to guard against counterfeiters.

THE GREAT AMERICAN PHILOSOPHY: "JUST DO IT"

> It's the only company that has successfully managed to sell a way of life with its products.[50]

We believe that *Nike*'s overall image – its commodity sign – is less about a particular commodity than the corporation itself. *Nike* has constructed itself as an icon that embraces a larger image system that possesses both a philosophy and a personality.

Since signs and icons do not exist in a vacuum, but in relation to one another, it is important to contrast *Nike*'s sign representations with those of competitors such as *Reebok* and *Converse* and *Fila* and *Asics* and *Adidas* and *British Knights* and *L.A. Gear* and *New Balance*. Perhaps *Nike*'s greatest advertising accomplishment has been its ability to attach the aura of a philosophy to its name via its sign and slogan. One aspect of the *Nike* philosophy emerges from how its ads communicate a philosophic identity embedded in the codes of its photographic style and tone. Yet, no serious deconstruction skills are required to recognize *Nike*'s basic philosophy in its most frequently stated maxim: "Just do it." *Nike* says its slogan "is cemented in consumers' minds as a rallying cry to get off the couch and play sports." More than just a slogan, "Just do it" receives almost daily mass media interpretation and affirmation. For example, the July 13, 1995 *USA Today* carried what seemed to be a press release: "Sponsor finds epitome of do it attitude." As *Nike* entered yet another sport, IndyCar racing, it sponsored race car driver Scott Pruett, in the Molson Indy in Toronto. Pruett, the story tells us, "was chosen for the 'Just do it' attitude he showed in recovering from a 1990 crash that left him with a broken back, knees and ankles. Ten months later, he won an International Race of Champions event at Daytona Beach, Florida." Pruett is quoted that "the values instilled in me when I was young – determination and perseverance – were the strengths I relied on during my recovery and return." A corresponding *Nike* campaign will "showcase people who have triumphed against disabilities through athletics."[51]

Why does "Just do it" resonate with so many people? It speaks to the restraint and inhibition in everyday life that keep people from the experience of transcendence. *Nike* provides a language of self-empowerment – no matter who you are, no matter what your physical, economic or social limitations. Transcendence is not just possible, it is waiting to be called forth. Take control of your life and don't submit to the mundane forces that can

so easily weigh us down in daily life. No more rationalizations and justifications, it's time to act. The phrase is wonderfully ambiguous. It hails all of us about any action that we have avoided, put off, or rationalized. The *Nike* philosophy challenges us to confront, and hopefully, to overcome barriers. Specific images encapsulate and honor this, such as the culminating scene in a spirited *Nike* ad called "A Time of Hope" in which a wheel chair marathoner exultantly rips opens his shirt as he crosses the finish line to reveal the superman insignia tattooed on his chest.[52]

Such moral lessons are hardly new to our culture: grit, determination and effort are frequently cast as enabling us to conquer all obstacles in our way. Nothing touches the heart of traditional American ideologies of individual achievement more than sports conceptualized as a level playing field for competition, because when the playing field is level, the individual may prevail. Contemporary advertising is replete with what we call motivation ads. Frequently these motivational stories rely on athletic metaphors. *Texaco* draws on the equivalence between the performance of Olympic athletes and the performance of its gasoline. *Champion's* solemn inspirational lyrics state that "it takes a little more to never say never." This genre of ads proclaim if you have "what is deep inside" and are willing to go the extra mile of hard work, you can become the best. If this ideological appeal is so pervasive, why then does *Nike*'s construction of it seem to stand out above the rest? We suspect the answer lies in the domain of aesthetic style and expression: it's not just what they say, but how they say it.

NOTES AND REFERENCES

1. B.G. Brooks, "*Swoosh*, the mark of success in '90s," *Rocky Mountain News*, October 13 1995, p. 12B.
2. Cited in Bethan Brookes and Peter Madden, "The Globe-Trotting Sports Shoe," www.oneworld.org/christian_aid/global_shoe.html: *Christian Aid*, 1995.
3. With no major competitor to challenge its commanding market position, *Nike*'s relationship with some retailers grew strained. Retailers who felt overly dependent on *Nike* began rooting for another shoe company to contest *Nike*'s market share. Jennifer Steinhauer, "*Nike* is in a league of its own, with no big rival, it calls the shots in athletic shoes," *New York Times*, June 7 1997, p. 21: 3.
4. Leigh Gallagher, "Industry retailers see *Swoosh* as double-edged sword; *Nike Inc.'s* dominance in the athletic footwear industry," *Sporting Goods Business*, April 1996, p. 8.
5. Jeff Mangum, "Wall Street heard a *swoosh* Tuesday," *USA Today*, July 10 1996, p. 3B.
6. Michael Lev, "Nike shoe obsession stirs up trouble," *The Oregonian*, November 1 1996, p. B1.
7. Jeff Manning, "Goal! *Nike* signs on Brazil's soccer team," *The Oregonian*, December 6 1996, p. C1, C6.
8. Linda Himelstein, "The swoosh heard round the world," *Business Week*, May 12 1997, p. 76ff.
9. See Stuart Hall, "Brave new world," *Socialist Review* 21, January–March (1991), pp. 57–64.

10. David Harvey, *The Conditions of Postmodernity* (Oxford University Press, New York, 1989), p. 159.

11. Miguel Korzeniewicz, "Commodity chains and marketing strategies: *Nike* and the global athletic footwear industry," in Gary Gereffi and Miguel Korzeniewicz (eds), *Commodity Chains and Global Capitalism* (Greenwood Press, Westport, Conn., 1994), p. 249.

12. Quoted in "The post-national economy: goodbye widget, hello *Nike*. (The new *Nike* economy: world without borders; part 1)," *Far Eastern Economic Review*, 159, (August 29 1996), p. 5.

13. Steven Goldman, Roger Nagel and Kenneth Preiss, "Why Seiko has 3,000 watch styles," *The New York Times*, October 9 1994, p. F9.

14. Alan Goldstein, "*Intel* trots out new products to stimulate market for PCs," *The Oregonian*, August 18 1996, p. E11.

15. *NIKE, INC.* 1996 Annual Report on Form 10-K, p. 1. All publicly traded companies are required by law to make the 10-K public filing with the Security & Exchange Commission.

16. Korzeniewicz, "Commodity chains," p. 247.

17. "The post-national economy," p. 5; Henny Sender, "Sprinting to the forefront," *Far Eastern Economic Review*, 159 (August 1 1996), p. 50.

18. Korzeniewicz, "Commodity chains," p. 252.

19. In Mark Clifford, "*Nike* Roars: All American, made in Asia," *Far Eastern Economic Review*, November 5 1992, p. 56.

20. Cited in Richard Barnet and John Cavenaugh, *Global Dreams: Imperial Corporations and the New World Order* (Simon & Schuster, New York, 1994), p. 328.

21. The exception to the rule here is *New Balance*, although even *New Balance* has some of its shoes manufactured in Chinese factories and gets all of its component parts made in Asian facilities. *New Balance* claims that on average 75% of labor costs go to US workers. *New Balance* has been able to keep some of its production in the US by limiting the number of styles and colors of shoe models, but it has also paid a price for this in terms of higher costs and lower profitability. See Jeff Manning, "The road less traveled," *The Oregonian*, December 1 1996, p. D6.

22. Brookes and Madden, "The globe trotting sports shoe;" Anita Chan, "Boot camp at the shoe factory: where Taiwanese bosses drill Chinese workers to make sneakers for American joggers," *Washington Post*, November 3 1996, p. C1.

23. Sidney Schanberg, "Six cents an hour," *Life* (June 1996), pp. 38–42, 45–8.

24. Donaghu and Barff and also Dicken do detailed mappings of the subcontracting network. Gereffi and Korzeniewicz offer some sense of the raw materials supply network as well as the production, export and marketing network. See Michael T. Donaghu and Richard Barff, "Nike just did it: international subcontracting and flexibility in athletic footwear production." *Regional Studies*, 24 (December 1990), pp. 537–52; Peter Dicken, *Global Shift*, 2nd edn (Guilford, New York, 1992); Gary Gereffi and Miguel Korzeniewicz, "Commodity chains and footwear exports in the semi-periphery," in William M. Martin (ed.), *Semi-Peripheral States in the World Economy* (Greenwood Press, Westport, CT, 1990), pp. 45–69.

25. Researchers at the global emerging markets fund of Robert Fleming uncovered what they call "*Nike* Indicator." "Analysis of *Nike*'s production pattern found that every country in which the company had produced sneakers had seen high, long-term economic growth." The report observes that *Nike* management selects its country sites not only because of low labor costs, but also uses criteria that assess political stability, quality of labor, infrastructure, government policy, customs duties, and quotas. Researchers claimed that when *Nike* departed from a country after having produced shoes there, that "Wage rates go up because workers have learned skills (like going on

strike). *Nike*'s departure indicates that the country is at a new stage of development."
See Andrew Gill, "Buying emerging markets? Use the sneaker indicator," *Reuters*,
1997. The migration of the Taiwanese and the South Koreans up the food chain of
footwear production does in fact lend credence to the argument that *Nike*'s presence in
an Asian locality leads to subsequent economic development in the region. The argument is that *Nike* provides the kind of light manufacturing capacity that paves the
way for heavy industry. This can be seen in the formation of Korean and Taiwanese
capital, but look at the form this model of development actually takes – authoritarian relations, the use of police and military forces to enforce labor peace. The corollary
of this argument that shoe assembly offers a steppingstone to development is that
Korean and Taiwanese capital now aggressively seeks to expand at the expense of
civil liberties and human rights.

26. An Asian diplomat quoted in Edward Gargan, "An Indonesian asset is also a liability,"
The New York Times, March 16 1996, p. 18.

27. *Andrew Young Report*, June 24 1997, http://Swoosh/intercom/anthony/findings.htm.
"*Nike* responds to Ambassador Young's Report on the *Nike Code of Conduct*," June 24
1997, http://Swoosh/intercom/anthony/response.htm.

28. Jeff Manning, "*Nike* cuts 4 factories from team," *The Oregonian*, December 1 1997, p. A1.

29. Gary Gereffi, "The organization of buyer-driven global commodity chains: how US
retailers shape overseas production networks," in Gary Gereffi and Miguel
Korzeniewicz (eds), *Commodity Chains and Global Capitalism* (Greenwood Press,
Westport, CT, 1994), pp. 98, 104.

30. See *Nike*, Inc. 1997 Annual Report, p. 38.

31. David Moberg, "Just doing it: inside *Nike*'s new-age sweatshop," *LA Weekly*, June 19
1997.

32. The most widely reported incident of abuse came from Vietnam where a female
Korean foreman beat fifteen workgroup ("team") leaders with a shoe sole to demonstrate her displeasure with their sewing (see Adam Schwarz, "Culture shock: Korean
employers irk Vietnamese workers," *Far Eastern Economic Review*, 159 (August 22
1996), p. 63). CBS News claimed the phrase "to *Nike*" has entered everyday usage in
Vietnam as a verb that means to take out one's frustrations.

33. Jeff Danziger, "The World According to *Nike*. USA – No work, $150 shoes. Indonesia –
Lots of work, no shoes," *Christian Science Monitor*, June 18 1996, p. 20.

34. Korzeniewicz, "Commodity circuits," 1994, p. 261.

35. Form 10-K for NIKE Inc. filed on 1997-08-30.

36. Ian Fisher, "*Nike* opens its glitziest retail store yet in New York," *The Oregonian*,
November 3 1996, p. D2.

37. Himelstein, "The *swoosh* heard round the world," p. 70; Marianne Wilson, "*NikeTown*
goes back to the future: dazzling effects and futuristic looks bring new creative spark,"
Chain Store Age Executive 67 (February 1991), pp. 82–3; Jennifer Pellet, "*NikeTown* takes
off," *Discount Merchandiser*, October 1991, pp 56–7; Rachel Spevack and Valerie Seckler,
"Innovations runneth over at *NikeTown* New York," *Daily News Record*, October 31
1996, p. 5.

38. Donald Katz, *Just Do It: the Nike Spirit in the Corporate World* (Random House, New
York, 1994), p. 198.

39. Laurie McDonald, "Selling high tech; marketing footwear," *Footwear News*, May 20
1996, p. 1.

40. Robert Goldman and Stephen Papson, *Sign Wars* (Guilford, New York, 1996).

41. Michael Donaghu and Richard Barff, "*Nike* just did it: international subcontracting and
flexibility in athletic footwear production," *Regional Studies*, 24 (December 1990), p. 541.

42. J.B. Strasser and Laurie Becklund, *Swoosh: The Unauthorized Story of Nike and the Men
Who Played There* (Harcourt Brace Jovanovich, New York, 1991), p. 125.

43. Korzeniewicz, "Commodity chains," p. 254. Davidson could not find a way to reconcile support and movement as Knight had instructed. "Support was static she explained, movement was the opposite." (Strasser and Becklund, *Swoosh*, p. 126). Instead, she recommended the shoe support be included in the shoe itself and the mark and the stripe be used to convey movement.

44. Strasser and Becklund, *Swoosh*, p. 126.

45. Ibid., p. 129.

46. Katz, *Just Do It*, p. 151.

47. Quoted in Brenda Lloyd, "Activewear firms banking on increased brand interest; Super Show," *Daily News Record,* February 13 1996, p. 4.

48. Bob Baum, "Athletic wear companies are pumping billions into the world's sports tank, fueling a proliferation of logos in places such as high school gyms and Olympic victory stands," *Chicago Tribune*, May 12 1996, p. 10C.

49. Ibid.

50. Joachim Schroder, purchasing director for Germany's Karstadt department stores cited in Himelstein, "The *swoosh* heard round the world," 1996, p. 76ff.

51. Beth Tuschak, "Pruett lures *Nike* on board at Toronto: sponsor finds epitome of "do it" attitude," *USA Today*, July 13 1995, p. 10C.

52. One of the first "Just do it" ads in 1988 also featured a wheelchair athlete, Craig Blanchette. Like *Levi's* and the *Bank of America*, *Nike*'s usage of a wheelchair athlete points to his/her signifying role in the cosmology of the emerging global capitalist system. The wheelchair person now signifies an inclusivity of spirit in a new stage of capitalism that ostensibly has removed all barriers of entry into markets and competitions.

2.

JUST METACOMMUNICATE IT

The way *Nike* has been able to make the *swoosh* stand out involves more than simply signing the right superstars. This chapter looks at how *Nike* developed the value of the *swoosh* by the **attitude it projects**, by the tones of voice it uses to address viewers, and by the way it appropriates and playfully reworks cultural imagery. But first, we want to briefly introduce our terminology for discussing advertising.

We view advertising as a system of **sign value production.** Stripped of its hype and glamour, advertising functions as a cultural mechanics for assembling and reinforcing the value of brandname icons. TV advertising, in particular, aims at building brandname identity, brandname differentiation, and brandname equity. We prefer the term **commodity sign** as a theoretical handle for talking about a brandname logo or icon. Advertisers try to link a product value with a cultural value to produce a sign value.[1] What would a shoe without a brand look like? What would a brand without an image be?

We could not have stacked the deck with a better example of this than *Nike* and its *swoosh*. Articles about *Nike* in the popular press almost invariably mention seeing the *Nike* logo plastered everywhere. "Other than *Coca-Cola,* I can't think of another company that has managed its brand as well as *Nike,*" said Steve Gelsi of *Brandweek Magazine.* "They have made the *swoosh*, sports and athletes inseparable."[2]

Advertisements are structured to boost the value of a product brand name (a commodity) by attaching it to images that possess social and cultural value (sign value). This can be written as a simple formula: brand name commodity + meaning of image = commodity sign. As the advertising industry has matured, advertisers have tried to devise the most efficient methodologies for assembling this currency of images and brands. Thus far, efficiency has boiled down to precise semiotic equations, into which disconnected signifiers (images) and signifieds (meanings) are fed, broken up, and then recombined to create new equations of meaning. Examples of this grimly mechanical process of cultural engineering dot the television screen

Chevrolet *truck*   +   *vital social relations in the American heartland*   =   *"The Heartbeat of America"/* Chevrolet *logo*

and magazine pages. Taking the *Chevrolet* example above, the flag and the dog are signifiers, while the vitality of the American heartland is a signified, and the *Chevrolet* logo and slogan is the cumulative Sign.

Consumer advertising works by removing meanings from context, and then recontextualizes those meanings within the framework of the ad itself. When viewers decipher ads they routinely accept the premise that signifiers and signifieds can be decontextualized, split up, and respliced arbitrarily to other signifiers and signifieds, similarly abstracted from their context. Contemporary advertising traffics endlessly in decontextualized, **free-floating** signifiers, combining and recombining them without limit.

This is the cycle of commodity signs: they are concocted, maxed out, and then disposed of to make way for the new fresh and different sign of today! And in a few years, some will be recycled and labeled as "retro." In the digital age, this process of slicing, dicing, and remixing signifiers and signifieds has not only accelerated, it has become the primary axis for commodity culture.

Taken as a whole, this circulation of signs and images in advertising has become a central feature of contemporary capitalism. But even as the circulation of images and signs became more and more pivotal to the economy in the 1980s, significant viewer resistance surfaced. Over the years, a growing proportion of television viewers grew weary, and wary, of the formulas devised by advertisers to keep the sign value assembly line rolling along. By the late 1980s, the clichéd formulas of advertising became so tiresome and tedious that viewers were clicking away with their remote controls. The body-politic of television audiences grew cynical and disbelieving. In response, leading-edge advertising agencies tried to find an aesthetic and a tone of voice that could distance themselves from the mainstream treatment of all cultural content as disposable. In so doing, a self-reinforcing loop of cynicism has been engaged.

Ironically, the semiotic equation for Guess *is all formula. Clothing + female sexuality framed in artsy black and white photography =* Guess.

Standardization of production in industry after industry has brought us into the age of parity products. From cars to sneakers, standardization has made it difficult to differentiate products. In today's consumer-goods markets parity products require signs and logos that add both difference and value to them. In the footwear industry, everything depends on having a potent, but differentiated, image. We can state bluntly that *Nike* captured a larger market share of the sneaker industry than did *Reebok* between 1987 and 1993 because they harnessed the power of Michael Jordan's image to better effect than could *Reebok* with their competing stream of imagery. We call these battles between brands **sign wars**.

As these sign wars intensified across the landscape of advertising, they have had an unintended side effect: they create cluttered image markets. And clutter undermines the very goal advertisers seek – differentiation of image. This tendency towards clutter and over-saturation drives advertisers to relentlessly scour the cultural landscape in search of fresh ways to stand out. As their sign wars become more pitched, and advertisers exhaust one category of signification after another in their obsessive hunt for profitable images, they push an increasingly rapid turnover of images. By the 1990s, this competition left no cultural stone unturned. When there is no clear way of differentiating products or even positioning strategies, all that is left is the style of signification, and this is where advertisers' competition turned. Style of signification can be varied through adjustments in the image-production process – e.g., tone-of-voice, color or black and white, wild new colors and tints, overexposure, fonts that mutate, split screens, quick cuts, no edits, airbrushing, no depth-of-field, etc. *Nike* advertising sets itself apart in this field of competition by the way it addresses viewers, by a distinctive photographic style, and by the way it appropriates and reworks moments of pop culture, positioning viewers as subjects who are media literate and capable of recognizing the commercial intent of advertising.

APPROPRIATION

Advertising works by appropriating, or drawing on, meanings from other referent systems. Any meaning system can serve as a referent for this appropriation: a song, a subculture, a celebrity, a television show, a piece of art, and so on, ad infinitum. While the obvious referent system for *Nike* is the celebrity athlete, *Nike* ads are also rich in allusions to popular culture. *Wieden & Kennedy* ad writers scour the cultural landscape looking for materials to weave into their ads. They have appropriated textual fragments ranging from the famous (Beatles) to the obscure (Buffalo Tom), from children's nursery rhymes such as "The Cow Jumped Over the Moon" and "Humpty Dumpty," to *Slam* magazine ("The In Your Face Basketball Magazine"), to musical genres of opera, punk, alternative, and gospel, to specific songs like "Search and Destroy" by Iggy Pop and the Stooges or a riff taken from Thelonius Monk. The scavenging might include quotes from Ralph Waldo Emerson and Sun-tzu, or the film persona of Dennis Hopper and Spike Lee, or the media celebrity of Denis Leary, James Carville, and Tyra Banks. And let's not forget references to classic film scenes lifted from *She's Gotta Have It*, *Beverly Hills Cop*, *Malcolm X*, and *Patton*.

The flow of meaning through ads is never finite or perfectly predictable, but always fluid and mutating. The appropriation of subcultural expressions tends to be layered – indigenous forms are interwoven with commodity forms. When this occurs, subordinate cultural meanings leak into dominant cultural meanings and vice-versa. While advertising incorporates and domesticates subordinate cultural forms, making them serve rather than resist dominant ideologies, the lower social strata may invert and contest privileged cultural codes. The complex interweavings prompted by the workings of commodity culture can be observed in a 1997 Nike *ad featuring Ruthie Bolton-Holifield, a member of the victorious 1996 US Olympic*

women's basketball team. Part of a series entitled "We are the games we play," the ad consists of Ruthie performing acappella, with her family offscreen calling out the response. From a large minister's family in small-town Mississippi, Ruthie Bolton-Holifield and her family sing together, both in church and at home. This song joins the social interplay of call and response, characteristic of African American religion with the chant form of the "jodie cadence" sung during military basic training drills. Cupping her hands around her mouth, Ruthie Bolton-Holifield calls out in song. "Mighty Ruthie!" From the other side of the room, off camera, a chorus of voices echo her, "Mighty Ruthie!"

Mighty Ruthie.
　　Mighty Ruthie.
She is infantry.
　　She is infantry.
Servin' our country.
　　Servin' our country.
I won a gold medal.
　　I won a gold medal.
We are number one.
　　We are number one.
Number one, the USA.
　　Number one, the USA.

"Mighty Ruthie" offers a glimpse into the vibrancy of grassroots culture in the US – spontaneous, genuine, and uncontrived. This is probably why Nike *placed its seal over it. But of course, the circulation of culture and the meanings of*

appropriation does not stop here. Once broadcast, this cultural production enters into a new phase. There are already reports of young girls mimicking "Mighty Ruthie," adapting the chant and its meanings to their own purposes.

　　Appropriation is the bread and butter of advertising. *Nike's* style of appropriation differs from the mainstream. *Nike* hails its viewers as hip, savvy, and media literate and so it draws on texts that signify these qualities. When *Nike* first brought out Spike Lee, he had completed his first full-length film, *She's Gotta Have It*, but was still unknown to most television viewers, and even fewer had reflected on the politics of his movies. Attaching the *Nike* name to this hot young director, *Nike* constructed itself as a company that recognizes and appreciates hipness. *Nike* hailed its viewers as the knowing few who might share an appreciation of the then-novel angle on urban culture in Spike's work. Moreover, *Nike's* appropriation tends to be symbiotic: *Nike* not only got a *swoosh* value boost for using Lee, Spike also got a boost in

Slam magazine calls attention to its use in a Penny Hardaway commercial. The copy reads:

"Did you see that?"

"See what?"

"That Nike *commercial with Penny and Little Penny. Nick Anderson is there reading SLAM."*

"Yeah, I liked it when Nick throws it down on the table."

"Thanks. What if I write the Sixth Man about seeing my magazine used as a prop in a Penny commercial?

Does that have any substance?"

"No."

"Hey, man. Think about it for a second. It's important."

"Okay...No, that has no substance."

"Really?"

"Well, let me ask you this: don't you think that kind of shameless self-promotion is, like, beneath you?"

"Well ..."

value after being joined to *Nike*.[3] Recognition of Lee as the character, Mars Blackmon, from his film also gave the viewer a sign value boost. The textual allusion thus connects the signified of urban hipness to both *Nike* and the viewer. Wearing a product signed by the *Nike swoosh* completes the circle.

Nike adopts texts in self-conscious ways, positioning viewers as active readers who can appreciate how *Nike* ads rework original texts. *Nike* (really *Wieden & Kennedy*) becomes perceived as a creator of culture, and not simply as parasite or culture-vulture advertisers that mechanically, and crassly, twist the meaning of the reference to suit their product. Lazy approaches to appropriation dot the screen. One recent instance has a domestic car maker adopting a 1960s sitcom theme song called "Green Acres" because it is now a nostalgia marker of an early exercise in intentionally bad TV. Oddly, the theme song that signals knowledge of television history and the ability to appreciate kitsch is now being used to express a lifestyle. In contrast to such blatant appropriation, *Nike* took children's nursery rhymes, such as "Humpty-Dumpty" and "The Cow Jumped Over the Moon" and playfully reconstructed the stories as animated drawings set to music.

Narrated as a black and white animated cartoon, "The Cow Jumped Over the Moon" is set to the jazzy lyrics of a song entitled "Destination Moon." The ad opens with a cow chewing grass. The moon smacks its lips and sticks out its tongue in a teasing gesture. The cow jumps at the moon, but she falls short, crashes to the ground and woozily dreams a *Nike swoosh*.

Nike's pastiche mixes a children's rhyme, animation, and jazz lyrics to form an original narrative. In the cluttered landscape of TV advertising viewers can appreciate creative appropriation.

But she thus awakes with a purpose and after donning *Nike* sneakers, the cow jumps over the moon, punches him in the jaw on the way past, and floats gracefully back to earth, leaving the moon seeing "stars" and the cow satisfied. This story is accompanied by the light and airy vocal stylings of a female singing voice reminiscent of Peggy Lee, whose lyrics suggest a flight of fancy, a romantic sexual interlude ("what a thrill you'll get riding on my jet") along with a retro feel, maybe 40s, maybe 50s.

Retro draws on a vague sense of history, but then empties it out, leaving primarily a signifier. The **pleasure** of viewing this ad comes from **interpreting** the narrative twist that *Nike* whimsically assembles. In this case, *Nike*'s sign value is boosted not because of the cultural allusions per se, but by the artful reworking of disparate cultural texts into an inventive pastiche that requires active viewer involvement. Because the ad is surprising in both style and content, it enables *Nike* to differentiate itself as a creative cultural bricoleur.

When a cultural text is appropriated it is not only recontextualized but also modified to meet the advertiser's agenda. *Nike* used Iggy Pop and the Stooges "Search and Destroy" as background for its commercial of Olympic athletes. Listening to Iggy Pop perform the song in the context of a 1970s British punk club obviously created a radically different experience with different pleasures and meanings than listening to it in your living room as the background for *Nike*'s commercial during the 1996 Summer Olympics. Though there may be a few who still hear the music as a punk anthem, this meaning is unnecessary to accepting it as merely a hard-driving background sound that gives an 'edge' to the images. By placing a part of a cultural text in a new location, new meanings and readings appear and earlier meanings disappear.

Transforming ideologies

What happens when the meaning of the original is radically modified to meet the agenda of the advertiser? This is particularly problematic when the author of the original had a political agenda. In the mid 1970s, Gil Scott-Heron recorded what would become classic pieces of 'political' music. As Nelson George observes on the Arista compact disc jacket, Gil Scott-Heron "has been cutting through the crap" as a "teller of uncomfortable truths." Two songs stand out in Gil Scott-Heron's opus: the first, "Johannesburg," addressed the condition of apartheid in South Africa in 1975; the second, called "The Revolution Will Not Be Televised," was a powerful and angry condemnation of the friendly fascism of consumerism and television as the opiate of the masses.

> *You will not be able to stay home, brother.*
> *You will not be able to plug in, turn on, and cop out.*

You will not be able to lose yourself on skag.
You will not be able to skip out for beer during commercials
because the revolution will not be televised.

Gil Scott-Heron's explicitly politicized music stood in stark opposition to the larger record industry

> where making records for a living is lying. Not big lies about politics, but little lies that suggest all that is happening on this globe is kissing and dancing. These are lies of omission that make pop music the playground of the jive and the banal.[4]

The lies of omission that Nelson George refers to could equally refer to the way advertising works. The imagery of people all over the globe "kissing and dancing" comes from advertising, and is precisely what *Nike* has positioned itself against in the majority of its advertising. And yet, a 1995 *Nike* ad reprised "The Revolution Will Not Be Televised" with modified lyrics now referring to the world of basketball, accompanying a slow-motion sequence of young basketball stars playing ball in an empty gym.

If you listened to Gil Scott-Heron in the late 1970s, you did so because you embraced his politics of opposition to capitalist America and its allies in the capitalist world-system, or you embraced his reading of the politics of mass culture. In this song he continuously juxtaposed the project of revolutionary change against the slogans of well-being drawn from commodity culture.

> *The revolution will not be right back after a message about a White*
> *tornado, White Knight, or White people. You will not have to worry*
> *about a dove in your bedroom, the tiger in your tank, or the giant in*
> *your toilet bowl...*
> *The revolution will not go better with Coke.*
> *The revolution will not fight germs that may cause bad breath.*
> *The revolution will not put you in the driver's seat.*
> *The revolution will not be televised.*

Only lingering memories of this cultural politics are aroused by the *Nike* appropriation and rendition of this song. Younger viewers, in particular, were probably less likely to make the connections to the political-economy of racism that Scott-Heron so eloquently rapped about. Still, though watered down, the song, recorded as a rap, conveys a tone of resistance against the power of that nebulous force called television. To make matters even more complex, *Nike* does appropriate the song to make a critical reflective statement about the hype of commerce applied to sports.

You will not be able to change the channel
you will not be able to catch the highlights on the evening news, enjoy it on tape delay
or adjust the contrast
because the revolution will not be televised.
The revolution will be led by Jason King, Jimmy Jackson, Eddie Jones, Joe Smith
*   and Kevin Garnett*
but it will not be followed by post-game up-close-and-personal interviews
because the revolution will not be televised.

The revolution is not fantastic.
The revolution will not give front-row seats to celebrities.
The revolution will not refrain from chest bumping.
The revolution will not begin with a laser show or a mascot or some sort of small
*   trampoline.*
The revolution will not be televised,
the revolution will not be televised.
And the revolution will not fail.
For as it fulfills the unfulfilled promise of Hank Gathers and Fred Wilson.
The revolution is about basketball
and basketball is the truth.

Ironically, the revolution to which Nike *refers* **must** *be televised for the talents of these young athletes to be transformed into* Nike *sign value.*

In contrast to those who cheapen sport by turning it into a circus spectacle, *Nike* positions itself as a lover of sport in its pure form – like you the viewer, an appreciator of the skills of a new generation of athletes. When *Nike* appropriates the tone of the original music poem, they adopt a sneering voice against the corrupting influence of television on sport and the crass commercialization engaged by the *NBA* with its spectacle of laser shows, mascots and cheesy trampoline stunts. At the same time, *Nike* positions itself **with** the Young Turks and **against** middle class codes of decorum that would restrict viscerally spontaneous displays of boasting – "the revolution will not refrain from chest-bumping."

"Winning isn't everything… cha, cha, cha"

In Jean Baudrillard's view, much of what we think we know about the contemporary world comes to us via the "simulacra" of the mass media. This "simulacra" is based on the distinction between a real world "out there" and a set of appearances governed by **codes**. In the simulacra the latter displaces the former and we gauge our notions of what is real by the codes that supposedly represent it. The term "simulation" suggests that distinctions between the original (the real) and the image (the representation) have become more and more hazy.[5] A recent set of *Nike* commercials revolves around actor-comedian Jerry Stiller's impersonation of Vince Lombardi commenting on *NFL* football in 1996. The musings by the ghost of Lombardi are actually a pretext for lavishing praise on *Nike*-signed *NFL* football players: Brett Favre, Deion Sanders, Barry Sanders, and Steve Young. In the advertising industry, the Lombardi ads are known as "entertainment" ads. The Lombardi campaign replaced *Nike*'s previous football campaign with Dennis Hopper playing an obsessive former referee drawn from a type of character that Hopper has played in films.

Lombardi signifies a traditional work ethic. When it came to winning, Lombardi was a no-nonsense coach known for his dedication to hard work, discipline, and iron will. In this series of commercials *Nike* constructs Lombardi as a traditionalist who can still recognize talent and has a deep knowledge of the game. *Nike* appropriates Lombardi as an icon of sports purism who is anti-spectacle. While "Lombardi" recognizes the greatness of the *Nike* athletes, the comedy in these ads expresses disdain for the technological apparatus of the spectacle. In each ad the ghost of Lombardi pokes fun at scoreboards with applause signs or helmets equipped with headphones.

Hey, get a load of this.
They put a radio in Steve Young's helmet.
Who do they think is playin' quarterback, Buck Rogers?
What are you going to tell a guy like Young he doesn't already know?
Hey Steve, you know that ball you're runnin' around with?
Well, toss it to Rice for Pete's sake.
Next thing, some knucklehead will want to hang an applause sign in the end zone
to let the crowd know when to cheer.

Deion dances in the end zone: "Cha, cha, cha."

The no-nonsense, all-business approach of Lombardi the authoritarian taskmaster has been dispatched in favor of a laid-back attitude towards the cartoon-style posturing of athletes like Neon-Deion Sanders: "If you ask me this Deion kid isn't showin' off, he's just havin' fun." Whoops, having fun was definitely **verboten** for Lombardi, and any player, especially a black player, who showboated and celebrated like Sanders does for the cameras, would have been off Lombardi's team in the blink of an eye.[6] Here, the ideological core of Lombardi has been hollowed out, and we are left with Lombardi's simulation. Appearance, dress, and mannerisms are copied as closely as possible, so that the look and the tone of Lombardi can now endorse what he opposed. This campaign exemplifies how appropriation cements a regime of simulation. What has been appropriated is not the biography of the man himself, but rather the media representations of him.

Like most *Nike* ads, these end with the *swoosh* as a signature. In the Lombardi ads, the signature *swoosh* takes on a pigskin texture. Stamping this *swoosh* across the scene of the simulated Lombardi commentaries reminds viewers of the **playful, tongue-in-cheek attitude** of these ads. This brings us to the subject of **metacommunication.** By the mid 1990s, most viewers in the US know the *swoosh* sign so well, that when the *swoosh* signature appears at the end it carries a lot of cultural baggage. Here, the metacommunication suggests a sensibility of playful irreverence, including irreverence towards inflated myths and legends like Lombardi. Is *Nike* pulling our chains here? Well, yes and no.

As "Lombardi" jokes about Barry Sanders' lost shoe, the pigskin swoosh *stamps the frame.*

TONE OF VOICE: METACOMMUNICATION AND SUBTEXT

It is no secret that *Nike*'s success in building up the popularity and value of its *swoosh* icon has been based on how it has presented celebrity superstars – such as Michael Jordan, Bo Jackson, Andre Agassi, Michael Johnson, Lisa Leslie, and Tiger Woods – whom it has under contract. But *Nike* has amplified the value of their image by the **attitude they project**, and the way in which it addresses viewers. The attitude it projects is bound up in the ways that *Nike* **metacommunicates** with viewers.

The concept of metacommunication refers to shared, but usually unstated, taken-for-granted assumptions about the nature of communication itself. It is communication about communication. Gregory Bateson defined metacommunication as the level of communication where "the subject of discourse is the relationship between the speakers."[7] Though these assumptions are generally unspoken, in daily life we may monitor this level of communication by tone of voice, or facial gesture, or body language. Only when we notice a split between this level and "the content level" or the report portion of a message does our attention become focused on the emotional politics of metacommunication.

In *Nike*'s ads, a recurring subtext concerns the relationship between the advertiser and the viewer. Indeed, sometimes the subject of the commercial is not the shoe at all, or what it can do, but rather a self-reflection about the world of other television ads that daily assault viewers with a mantra of consumption based on false assumptions. The most conspicuous false assumption that ads position viewers to make concerns the suggestion that products can make the viewer equivalent to the model (or spokesperson) shown in the ad. This is one of those assumptions that most viewers know to be untrue, but whose seductive powers repeatedly lure them back.

Being positioned to play out this assumption for the benefit of advertisers eventually prompts anger among a portion of viewers. *Nike* ads recognize this anger, and its correlate, resistance to listening, and have built its advertising strategies around denying such assumptions. Hence, a key relationship in *Nike* ads is between *Nike* as an advertising voice and the spectator's sense of identity. This relationship takes place primarily as metacommunication.

Separated from the context of the commercial this scratched frame is meaningless.

Nike's style of metacommunication is most evident in its ads that project "irreverence," but it is no less important in ads that convey a sense of the "inspirational." Copywriters at *Wieden & Kennedy*, routinely comment that their overarching aim is to produce commercials that treat the viewer with "respect" as an "intelligent peer." They resent, along with their audience, the insulting way most ads speak at viewers. *Nike's* style of metacommunication was revealed to us when we interviewed a *Wieden & Kennedy* copywriter about an ad called "A Time of Hope" (see Chapter 3). When asked why *Wieden & Kennedy* had used heavily scratched high-contrast film sandwiched between the primary images, he replied that it was no big deal. He merely wanted to avoid having the ad "feel like a generic *Pepsi* commercial with a seamless sensibility." The scratches signified to him, and to viewers, a "rawer, edgier" tone and a more jarring textual climate. What was to him an unremarkable moment, was to us a powerful example of metacommunication at work.

The style and personality of metacommunication in 1990s' advertising have become a key to building a highly valued brand image. Advertisers no longer differentiate themselves simply by the objects or services they sell us, or by the content of their images, but by the style or aesthetic of their pitch. They differentiate themselves by how they tell a joke, or by the photographic aesthetic they adopt, or by the tone of voice they employ.

When we encounter an advertisement or a commercial we engage in a "decoding" activity. This does not mean that we will necessarily decode what has been encoded, but rather that we recognize that the ad we have encountered requires our interpretation. So, how do we recognize an ad when we see one? How do we distinguish something as a TV commercial rather than as a news item or a sitcom or a public service announcement? Most of the time we recognize the "look" of ads almost instantly because of how they are structured and shot. Our tendency as TV viewers and magazine readers is to look for markers that provide clues to the agenda or "purpose" of the image so that we can get a handle on how to interpret it. Perhaps, we recognize a particular kind of announcer's tone; perhaps we recognize a particular kind of camera work; or a style of editing that we associate with the agenda of advertisements. There are also formal rules of structuring ads that we referred to above as formulas. Jaded viewers can usually recognize an ad quickly enough that if they have a remote control device in their hand, they can move on before being exposed to the irritating formula. As a result, advertisers in the 1990s have been compelled to search for tactics that might re-engage jaded viewers.

Once we recognize and identify that something is an ad, we then go on to decipher it. Some of this decoding is mechanical, like following the rules of a formula or a recipe. But a significant part of the decoding process goes well beyond these rules as we interpret the significance of an image.[8] The *Wieden & Kennedy* writer spoke of how scratches in the video **signified** a "rawer, edgier" tone. The language of signified and signifier is the language of semiotics, which is an analytic approach to the study of how things mean. The signified is the meaning we draw from a scene, while the signifier is the thing that "gives off" the meaning. In this case, the scratches made up a signifier, while the signified was a sense or feeling of "edginess" about the whole of the ad.

John Berger captured advertising's underlying commodity narrative as follows: "The spectator-buyer is meant … to imagine herself transformed by the product into an object of envy for others, an envy which will then justify her loving herself."[9] Consumer-goods ads typically tell stories of success, desire, happiness, and social fulfillment in the lives of people who consume the right brands. Interpreting the stories told by ads is always conditional on how they address, or hail, us – how we are positioned and how the commodity is positioned. When ads hail us, they **appellate** us, naming us and inviting us to take up a position in relation to the narrative of the ad. In this way, ads greet us as individual viewers with what seems to be our own "**alreadyness**" – our own ideological assumptions and personalities.[10]

Over the years, thousands of ads for consumer items have invited us to identify in this way with the model on screen. They do so by literally naming and inviting us into the ad with a "hey you" slogan. *Sears*, for example, has been running a TV campaign that sings, "here's looking at you …" This kind of advertising encourages viewers to imaginatively invest in a process of identifying with the image of the objectified model on screen. Another frequently used form of address leaves the "you" part of the address tacit in a command or imperative form, such as "Life is a sport. Drink it up." These lines, taken from a recent *Gatorade* campaign, can be instructively contrasted with *Nike* advertising. The *Gatorade* commercial consists of a collage of fully decontextualized scenes of human movement, assembled as a rapidly moving, rapidly cutting sequence choreographed by a vaguely African-inspired musical rhythm, all while the male voice-over hails viewers with motivational slogans such as "You gotta want it so bad, you can taste it."

Gatorade attempts to disguise a trite advertising formula with the rhythm of the African music and the slick editing movement. The ad is built around a pattern of abstracting snippets of activity from any meaningful context, for the sole purpose of using these scenes to testify to their stated slogan, "Life's a sport … drink it up." The *Gatorade* slogan draws an **equivalence** between drinking a container of *Gatorade* and this glorified imagery of the fullness of life. To reinforce this equivalence throughout the ad, *Gatorade* tinted the scenes orange with greenish objects dotting the foreground. This combination replicates the colors of the *Gatorade* packaging to visually reinforce brand identification with the colors of the *Gatorade* container. Piling redundancy on redundancy, in the closing scene, the slogan is

written out on-screen, with the orange and white *Gatorade* lightning-bolt insignia forming a punctuation mark, just in case we might have missed the equivalence already drawn.

How do *Gatorade* ads differ from *Nike* ads? Well, actually most *Nike* ads draw on roughly the same structural pattern. They abstract the meanings of images, recontextualize them and then draw a relationship of equivalence between that meaning and the meaning of the *swoosh*. Yet, the *Nike* ads are far less **transparent** in how they urge us to follow and execute these reading rules. The difference in transparency between these ads lies at the meta-communicative level. *Nike* ads do not use comparable video or photographic codes, nor do they attempt to over-orchestrate meaning – instead, *Nike* ads tend to let viewers be actively involved in making sense of the ad – making it appear as if they are the ones doing the meaning construction. Notice the difference between *Gatorade's* slogan, phrased in the imperative voice, "You gotta want it …" as opposed to the volitional *Nike* injunction "Just do it" because it is a matter of will.

Rather than fully repress its own part in the commodification process, *Nike* chooses to draw attention to its own involvement by means of parody and exaggeration. In contrast to the subdued sincerity of their black and white ads, *Nike* frequently uses entertainment-style ads to flex their irreverent attitudes. In these ads, *Nike* may rely on exaggerated and oversaturated colors, satirical humor, and expressionistic editing to play with the contradictions of the celebrity athlete – that media hype, sneaker contracts, and advertising have invaded their lives. This metacommunicative style not only addresses the ambivalence of the celebrity athlete but also sets *Nike* apart on a higher moral plane. *Nike* pokes fun at the commercialization and spectacularization of sport by making fun of its own contributions to the society of the spectacle. In a world where the excesses of commodification are visible everywhere, *Nike's* approach is to acknowledge the almighty dollar bill and joke about its tyranny.

Saturday Night Live *comedienne Jan Hooks plays the role of therapist for* Nike *athletes who can't handle being fast.* Nike's *use of humor expresses a non-commercial attitude towards its stable of athletes while it takes a satiric jab at the feel-good therapeutic ethos.*

HAILING SPORTS SUBCULTURES

Nike has become synonymous with sport culture, or more precisely, sports cultures. *Nike* organizes its marketing, design and development around sport categories. In the *Nike* organizational culture, people pride themselves on **connecting** with athletes in terms of the authenticity of specific sports and their cultures.

Even though a significant portion of *Nike's* sales go to non-athletes, *Nike* sees itself as producing products for athletes, as a company in touch with the concerns and interests of athletes and the subcultures with which they identify. Hence, in addition to featuring premiere athletes from specific sports, *Nike* ads also capture the nuances and details of the sport that connote a tone of insider authenticity. When asked about the non-athlete portion of their market, *Nike* employees invariably respond that this is gravy, but never, ever informs the way *Nike* addresses its target audiences. Indeed, watching *Nike* ads often presumes that viewers have access to a body of shared cultural capital. By addressing viewers as sports insiders, *Nike* hails them as members of a select group. The boundary drawn around the "we-ness" of the community includes *Nike* and those who get the joke, or share the concern, or recognize a player.

Originally, *Nike* produced runners' shoes before moving into basket-ball. Subsequently, as *Nike* has grown, it has looked to translate general demographic characteristics into meaningful sports categories. Moving from women's sports as a general marketing category, *Nike* now addresses women basketball players differently than women who run or who play tennis or golf. In a comparable manner, *ACG* – *Nike*'s outdoors category – becomes subdivided into hikers, mountain bikers, and climbers. By direct-ing advertising at specific sports cultures *Nike* both embraces niche mar-keting while also affirming its own ideology, that it is a product-driven corporation that responds to the specific needs of athletes. Paradoxically, while *Nike* defines itself as product-driven, its television advertising is not. Its commercials rarely demonstrate products or give product information. Rather, *Nike* ads concentrate on hailing viewers about the aesthetic and dis-cursive practices of each sport subculture. *Nike* focuses on the subcultures of sport – those already existent communities of meaning that share values, linguistic codes, rituals, jokes, heroes, concerns, commodity signs, and net-works. When *Nike*'s marketing and advertising decision-makers do their job well, *Nike* appears to "speak the voice" of these subcultures as an insider, speaking to other insiders who share a set of recognized signs. The humor, tone of voice, and issues addressed in these ads give *Nike* an authentic voice. This permits *Nike* to insert itself as a legitimate part of that sport subcul-ture. In this sense we see *Nike* advertising constructing sports as cultural practices and then inserting the product, the *swoosh* and *Nike* philosophy into those practices.

The process of hailing a collective sport subculture rather than just an individual is nowhere made as clear as in the opening lines of a 1997 cam-paign focused on the authentic core of basketball. The ad opens with an African American narrator declaring:

Nobody owns us, man.
When I say us, I mean ballplayers.
nobody owns us, you understand?
And nobody can own basketball …

If the subject already considers him/herself as part of this community, they are invited to consider this as their discourse. This approach to hailing creates both a sense of exclusivity (I am one of the elect, a self-identified ballplayer who having played the game can connect to what is being said) as well as a sense of populism (the authenticity and interests of the grassroots game aligned against the fat cats who want to control everything that is good and decent). Now, it might be argued that this ad is disingenuous insofar as *Nike* appears to be taking the side of those who oppose the commodification of basketball. So be it – that is how the hailing process is tied into questions of ideology.

In the interest of highlighting how the hailing process is tailored to fit the sport subculture in question, let us now look briefly at how *Nike* addresses the distinct market niches of hockey, soccer, and skateboarding.

Nike's hockey campaign consists of comic ads in which a manic ex-goalie harbors a grudge against *Nike NHL* stars for ending his career as a *NHL* goalie. Each ad depicts him wearing his full hockey gear as he tries to move into civilian life – staffing a psychic hot line, working at a fast-food counter, and mopping a floor as a janitor (a "custodial engineer") all the while slipping in and out of bitter diatribes as he relives his inability to stop the shots of *Nike* stars such as Sergei Fedorov. In each ad an unsuspecting consumer or passerby becomes the target of his out-of-control harangues. Each harangue is, however, punctuated, by a touch of humor aimed at the audience. Thus, after the goalie's tirade has intimidated two young boys who are backing away from the fast-food counter, he calls out after them, "Hey, I was the employee of the month." This depiction of a crazed goalie who obsessively lives and breathes hockey derives from one of the nuances of hockey culture, where goalies are often cast as borderline psychotic personalities, who have to be a little bit "off" to play a position that pits the goalie versus the world.

Poke check!
Couldn't stop him.

A flop!
Couldn't stop him.

Butterfly!
Couldn't stop him.

Kick save!
Couldn't stop him.

Nike creates a visual joke by placing a goalie in full gear in the role of a custodian. Here, he relives his failure to stop Sergei Fedorov by demonstrating saves to a businessman waiting anxiously for an elevator.

But shift to soccer and *Nike* addresses soccer athletes in an entirely different tone of voice. In its soccer ads *Nike* celebrates the dedication of the unsung underpaid athletes of the sport while needling the American mass media for not giving soccer the coverage it deserves. In one ad, rain-soaked and covered with mud and sweat, a player named Brian McBride provides the voice-over for soccer highlights strung together using hyper-real codes.

Our football has no Primetimes nor Ministers of Defense
Our football never stops, not for injuries, not for commercials.
Our football championship isn't won
by beating another city in our own country.
It is won by beating every nation on earth.

By stressing the plural possessive of "Our football" *Nike* hails soccer players as members of a pre-existing soccer community with what seems a statement of identity. It is not that other game of football with its commercial breaks, its nicknames, and frequent stoppages of play. *Nike* frames soccer players as unconcerned with either money or fame, but who play because of their dedication to their sport. By constructing soccer as a global non-commercialized sport discriminated against by the network television executives of North America, *Nike* boosts the cultural capital of soccer players. While the ads hail soccer players as willing to labor in obscurity, the ads also suggest a touch of irritation and annoyance about the lack of attention and compensation. This ambivalence has a purpose here. By recognizing soccer players for their non-commercial love of their sport, *Nike* also positions itself as recognizing and acknowledging dedication. By acknowledging the sense of unjustified exclusion from the media, *Nike* can be seen siding with the players against the "big guys." Ironically, if soccer gets increased recognition, commercial time-outs may quickly become parts of the game, so will big name stars, and increased *Nike* sales.

To address skateboarders *Nike* exploits a central issue to skateboard culture – the prohibition of skateboarding in public places. During the 1997 X-Games *Nike* aired commercials created by *Goodby, Silverstein & Partners*, a San Francisco advertising agency, that depicted golfers, runners, and tennis players being hassled for participating in their sports. In one ad a security guard harasses two adult couples playing doubles tennis. The security guard is full of his own authority, so that the emphasis is precisely on the abuse of authority. When one of the players throws his racket, the security guard yells, "Hold your horses there, McEnroe. Do you see the sign?" "Tennis prohibited" signs are plastered around the court. As one couple bolts and tries to escape by climbing the chain link fence, the guard reacts, "Hey, hey, hey, hey! Off the fence. Couple of monkeys up there. Game over. Tonight's done. Jackasses." On the screen *Nike* copy speaks for skateboarders as it poses the question, "What if we treated all athletes the way we treat skateboarders?"

Making inroads into skateboard culture will be a difficult task. Associated with punk ideology and style, skateboarders have been distrustful, and even downright hostile toward all that smacks of corporate America. *Nike*'s skateboard ads hail the youth who might be skateboarders not as an alternative lifestyle group but as athletes. *Nike* speaks to this group by speaking for it. The use of mainstream middle class sports and older athletes integrates class and age into *Nike*'s critique of both hypocrisy and

authority. Classifying skateboarding as a sport not only legitimizes skateboarding but also positions *Nike* as a corporation that sides with those who are treated unfairly. Note finally, not just what is included in the hailing process, but what has been left out. What is absent in these ads? Skateboarders. Unlike the ads in a skateboard magazine such as *Thrasher*, which address this audience with anti-establishment copy, signs, and images, the *Nike* ads have excluded the wider relations of alternative culture and its references to punk, drug use, zines, etc. These *Nike* ads hail skateboarders, and align with their interests, even while expunging the threatening (to the middle class) ideological components of this subculture.

ADVERTISING AND THE KNOWING WINK

One offbeat Miller Lite *campaign featured an advertising character named Dick, who sportively exposes the underlying semiotic formula for commercials. The key to the "advertising concept" as indicated on the screen is to start and end with the "Miller Time" and then virtually any material that comes to mind can be sandwiched in between.*

Ads adopt a "tone of voice" and an "attitude" in addressing viewers. Until the late 1980s, few advertisers drew attention to their form of address. What changed this? "The nature of a relationship must be metacommunicated, but in a power relationship an authority may attempt to falsify the metacommunication." In other words, an advertiser usually seeks to position the viewer in relationship to the brand product. In marketing jargon, positioning the viewer is as important as positioning the product. However, the exercise of power in relationships tends to elicit anger over time. Eventually, the viewing subject who has been positioned, becomes aware of it and becomes resentful.

When audiences grew resistant to being positioned by the command structure of advertisements, an avant-garde of risk-taking advertisers countered viewer disenchantment by drawing attention to the usually tacit assumptions ads position viewers to accept. These advertisers sought to disarm resentment by acknowledging that advertising usually positions viewers in a manipulative way. By bringing this relationship between advertiser and viewer to the surface of the ad, and acknowledging the agenda of advertising, these advertisers try to exempt themselves as different from the rest.

Levi's brought the "knowing wink" to prime-time television advertising in the mid 1980s when they acknowledged the bogus character of fashion advertising that implied a desirable individuality could be gained through the act of consumption. The wink was subsequently imitated by other advertisers and modified until it too reached the level of banality. Within a few years, the wink had become overtly self-conscious. The Joe *Isuzu* campaign is probably the most famous attempt to self-consciously foreground the issue of falsified messages in advertising while joking about this process. This foregrounding makes it a metalanguage that speaks to a higher level of spectator sophistication about advertising codes. It does seem ironic, however, that as spectators come to distrust the manufactured simulacrum of television advertising, advertisers try to appease this by offering ads that reflect harshly on the subject of advertising itself.

Around 1988 the reliance on self-reflexivity in ads escalated. During the early 1990s a new type of commercial emerged, layered in levels. No ads are better recognized for this amalgam than those done for *Nike* by *Wieden & Kennedy*, who unveiled another classic of metacommunication, intertextuality, and self-reflexive awareness during the 1993 Baseball All-Star game. Called "Boys in the barbershop," this ad built on references to *Nike*'s prior "Bo knows" series of ads. Set in a small town barbershop to connote a reminder of a social space where men talk sports and politics, the ad opens with the men staring at a mockup Bo commercial on the barbershop TV. This is the commercial within the commercial. The music that accompanies Bo's workout has the same repetitive beat as the "Bo knows it's got that Air Thing" music from one of *Nike*'s previous ads about Bo in Las Vegas. An old-timer mutters, "This *Nike* commercial is boring." On the screen, Bo can be seen doing squat thrusts as a second man remarks in deadpan tone, "It's just Bo in a gym." A third man declares that "I can do that." Bo's doing nothing we can't do. In turn, they continue to critique the *Nike* ad.

Man #4: *Where are the dancing girls?*
Man #3: *Where's the singing?*
Man #1: *I miss the montage style of editing.*
Man #2: *It's just Bo in a gym.*

The men's voices wander from deadpan to flattened numbness and disbelief. Their comments again refer viewers back to Bo's Chorus Line commercial with dancing girls and a Vegas showtune. They lament the absence of these elements in the current campaign. The comment, "I miss the montage style of editing," contrasts Bo's exercise and work ethic with the glitz and tricks of the television spectacle. Comparing the space of the barbershop with the space of the ad makes for a wryly delivered joke, as the men state their preference for the "entertainment" ads that enliven their otherwise dull and uneventful lives. The device of an ad within the ad offers us a glimpse at what is supposed to be the underlying *Nike* philosophy, while the jokey part of the ad itself offers meta-commentary about the difference between true sport and the spectacle.

By calling attention to its own spectacle *Nike* calls into question the authenticity of that spectacle and advertising's manipulation of excitement. The ad draws to a close as the old-timer comments that "only a *Nike* commercial in a barbershop would be more boring." The barber replies, "Even *Nike*'s not that dumb." At this, the camera scans back to the television screen and there is a pause in the music. Bo looks up from his workout as if he has been listening to their conversation. His look, an ironic glance shared directly with us, the viewing audience, suggests that "well, I dunno – *Nike* could indeed be that dumb." Bo knows. Wink, wink. It is this look which summa-

rizes what we mean by the "knowing wink." *Nike* isn't just a shoe anymore, or even a collection of superstar athletes, it's an attitude – it's an ironic awareness that Roland Barthes called "the second degree."[11]

Nike has cultivated this ironic and reflexive awareness about the role of ads in such a way that *Nike*'s profile of self-awareness has become part of *Nike*'s identity. *Nike* advertising has, since the Spike Lee and Michael Jordan ads, been able to distance *Nike* from their own commodity rhetoric – e.g., "it's gotta be the shoes." They consistently joke about their slogans, as if to say – "our primary message to you is still that the capacity to change and develop as a person must come from you. Hey we just sell good shoes with an attitude."

The ironic winking encourages reflexivity and constructs *Nike* as self-effacing company with a sense of humor. They don't take themselves too seriously. The "Bo knows" Las Vegas commercial embraced the contradiction that always lurks underneath the construction of celebrity athletes who are supposed to be authentic. In what appears to be a big-budget musical extravaganza with orchestra and costumed dancing girls, Bo plays the role of superstar singer/performer. The chorus, "Bo knows it's got the Air Thing" refers to the "Bo knows" series of ads and presents itself as a form of *Nike* self-mockery. After a few seconds of the singing, Bo yells "Stop," before blurting out, "this is ridiculous. I'm an athlete, not an actor. Let me out of this thing. I have rehab to do." Suddenly he climbs through the TV screen into a middle class family den. As he passes through, he matter-of-factly admonishes the boy not to watch too much TV, while the boy can be heard saying, "great shoes." A montage shows Bo weightlifting, swimming and bicycling. In the middle of this, the big musical production number can once again be heard faintly in the background. Bo stops his workout to object, "Hey, where's that music coming from?" The ensuing scene shows Bo scolding a large screen bearing the *Nike* logo: "You know I don't have time for this." But the final shot completes the joke, as the scene cuts to George Foreman loudly declaring, "But I do! Hit it!" And the chorus resumes their song and dance with Big George who happily participates in the spectacle and hype. Bo's role in the narrative is to critique the logic of the spectacle, insofar as it moves him away from his real identity as athlete to an inauthentic self (the entertainer). *Nike* has executed an ad "analyzing the essence of hype and the inevitable cycle of mega-celebrity: mass adulation, giant commercial deals, overexposure, death and revival as self-parody."[12] Having Bo speak directly at the *swoosh* sign shows that *Nike* can laugh at itself and participate in its own self-critique.

Nike ads almost always end with the *swoosh* overlaying or replacing the final scene. This is obviously *Nike*'s way of **signing** its ads. Since *Nike* so often runs ads without any obvious indication of selling shoes, it is important to identify which corporation brought you the image or the narrative or the joke you've just watched. Without such an identifying mark, we might wonder what the agenda of this piece was. In the case of *Nike*, where the name has disappeared, replaced by the logo, the *swoosh* sign not only signifies *Nike*, it also supplies a missing piece of the narrative, another clue about how to interpret what has already been seen. For these reasons, we consider the *swoosh* at the end a **punctuation** mark. It locates, orders, and closes the narrative, signs the ad, and hails the viewer goodbye with a wink and a nod.

EXPOSING COMMERCIALISM?

The *Nike* print and Internet campaign prior to the 1996 Atlanta Summer Olympics addressed viewers in exaggerated terms about what advertising, marketing, and promotion do to sport and sport culture. *Nike*'s multi-page, fold-out ad appeared in *Rolling Stone* and *Sports Illustrated*. The same material was delivered differently, with crude movement and sound, at *Nike*'s Olympic Internet site. The tone of the ad was both hyper-irreverent and sarcastic. The slogan, or should we say, the anti-slogan, of the *Nike* campaign was: "We don't sell dreams. WE SELL SHOES." The ad opens with Max, a "clever corporate icon created to help explain the new technology of Air Max cushioning from *Nike*," self-consciously spouting off about his function.

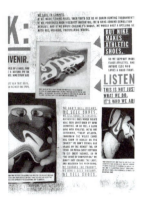

> In an effort to foster a somewhat tenuous feeling of good will between you, the target market, and my employer, the *Nike* corporation, I have been rendered as an innocuous anthropomorphic icon with protruding eyes and sneakers.

In the Internet version, the obnoxious talking icon (a parody of the Atlanta Olympic Games mascot, the Whatzit) is suddenly interrupted when a large foot squashes it, à la the cult classic movie short, "Bambi meets Godzilla." This is followed by:

Don't insult our
Intelligence.
Tell us what it is.
Tell us what it does.
And don't play
The National Anthem
While you do it.

Throughout the multi "page" ad, *Nike* snidely attacks rival marketers: "If you put an officially licensed logo on a box of cupcakes in anticipation of world class competition you are a marketer." The execution of the ad is intentionally crude and un-slick – simulating the look of an alternative zine. Here *Nike* stakes out the antithesis of *NBC's* approach to Olympic broadcast coverage. *NBC* turned every event into sappy emotional stories about overcoming personal adversity. The editing room became far more central to the story they told than the actual Olympic events themselves. Schmaltzy mood music and a gauzy feel to the video framed every story. By contrast, *Nike's* "Search and Destroy" campaign had a visceral feel, driven by both the "roughness" of the music and the imagery. While the print and the Internet campaigns focused on blatant self-conscious statements about the cultural conditions of interpreting ads, the TV campaign drove the point home minus the self-reflexivity.

Nike advertising has relied heavily on the metacommunicative dimension to address some of the fundamental cultural tensions and contradictions that come with the territory of being the biggest shoe company: How can they reconcile in the public mind the issue of corporate size vs. empowerment? The advertisers at *Wieden & Kennedy* sensed that they must buffer *Nike* from the logic of the spectacle, the logic of commercialism, and the logic of advertising, even though they are enmeshed up to their ears in these logics. Though this flavor of *Nike* ads engages us by being self-reflexive about underlying agendas, they do not actually promote much serious reflection on these subjects – instead, these narratives of irreverence aim solely at reinforcing the value of the punctuation mark: the *swoosh*.

In summary, *Nike* ads draw attention to metacommunication in order to distance *Nike* from the processes of commercializing sport and thereby legitimize its own contradictory commercial practices which contribute to the corruption of sport. Further, this approach self-consciously differentiates *Nike* from competing advertisers by conveying the impression that *Nike* occupies the higher moral ground in sports (for example, the distinction drawn between others who are characterized as "marketers" and *Nike* who is defined as an "innovator" of athletic technology). Third, this approach creates space for constructing sport as a personally empowering activity, something that is essential to future *Nike* markets and earnings. Finally, drawing attention to the underpinnings of metacommunication allows *Nike* to continue representing itself as a self-reflexive corporation with a thoughtful philosophy. Though *Nike* has become the Goliath of the industry, it still wants to appear like David.

NOTES AND REFERENCES

1. The concept of a political economy of sign value has gained weight in recent years thanks largely to the reception of Jean Baudrillard's writings. For more on the political economy of sign value in relation to advertising see Judith Williamson's *Decoding Advertisements* (Marion Boyars, London, 1978); Jean Baudrillard's *For a Critique of the Political Economy of the Sign* (Telos Press, St. Louis, 1981); Robert Goldman's *Reading Ads Socially* (Routledge, New York, 1992); and Robert Goldman and Stephen Papson's *Sign Wars* (Guilford, New York, 1996).
2. Cited in Gene Yasuda "Making Penny a Show-Biz Star," *The Orlando Sentinel*, October 29 1995, p. A1.
3. "Suddenly, he's everywhere – Spike the director, Spike the *Nike* endorser, Spike the guest editor. But the real-life alter ego of Mars Blackmon is more than the conscience of a racially divided society. His emergence as a product pitchman tells us something about marketing" ("Spike, The Phenomenon," *Adweek's Marketing Week*, July 16 1990, p. 4).
4. Nelson George, liner notes: *The Best of Gil Scott-Heron* (Arista, New York, 1984).
5. See Jean Baudrillard, *Simulacra and Simulation*, translated by Sheila Faria Glaser (University of Michigan, Ann Arbor, 1994); William Bogard, *The Simulation of Surveillance* (Cambridge University Press, Cambridge, 1996); Douglas Kellner, *Jean Baudrillard: From Marxism to Postmodernism and Beyond* (Stanford University Press, Stanford, CA, 1989).
6. See John Fiske's *Power Plays, Power Works* (Verso, London, 1993) for how the end zone dance of African American ball players represents the struggle between discipline and expressivity.
7. Gregory Bateson, *Steps to an Ecology of the Mind* (Ballantine, New York, 1972).
8. Interpretation is an open process that can produce multiple meanings. Ads may be read against the grain of the text, or readings may vary by the level of intertextual knowledge and savvy brought to the reading. *Nike* constructs ads that can be enjoyed without much background knowledge of specific advertising texts. But they can be appreciated much more if the viewer does recognize textual allusions and references to other mass media pieces both within and outside the sphere of *Nike* discourse.
9. John Berger, *Ways of Seeing* (Penguin, New York, 1972), p. 134.
10. Williamson, *Decoding Advertisements*, p. 51.
11. Roland Barthes, *Roland Barthes*, translated by Richard Howard. (Hill and Wang, New York, 1977).
12. Barbara Lippert, "*Nike* learns to use overexposed celebs," *Adweek's Marketing Week*, July 15 1991, p. 29.

3.

NIKE AND THE CONSTRUCTION OF A CELEBRITY DEMOCRACY

A tension between the desire for individual glory and the desire to be a part of an egalitarian and democratic community runs throughout American sports culture. In this chapter we examine apparently opposing poles of *Nike* commercials. While the Michael Jordan, Penny Hardaway, Deion Sanders, and Ken Griffey, Jr. ads encourage viewers to identify with heroes and athletic superstars, *Nike* ads such as "Revolution," "Instant Karma," and "A Time of Hope" conjure up a community of equals who play for the love of the game rather than for record performances or celebrity status.

Sports talk embraces both the language of individualism and the language of community. While celebrating the heroic individual who performs great feats, it also rhetorically endorses commitment to others through teamwork. Still, the elevation of individual athletes into big-name celebrities dominates sports discourse. The language of individuality finds its pinnacle in the language of heroes. *Nike* built its brand identity upon such hero worship. The power, indeed the value, of *Nike's swoosh* depends upon the athletes *Nike* signs to contracts. *Nike* transforms athletes into cultural heroes. After losing ground to the *Nike* strategy of turning star athletes into sign value, *Reebok* has countered with its own superstar signees – Shaquille O'Neal, Frank Thomas, and Allen Iverson. *Adidas* has made its move by signing future stars: Kobe Bryant and Tracy McGrady.

In a society so addicted to individualism, athletic heroism serves the market economy well. Developing heroes into sign values is, however, a risky business. Visual representations of athletes are driven by the logic of the media and its markets. Nurtured to increase sales, these representations exaggerate by being one-sided. However, heroes are also real people who don't always meet audience expectations. The expectations of image collide with news of how heroes sometimes actually act. Celebrity athletes spit in the face of umpires (Roberto Alomar), get injured (Bo Jackson), become implicated in scandals (Michael Irvin), dog it (Derrick Coleman), perform ordinarily (Harold Miner) or gamble (Michael Jordan). And, when images of

Pakistani children making *Nike* soccer balls flooded the news, *Nike* itself became vulnerable to the disparity between its self-representations and the photorealist record of its production practices.

Heroes are supposed to act from idealistic motives; the celebrity, however, is a paid endorser. Heroes do it for the love of the game and for the community they hold dear. But, in the sports era of free agents, with teams jumping to more lucrative markets, labor strikes, hold outs and arbitrations, it is difficult to convince increasingly suspicious audiences that a professional athlete is pure of heart. While the hero transcends human limitations, the hero must also act in behalf of the greater good. Where people experience commercialism as a calculated assault, *Nike* must construct representations which counter this trend, and this is no easy task when the promotion of heroes edges advertisers toward promoting self-aggrandizing individualism. When self-centered motives are ascribed to an athletic hero, the celebrity's sign value may be weakened. While keeping alive the glory and reward for individual achievement, *Nike* has also tried to construct a language which articulates our desires for fraternity and sociability.

THE AMBIVALENCE OF HERO WORSHIP

Any discussion of hero worship and *Nike* must begin with Michael Jordan. In 1984 *Nike* signed Jordan to a $2.5 million contract over five years. *Nike* took a risk investing in this young athlete at a time when *Nike's* economic performance was under pressure. *Nike's* earnings had declined 65% and in December of 1984 *Nike* laid off 400 employees. For a small company in economic difficulties, signing Jordan to a contract this size was a gamble. What if Jordan got injured? What if Jordan didn't perform as expected? *Nike* management, however, was so confident in Jordan's abilities that they went beyond the traditional endorsement strategy and created a line of shoes named Air Jordan. To increase Jordan's incentive in promoting *Nike*, the firm paid him a royalty on shoes and apparel that carried his name. In April 1985 *Nike* aired its now-famous "Jordan Flight" commercial. To the sound of revving jet engines Jordan moves towards the basket. As the engines reach the roar of take-off velocity, Jordan explodes into the air. Legs apart, Jordan seems suspended almost indefinitely. "Who said a man was not meant to fly?" This commercial not only propelled Jordan into the air but also restored *Nike* as a growth corporation. When Air Jordans hit the stores in April of 1985, *Nike* could not keep up with demand. The Air Jordan line sold over $100 million in its first year. Jordan's sign value continued to rise and with him *Nike*. Jordan would later comment that, "What Phil and *Nike* have done is turn me into a dream."[1] The theme of human transcendence conveyed by the image of Jordan in flight became fused with the *Nike swoosh* reinforced by its "Just do it" tagline.

In this comic commercial CEO Jordan inspects and boxes each shoe. In the marketplace, Nike's strategy has been to produce fewer Air Jordan shoes than it can sell.

Advertising, in general, amplifies a culturally ambivalent relationship between identity and hero worship. Athletic heroes represent prevailing societal values, particularly those linked to the triumph of individualism. Sports discourse has become so heavily loaded as the discourse of morality that the athlete superhero has been turned into a hyperinflated signifier of the benefits of hard work and the achievement ethic. Because many athletes emerge out of lower classes, the superhero image lends credibility to a functioning American Dream. Consequently, in contemporary American society the star athlete's representation emerged as an over-idealized role model for childhood and adolescent cultures. Think of *Gatorade*'s campaign tagline, "I want to be like Mike," where the desire to identify with the superstar turns into a conformist urge. There is, indeed, a psychological risk in over identification with the celebrity athlete. Recall the feminist critique of women's advertising and how the tantalizing, yet unattainable beauty ideals held out to women spur on feelings of inadequacy, obsessions of regulating body weight and the diseases of anorexia and bulimia associated with the gap between the glamour of the model and the everyday. The celebrity athlete always speaks to what one wants to be, as well as what one is not. In *The Culture of Narcissism*, Christopher Lasch suggested that constant media exposure to celebrity culture cultivates a dark underside of individualism: anxieties about inferiority fuel compensatory grandiose fantasies of unlimited fame and success.[2] Films such as *The King of Comedy* and *The Fan* explore how self-identity can become warped when the fan over-identifies with representations of celebrity.

One way to defuse the underlying mix of anxiety and anger associated with the relationship between the fan and the star athlete is the use of self-reflexive and self-deprecatory humor in ads. While the "Flight" commercial established Jordan as the premier sports celebrity of the *NBA*, it was the ensuing campaign that gave both Jordan and *Nike* personalities. Its new advertising agency, *Wieden & Kennedy*, developed a self-referential intertextual style for *Nike*. In terms of a personality quotient, *Nike* sold authenticity by developing a playful relationship between its athletes, the media, the audience, and itself. In the "Mars" campaign Spike Lee played the character Mars Blackmon from his film *She's Gotta Have It*.

In one early ad, Mars asks, and answers, a now famous line in advertising history. With Mars' face almost pressed to the camera, Michael Jordan stands in the background, arm around Nola Darling, while Mars peppers them with questions about why she likes him. "Is it the shoes?" "No Mars," replies Jordan. "Is it that he's 6′ 6″ and the best dunker in the universe?" "No Mars," repeats Nola. Finally, Mars declares, his face thrust into the camera, "It's gotta be the shoes! Please baby, please baby, please Mr *Nike*, you gotta hook me up [with some of these shoes]." In this series of ads, Mars playfully addresses assumptions about the relationship between advertising, commodities, and people.

Most advertising, of course, presumes that one can obtain an identity with the commodity advertised. In athletic shoe advertising, countless ads associate their brand with images of speed, success, and the admiration of beautiful women. *Nike* commercials playfully raise the usually unspoken assumptions concerning the relationship between commodities and identity so that *Nike* can distance itself from such philistine attitudes. In this way, *Nike* disavows the spectacular function of the shoe. It both joins and separates the superstar's performance from its product. *Nike* openly acknowledges its product will not endow us with the power to magically perform like Jordan, even while teasing that "it's gotta be the shoes." Particularly with young, media literate consumers, *Nike's* authenticity quotient went up.

As Jordan's career and legend progressed, *Nike* continued to associate Jordan with themes of transcendent skill and iron determination while keeping him human. *Nike* balanced Jordan's celebrity with humanity by casting Jordan in moments of self-reflexivity that alternate between serious and humorous. During the 1997 *NBA* play-offs *Nike* aired two ads featuring the inner voice of Michael Jordan musing about what it takes for him to excel as an athlete. Shot in slow motion, one ad takes us backstage to follow Jordan's pre-game route from his car into the arena, making his way past admiring fans and employees via the players' entrance. Looking like a *GQ* model, Jordan is dressed for success while his inner voice reflects on his willingness to risk failure as a necessary prerequisite to his success.

I've missed more than 9,000 shots in my career.
I've lost almost 300 games.
26 times I've been trusted to take the game winning shot and missed.
I've failed over and over and over again in my life.
And that is why I succeed.

Jordan glides through this commercial with kingly grace. Here, regal wisdom replaces athleticism

In a second ad, a sweat-drenched Jordan sits on a weight bench reflecting on the sports talk that surrounds him. This time Jordan speaks directly to the audience about how criticism motivates him to accomplish still more. The combination of slow motion and rich black and red color tones reinforces the reflexive moment. In the *Nike* philosophy talk is just talk – you've got to be able to back it up.

> *Challenge me*
> *doubt me*
> *disrespect me*
> *tell me I'm older*
> *tell me I'm slower*
> *tell me I can no longer fly*
> *I want you to*

Jordan embraces "doubt" and "disrespect" as new sources of challenge to motivate himself. Jordan is more than the premier athlete of the decade, he is also the premier global celebrity. "Jordan long ago ceased to be a mere athlete. He transcended his sport and became a global figure, an avatar of cool integrity, and exemplar of masculine confidence and grace" largely because *Nike* constructed him that way.[3] The ads express Jordan's success as an attitude composed of intensity of purpose and desire, focus, and confidence. Moreover, these *Nike* ads highlight Jordan's inner voice. His introspective reflexivity separates him from other athletes, framing him as a sophisticated muse – a man who knows himself and appears at one with himself, a man who demonstrates that the exercise of will enables transcendence of circumstance.

In contrast to these motivational discourses, *Nike* also presents Jordan in ads colored by self-reflexive humor in which the star of the commercial is not Jordan's ability but his confident demeanor and self-effacing personality. When Jordan returned to the *NBA* after his self-imposed retirement from basketball to try his hand at professional baseball, *Wieden & Kennedy* composed a spot in which Jordan is shooting foul shots in a gym. In a closeup shot Jordan glances at the camera. "I had this dream. I retired." Spliced in is a cut from his retirement speech, "It's time for me to move away from the game of basketball." In 1940s film montage style, the front page of a newspaper spins into focus with a headline that reads, MICHAEL CALLS IT QUITS. Jordan's voice-over narrates a montage of scenes – a press conference, playing baseball, eating at a diner, riding a bus – "I became a weak-hitting AA outfielder with a below-average arm. I had a $16 meal per diem. I rode from small town to small town on a bus." The spinning newspaper returns with the headline I'M BACK followed by shots of Jordan playing basketball. "And then I returned to the game I loved. I shot 7 for 28." The dream-like sequence ends and Jordan is alone

After riding the bus to nowhere, Jordan bought a bus for his minor league team.

again shooting foul shots. As Jordan shakes his head in disbelief, he asks "Can you imagine it? Nah!" Jordan is willing to make fun of himself, his foibles, and his failure as a baseball player. His status as a superhero is enhanced by such self-reflexive humor that speaks more to Jordan's personality than his ability. *Nike's* willingness to joke at Jordan's expense positions it as a corporation that enjoys its relationship with its athletes and its fans.

(Re)creating the modest celebrity: Jordan's "Air" apparent

There has been speculation that basketball's rapid growth as a world sport might someday elevate it above soccer in popularity. The spectacle of the Dream Team at the Barcelona Olympics was constructed by the *NBA's* marketing machine as it reached out to become a global network. The growing power of basketball as a global sport necessitates that *Nike* maintain a clear cultural dominance in that sport. As the retirement of Jordan looms on the horizon, and *Adidas* and *Fila* aggressively sign young stars, *Nike* must develop a new marquee celebrity athlete. *Nike's* rising new star, Anfernee "Penny" Hardaway appears to be Jordan's heir apparent. In October 1995 *Nike* brought out its "Air Penny" basketball shoe.

Nike introduced Hardaway in a "biographical" commercial. In a soft spoken voice, Hardaway expresses his appreciation of his mother and grandmother, the Boys and Girls Club, and the opportunity to play at Memphis State University. He talks about practice and hard work. This homegrown hero rooted in his family also reflects a sense of Southern civility. *Nike* presented Hardaway as a hard-working athlete, respected for his ability, but most importantly, humble before the world. In a second commercial Hardaway meets the press. He sits under a bright light as if being interrogated by the police. Five microphones jut into the frame and the press fires questions at him so fast he has no time to answer. As the questioning continues, the questions become increasingly absurd.

"Penny, this is your first time to an NBA *final. Are you scared?"*
"Penny, if Houston double teamed you would you still be able to play?"
"Houston is known for their quickness, so is your team, Orlando. Will that eliminate speed as a factor in this series?"
"Penny, when you played against Tim Hardaway did it get confusing?"
"Houston is a different team than Orlando. Is that a fair question?"
"You scored a different number of points in every playoff game so far. What's the strategy?"
"If you win who deserves the credit?"
"What do you think about at the free throw line?"
"What do you think about right now?"
"Hey Penny, an NBA championship ring, would you wear it?"

The media interrogates Anfernee Hardaway, a.k.a. Penny.

"Penny, you wear a size 14 shoe. Does that decrease your chances for a traveling call?"

Frustrated, Hardaway sits stoic in his silence, impassively staring in disbelief. With the hint of a sigh the "Just do it" line appears on the screen. This *Nike* spokesperson is mute; he's a player not a spokesperson. This is another of *Nike's* metacommunicative moments where *Nike* constructs itself as a sign of performance. *Nike* hails us by not actively hailing us. This *Nike* athlete doesn't talk about his performance; he just does it.

How does an advertiser make a quiet non-verbal spokesperson an effective celebrity icon? How does it allow Penny to speak without turning him into a marketer? How does it keep Hardaway pure in a commercial? The ad's creator, Stacy Wall points out that "by creating a foil for Hardaway, we allow him to be the true athlete that he is at the same time we've created someone who can say: 'Pay attention to Penny. He's real good.'"[4] Enter Little Penny – an alter-ego big-mouth, a sidekick, a look-alike mannequin resurrected from a proposed commercial that *Wieden & Kennedy* had opted not to use. Little Penny is *Nike's* voice (as performed by Chris Rock) of pure irreverence. In one ad, Hardaway and Little Penny are watching TV, and a *Nike* commercial comes on with Hardaway dressed in a glittering gold suit, dancing and selling *Nike* shoes. Hardaway appears flabbergasted as Little Penny wisecracks, "Well, I guess Spike Lee wasn't available." The "Hardaway" within the frame of the mockup television ad, is the inauthentic, commercialized, that's-entertainment Hardaway – what sports marketing does to athletes. The embarrassed "Hardaway" outside the frame is the authentic Hardaway. Nevertheless, they are both constructions. The authentic Hardaway is no less a cultural fabrication than the inauthentic, wooden one. *Nike's* playfulness in presenting Hardaway as a showbusiness cartoon, but with a self-reflexive wink, is *Nike's* sign of itself.

Another commercial opens with Little Penny, dressed in a miniature Orlando Magic uniform and wearing headphones, sitting on a locker room bench. As the taciturn Hardaway ties his shoes, the mannequin engages him in pre-game locker room chat.

Little Penny: *Hey, Penny whadda ya' call those shoes anyway?*
Hardaway: *Air Penny.*
Little Penny: *So who do you guys play tonight anyway?*
Hardaway: *Minnesota.*
Little Penny: *Los Lobos! I guess you're goin' for the big numbers tonight. I want you to go inside then outside. I'm sensing a triple double. I want ya' to say hello to my man Kevin Garnett. We went to high school together. Just tell him Little Penny from the science class says hello. Can you do that for a brother?*

Here, Little Penny and Hardaway watch the exaggerated spectacle of advertising. This commercial uses the same falsified metacommunicative structure Nike *used in the Bo Jackson campaign.*

Little Penny trashes the Timberwolves in Orlando's locker room.

Little Penny shows no respect for the opponent and talks trash – "Los Lobos," "big numbers tonight." His stream of inflated hype continues as he claims to be a high school chum of Kevin Garnett. And he talks black: "my man Kevin Garnett" and "can you do that for a brother?" Yet this dynamic, clever, quick-thinking verbal style is a non-threatening discourse because it is delivered by a mannequin. Hardaway's reactions express discomfort with the conversation. Looks of "why me?" and "How do I get out of this conversation?" cross Hardaway's face. In this campaign the condescending arrogant trash-talking mannequin serves as the perfect counterpart for constructing Hardaway as a soft spoken, respectful, unassuming athlete.

In the "Party" ad the relationship between Hardaway and Little Penny mimics a parent/adolescent relationship. Hardaway is on the road calling from his hotel to make sure everything is OK at home. Little Penny answers the phone, dressed in a bright red satin Hugh Hefner-type bathrobe, "The Hardaway residence." Behind Little Penny is a wild party with music blaring and people dancing. Hearing the background noise, Penny asks suspiciously, "Are you having a party?" "Party," replies Little Penny, "I'm just sitting here reading a book." Little Penny immediately shifts the conversation, "Caught the game last night. Let me just put it this way. You're the best player in the *NBA*. I mean those spin moves and the dunks. Oh! Too vicious! I had to go outside to do some tai-chi to calm myself down." As the conversation continues the party appears increasingly out of control. Hardaway recognizes Little Penny's attempt to redirect the conversation into hyperbole. "Man, you are having a party. I swear if you and your sloppy friends are messing up my house …" Meantime, a woman kisses Little Penny on the cheek. "Oh thanks baby! I'll meet you out by the pool. Hey! hey! I can't talk now." Uttering something unintelligible as if static on the phone line was garbling their conversation, he hangs up.

In his Hugh Hefner bathrobe, Little Penny cajoles Hardaway.

Each ad is similar in structure. Little Penny tries to manipulate situations for his own personal satisfaction, cajoling Hardaway with adulation and flattery. As a character, Little Penny functions to raise Hardaway's sign value by singing his praises, supported by highlight footage of Hardaway driving to the basket and dunking cut into the ad.

Always looking for the angle, Little Penny is a transparent hustler looking to score with Tyra Banks or do a film deal with Spike Lee. Hardaway distances himself from this style with looks of embarrassment. Little Penny is invariably a source of grief for Hardaway. Each ad ends with Little Penny continuing his self-promotional chatter.

You know what your problem is.
You're too modest.
Hey, I give good quotes.
And you can print this on the front page.

Anfernee Hardaway, best player in basketball, guarantees championship.
Guarantees.

While Hardaway is the modest celebrity who just plays ball, Little Penny is the classic hustler who is always looking for an angle to attain money, fame, and women (Tyra Banks). Nike pokes fun at media fantasies as it simultaneously creates them.

Why Hardaway? Why not Gary Payton or Alonzo Mourning? While Hardaway is one of the premier players of his generation, we might look beyond basketball ability to personality, style, charisma, and how these elements can be used to construct a public presence. Stacy Wall of *Wieden & Kennedy* describes Hardaway: "On the court, he's an aggressive, phenomenal player, but off the court he's so soft spoken. It's just not in him to trumpet to the world that he's the best player on the planet." Erin Patton, *Nike's* public relations manager for men's basketball, observed that "If sports has a tarnished image, Penny's a shining example of what an athlete should be."[5] *Nike* recognizes that in a sports world tarnished by constant excesses of commercialization, its marquee athlete must appear to be pure. While Charles Barkley can harp on not being a role model and Deion Sanders can be constructed as the incarnation of the spectacle itself, Jordan's heir must appeal to mainstream middle class audiences by signifying the moral and the motivational functions of sport. No trash-talking players are acceptable for this role.

Nike's construction of Hardaway as their lead celebrity is designed to appeal to a general audience. In the world of trash-talking braggadocio, Hardaway just plays the game. He's a player not a talker. Hardaway doesn't display black cultural codes or use black language structures. This is not to say that *Nike* doesn't niche market along racial demographics, but that its flagship celebrities have to appeal across racial and ethnic boundaries. Remember that most people don't buy *Nike* shoes for use in the sport for which they were designed. The white middle class has the disposable income to buy shoes as well as other apparel products from *Nike*. While *Nike* garners media attention when it occasionally transgresses bourgeois moral boundaries, its center remains organized around conservative bourgeois moral codes. The trick is to find black athletes who have mass appeal to both black and non-black audiences. Using Little Penny as a device to structure the ad allows black cultural codes to enter the frame without overwhelming it.

The Little Penny campaign is often compared to the Mars Blackmon campaign because each represented blackness outside the persona of the star athlete. When the subject is Jordan or Hardaway, *Nike* avoids treating blackness strictly as race, but rather as a matter of ethnic humor. Consistent with this pattern, when *Nike* did run a series of ads that dealt directly with the issue of racism, they engaged Spike Lee (already associated with *Do the Right Thing*) rather than Michael Jordan to address the divisiveness of racist language. The presentation of Hardaway in relationship to Little Penny mirrors the construction of Jordan in relationship to Mars Blackmon.

Hardaway's representation, like that of Jordan, allows *Nike* to hail not just a broad American audience but a multi-racial global audience. There are those who see this construction of blackness as problematic.

> Jordan is not an example of racial transcendence, rather he is an agent of racial displacement. Jordan's valorized, racially neutered, image displaces racial codes onto other black bodies: be they Mars Blackmon, Charles Barkley, or the anonymous urban black male who the popular media seems intent on criminalizing. *Nike*'s promotional strategy systematically down played Jordan's blackness by contrasting him with Spike Lee's somewhat troubling caricature of young, urban, African American males, Mars Blackmon … The contrast fortified Jordan's wholesome, responsible, all American, and hence non-threatening persona, and became the basis of his hyperreal identity which was subsequently embellished by the multiplying circuits of promotional capital which enveloped him.[6]

There are a series of related assumptions underlying this critique of race representations that demand closer examination. Viewing Jordan's persona as a completely market-driven identity in which Jordan's blackness disappears from view in relation to Mars Blackmon assumes that Jordan's own subjectivity and biography have been emptied out in the marketing process. What has been distilled out, this argument suggests, is "threat." This rests, in turn, on a dubious equation of "racially neutered" with "nonthreatening persona." What does a "threatening persona" have to do with blackness? If Jordan does not come across as representing sufficient blackness, perhaps that is because "blackness" is constructed on television in the stereotypical expressions and postures associated with the lower classes. If Jordan comes across as unthreatening, perhaps that is because he grew up in a largely middle-class background. It would seem that on television at least, the signifiers that we most closely associate with blackness have to do with the codes of social class more than race.

This critique also fails to acknowledge how black viewers might view Jordan as embodying "the deepest fantasies black men have of themselves," manifesting decency as well as strength. Nelson George argues that like great black athletes who have preceded him, "Michael Jordan's movements, boldness and skill allow African-American men to see the best of themselves projected in the symbolic war of sports."[7] George may push the argument a bit too far, but it is worth noting his claim that black Americans "need" Michael Jordan – they need access to the "purity and strength" he displays on the basketball court.[8] Even after Jordan's representation has been worked through the "circuits of promotional capitalism" it still offers portions of the black community a symbol of empowerment and dignity. Displacing racial codes is very different from the erasure of race. The latter does not, and cannot, occur in a racist society. Rather, as Michael Dyson has observed, the construction of Michael Jordan as a celebrity icon is tightly woven into a knotty tangle of meanings that orbit around the subject of race in American society.

> Though basketball is anchored in the metaphoric heart of African-American culture, Jordan has paradoxically transcended the negative meanings of race to become an icon of all-American athletic excellence. In Jordan, the black male body, still associated with menace outside of sports and entertainment, is made an object of white desire. And black desire finds in Jordan, through his athletic ability, the still almost exclusive entry into wealth and fame. He has become the supreme symbol of black cultural creativity in a society that is showing less and less tolerance for black youth whose support sustained his career. Jordan reflects black culture's love affair with spontaneity and improvisation, its brash experiments with performance, its fascination with those who exceed limits. Jordan's embodiment of these black cultural elements has created in American society a desire to, in the words of the famous *Gatorade* media campaign, "Be Like Mike."[9]

The *Gatorade* campaign sought to draft on the coat-tails of Jordan's *Nike* image. What's more, this urging to "Be like Mike" [drink *Gatorade*] is the kind of copycat, advertising slogan that *Nike* advertising scorns: the kind of advertising that magically places the desire for a standout identity in the passive consumption of a brandname. Nevertheless, through his agent, David Falk, Jordan has long since made the decision to maximize his endorsement value with sponsors. The logic of this game – trading commercial endorsements for lucrative fees in the millions of dollars – invariably lends itself to a stress on having desirable consumer items. Given this trail of market calculations it is not surprising that "Black youth learn to want to 'live large,' to emulate capitalism's excesses on their own turf."[10]

Considering hero worship along the dimension of race magnifies the cultural contradictions between media-stimulated fantasies and the material conditions of inequality in everyday life. Quite beyond any intentions of *Nike* or Jordan, Jordan's imagery now stands at the intersection of celebrity, blackness, masculinity, and desire. Jordan's image has been invested with so much that it now has a life of its own. The complex social and cultural contradictions between race, class, gender, and the promotional circuits of hero worship and identification would require a book in themselves. Do fantasies of hero identification help motivate low-income youth to overcome their circumstances? Or, are they just another way of keeping those youth locked into desires for material acquisition? We do not have ready answers to these questions, although we are quite sure that in the real world, there are no either–or scenarios.

THE MULTIPLE PERSONALITIES OF *NIKE*

Nike names its shoes after a select group of marquee athletes: Air Jordan, Air Penny, Air Swoopes, Air Pippin and soon, a Tiger Woods line. Jordan's "star power" vaulted *Nike* to the top of the athletic shoe industry as well as the sports industry in general. Penny Hardaway is Jordan's heir apparent, and Sheryl Swoopes was *Nike's* first female basketball star as it positions itself in the booming female athletic market. But, there are lesser gods in *Nike's* stable – each with their own distinct abilities and personalities, each with their own market niche. Phil Knight understood that brand value is not just about a product but about a sign, so that *Nike's* representations of athletes tied fans to the consumption of its products.

> People don't concentrate their emotional energy on products in the way fans abandon themselves to the heroes of their games. But great products that were necessary to great athletic figures, Knight reasoned, could create customers who were like fans. "Nobody roots for a product," Knight would say; the products needed to be tethered to something more compelling and profound.[11]

In *Decoding Advertisements*, Judith Williamson casts the issue theoretically:

> it is the first function of an advertisement to create a differentiation between one particular product and others in the same category. It does this by providing the product with an "image"; this image only succeeds in differentiating between products in so far as *it* is part of a system of differences. The identity of anything depends more on what it is *not* than what it is, since boundaries are primarily distinctions: and there are no "natural" distinctions between most products [emphasis in original].[12]

Consider the *Nike* ad that presents Charles Barkley and Michael Jordan in an exaggerated bragging contest about their shoes, set up as a comic version of this differentiation process at work. When Barkley boasts, "Hey Mike, I got my own shoes with my own initials on it," he is bragging about his sign value. To which Jordan retorts, "Yeah! Well I have my own shoes with my own name on it." "My shoes got straps." "Laces." "Black." "White." "White's wimpy." "*Nike* Air." "Mine's got more." The representation of the athlete (both personality and performance) is attached to a particular product. Each athlete acts as a signifier for a personality or performance trait (the signified) that is joined to a particular shoe.

Using humor Nike *pokes fun at sign value while still differentiating and promoting it.*

Differentiation doesn't just refer to niche markets, it also describes the relationship between competing commodity signs. When we say that Jordan increased *Nike's* sign value, we mean that representations of Jordan increased the value of the *Nike* name and icon. What differentiates *Nike* most from *Reebok*, *Converse* or *Fila* are the *ways* in which *Nike* represents its athletes. Industry watchers readily agree that *Nike* has achieved a degree of authenticity that its competitors have not. When *Nike* represents an athlete in its commercials, there is a sense we are getting the real thing. *Nike* seems to respect its athletes as people, permitting them to display their own personalities.

This appearance is not accidental. In constructing the Penny Hardaway campaign, *Wieden & Kennedy* spent hours interviewing Hardaway. "They asked me everything – the things I like to do, the movies I like to watch."[13] Constructing Hardaway as a modest athlete has an authentic feel because it resembles Hardaway's personality. Likewise, the Barkley – "I'm not a role model" – commercial, although controversial, signified *Nike's* respect for the personality, style, and unmuzzled autonomy of Barkley. By playing off of its athlete's personality traits, even if it means transgressing acceptable boundaries, *Nike* creates a feeling that it allows its spokespersons sufficient space to speak authentically. They are presented as individuals who are part of the *Nike* community and not just pitchmen in the *Nike* stable. The range of personalities which *Nike* offers creates numerous routes to the *Nike swoosh*. In fact, *Nike* has pursued the premise that many consumers liked to be hailed by anti-heroes as well as heroes.

> Consumers seemed to respond best to athletes who combined a passion to win with a maverick disregard for convention: "Outlaws with morals," in the words of Watts Wacker, a Yankelovich consultant who has worked with *Nike*. Steve Prefontaine, the University of Oregon track star who regularly tilted with the NCAA and other regulatory bodies, was *Nike's* first effective sports icon. Later, when the company began producing shoes and apparel for other sports, tennis brats John McEnroe and Andre Agassi, along with basketball bad boy Charles Barkley, fit the mold perfectly.[14]

In "Barkley of Seville" Nike *parodies opera in an elaborate spectacle. Reacting to a foul call Barkley "accidentally" kills the ref.*

Each *Nike* athlete signifies a particular personality trait. Taken together their representations signify authenticity. Rather than thinking of differentiation as a way of distinguishing products from one another, we might think of it as the process of creating multiple routes to *Nike's swoosh*. In practical marketing terms, differentiation enables consumers to connect with specific product niches while also valuing anything with a *swoosh* on it. In this sense, *Nike* has both multiple personalities and a coherent identity. *Nike's* athletes have styles and personalities which provide different entry points to the *Nike* totem group.

A 1996–1997 ad campaign features commercials that define and differentiate the range of meanings available via *Nike's* stable of basketball stars –

Scottie Pippen, Gary Payton, Damon Stoudamire, Kevin Garnett, and Jason Kidd. Assembled like music videos, these ads arrange highly idiosyncratic signifiers together to create a puzzle-like montage that requires interpretive "labor" on the part of the viewer. Each ad consists of a mysterious amalgam of signifiers drawn from a variety of referent systems including the animal kingdom, the vaults of pop culture kitsch, and music genre. For example, the Scottie Pippen ad opens, almost dream-like, with Pippen dressed in a long black coat walking along a pole that extends out from a skyscraper creating a sense of vertigo, while an announcer intones, "Ladies and gentlemen, Thelonius Monk." Pippen is surrounded by a flock of cawing crows, obviously matted into the background. And so the ad unfolds dissociatively, incongruent image followed by incongruent image, set to breaks or ruptures in the musical soundtrack. The only other spoken comment, situated over game footage of Pippin dunking, seems somehow to connect Monk with Pippin: "to imply the missing note that is in between." When the ad concludes with a shot of a stylized painting of Pippen dressed in a suit holding a basketball in his hands, a crow on his shoulder, and a cheetah and smokestacks in the background, this seems to be yet another clue confirming that perhaps we have just watched a portrait of Pippin. But now we must decipher it.

The commercials from this campaign don't tell stories per se, but overlay a series of symbolically packed visual metaphors. Deciphering the puzzles permits viewers to differentiate these athletes from one another.

Knowledge of Pippen's personality and style of play can supply clues to making sense of the odd jumble of signifiers: crows; Thelonius Monk; a streaking cheetah; a simulated bullet ripping through paper in slow motion; an alarm system, called "Silent Assassin"; shoe shoplifting. The arrangement of signifiers is ambiguous and obscure enough to create space for viewers to invent interpretations, to read the symbolic text attentively. As viewers we reason to ourselves that all these are clues to a jigsaw puzzle that has "Scottie Pippin" as its answer. OK, so Pippin is a great basketball player, so

Nike *associates signifiers of alternative culture with Seattle's point guard Gary Payton in a rapidly edited commercial styled after music videos.*

"I am the king! I am the king!" chants the narrator. "What does this mean? What does this mean?" chants the viewer. Formulaic ads that offer solutions are boring. In order to involve commercially saturated viewers this series doesn't offer solutions.

hmmm let's see, how does he stand out. Well, he's known for his defensive skills, his ability to steal the ball – perhaps that's why the images of the crow or the alarm system that can't prevent theft? The cheetah – well that seems easy enough, it is super quick and it finishes off its prey. But the Thelonius Monk reference is more enigmatic. Perhaps Pippin enjoys Monk's cerebral jazz? And the reference to Monk's comment, "to imply the missing note that is in between" can be stretched to conjure up Pippin's crucial relationship with the absent Michael Jordan on the basketball court. The point here is not that we have finished interpreting this ad, but rather that we have explored the text. Indeed, by ad's end, we are aware that this brief deconstructive odyssey has left us with surplus signifiers and references that we can't entirely fit into our scheme of meaning. This is also what happens to us when we view the Gary Payton ad. After viewing the ad at least two dozen times, while we can readily place Payton in relation to punk music (he plays for Seattle) or to the reference "fringe agitator" since he disrupts opponents' games from his guard position, the reference to "July 4, 1910" juxtaposed against a gray sky and a skyscraper completely baffles us.

In her primer on decoding ads, Judith Williamson observes that "ads produce a universe of puzzles – one that we cannot move in without 'deciphering', one that requires us to stop and work out a solution."[15] The *Nike* ads mentioned above present an elaborate hermeneutic puzzle. Because the images are placed in unusual ways that do not fit with the customary codes governing television messages, the ads focus the viewer on connecting the meaning of the parts to that of the whole. This challenges the viewer on several levels: discovering the thread or underlying theme; recognizing the cultural identity of the featured athlete; and constructing the significance of this or that oddly dangling signifier. When students watched the Damon Stoudamire ads, they kept asking questions like "why is there a child's drawing of a crown in there" or "what does that have to do with Stoudamire?" Even students familiar with the player and his sports-page defined persona were perplexed. The pleasure of watching what seem to be schizophrenic texts is trying to solve the riddle. While Williamson argued in 1978 that readings of ads tend to be guided along "carefully defined channels," noting that "a puzzle has only one solution," contemporary ads now encourage multiple solutions that are contingent on the interpretations supplied by the viewer.[16] Ads with simple solutions are boring. They don't engage or hold viewers. Ambiguity creates interpretative space and promotes viewer involvement and investment in the ad.

THE COMMUNITY OF SPORT AND PLAY

The contradiction between the desire for individual glory and the desire to be a part of an egalitarian and democratic community of others plays itself out throughout American culture. In *Habits of the Heart*, Robert Bellah and his associates addressed this tension between unbridled individualism and the desire for community. Bellah argued that American cosmology celebrates individual success to such a degree that it fails to give adequate voice to the need for communal belongingness. Without an historically grounded community, decisions, values, and moral codes are driven by privatized self-interests and personal feelings and desires. With the disappearance of real communities of memory, the desire for community becomes expressed as nostalgia. Nevertheless, the yearning for community remains.[17]

While much of *Nike* advertising addresses the autonomous individual, a surprising number of spots also dwell on the social character of sporting activity. In recent years, *Nike* ads about rugby in the snow, tennis in a NY City street intersection, and kid's street hockey have pivoted on the social side of sport. A car horn beeps and a kid hollers "Car!" Thus begins a street hockey commercial patterned after the Dr. Seuss story, *And To Think That I Saw It On Mulberry Street*. The kids clear the goal nets off the street to let the car pass and then resume playing. Moments later a kid yells "Motorcycle gang!" and a group of bikers pass through. Next a kid yells "Marathon," and a marathon passes by. This is followed by "Parade!" complete with marching band, floats, cheerleaders, and a beauty queen blowing kisses. Finally, a kid yells "Stampede" and a black frame appears with "Just do it" bouncing up and down to the ground-shaking stampede in the background. The musical background is lively and upbeat, punctuated by the "whack! whack!" of slapping the puck. The ad's humor is based on exaggerating the social experience of kids' informal play. Though the ad speaks to kids, it also nostalgically engages older audiences about that time in their lives when the spontaneous community of childhood games battled cars for control of the street. Most importantly, the spontaneity of play transcends social conventions. Similarly, a Sampras–Agassi tennis commercial plays on this social control of the street. Sampras instructs a NYC cab driver, "Looks pretty good. Stop right here." He and Agassi hop out, stop traffic and set up a net. With punk music defining the background they aggressively overhit balls at one

Sport transforms the street into an instant community.

another on their hastily-assembled street court. A crowd gathers and cheers them on. In this ad the pleasure of sport takes place as a form of transgression. Play transcends the socially proscribed use of urban traffic space, and an instant community is born. City workers, pedestrians, automobiles all stop, taking a moment to share the pleasure of disobeying the repressive order of everyday routines, until a city bus comes barreling through the net, ending the break and restoring order. Rather than view these as merely amusing yarns, we take these to be parables reflecting *Nike*'s philosophy. These ads portray space and time as social constructs that can be overcome by the will to play. The spirit of sport restructures social space, carving out conviviality in the most unlikely places – marking off a rugby field by spray-painting red lines on a blanket of snow; children's informal play communities carving out space for play wherever the opportunity presents itself; or the forcible seizure of a traffic intersection governed by laws and regulations to create a fugitive tennis court as a theater for the passion of play. The latter of course assembles not a community of players, but a community of spectators brought together by the staging of *Nike*'s guerrilla theater.

Celebrating the game

"The game" refers to that which is sacred in sport. The game is pure and simple. At its basic level it is a set of rules that govern relationships and performance. Within this set of rules everyone is equal. It does not matter who you are but what you do. As soon as one enters the circle of the game, one's ability and determination magically displace class, race, gender, and age. The game is the pure form of sociality – play. Like society, the game has a history and a future which transcends the individual. On playgrounds, in parks, in school yards, in stadiums, and on TV the game not only empowers the individual but also represents a space in which community still exists. The "love" for the game recognizes a world greater than the individual.

In our society there are two recognized threats to the game – commodification and spectacularization, or more concretely, money and the media. These forces are seen as intrusions into the essence of the game, the pure form of sociality. Here, there is an odd congruity between *Nike*'s position and the sociological approach of Robert Bellah. Both "theories" – Bellah's and *Nike*'s – disregard capital as a force that structures privatized lives. And yet, each in its own way recognizes the pernicious impact of markets on culture and community life. Like Bellah, *Nike*'s solution to this dilemma is idealist. Bellah speaks to desires for secular re-spiritualization. *Nike* similarly poses the activity of sport as highly spiritualized: the means of finding oneself and belonging to a community of others.

The celebrity athlete embodies the conflict between the sacred (the game) and the secular (commercialization). Representations of the super athlete signify human transcendence, but those representations are constructed by media, sport corporations, and advertisers to serve their own materialistic ends. The athlete as a celebrity is a threat to the pure form of the game. Bigger contracts and proliferating endorsements prompt fans to suspect that money rather than the love of the game is the prime motivation. Consequently, the athlete must be regularly purified of his/her materialistic motives. When Michael Jordan retired from basketball to play minor league baseball, *Nike* used the opportunity to celebrate Jordan's purity of soul and motives by humorously casting his retirement as a consequence of his desire to preserve his deep love for the essence of basketball, the game. The tongue in cheek comments on Jordan's retirement made by members of the professional basketball sports fraternity provide the narration for the ad which tracks Jordan in various disguises – wearing a beard, a wig, goggles, a trench-coat – as he plays basketball with minor league teams like Las Cruces, Gary, Billings, and the Crawfish.

John Thompson: *If Michael is out there still playing, the message is clear. Here is the guy who is the greatest player of all times letting nothing stand in his way doing what he loves to do. And that's just play basketball.*

Marv Albert: *I think he had to get away from everything. It all overwhelmed him. I can understand Michael playing in disguise.*

Michael Irvin: *You can't blame the man. This man just wants to play the game.*

Ahmad Rashad: *I think that he got so tired of the hype and so tired of the media that he wanted to find a place that he could play and really have fun.*

Dan Majerle: *I think that he's a little bored. I think he wants to come back for the competition. And he wants a chance to come out and score some points and play against his old friends again.*

David Robinson: *I think that Mike is doing this just to get away from the insanity of pro basketball – the hype.*

B.J. Armstrong: *The pressure.*

Marv Albert: *The media.*

Dennis Rodman: *The refs.*

Spike Lee: *The commercials.*

Chris Webber: *Nah! I think he's scared of me.*

Harold Miner: *Or maybe Mike is doing this just because he wants to be a player again.*

Can you identify this mystery athlete?

Nike encourages an exaggerated self-awareness when these commentators speak directly to the camera (to us) as they speculate on why Jordan retired from the *NBA* – because of the hype, the media, the commercials, the pressure, all answers that focus on the commercialization and the spectacularization of sport. When Spike Lee holds up a pair of shoes and blames commercials for Jordan's retirement, *Nike* playfully critiques itself. By poking fun at itself and its role in creating the hype and spectacle that drove Jordan from the *NBA*, *Nike* hails the cynical viewer and then deflates both criticism and cynicism by humor. This is another example of the knowing wink. Throughout the commercial *Nike*'s icon remains pure. Jordan, the king of sign value, is shown transcending the hype because his love for the game remains strong. What does Jordan want to do? Just play the game, to be a player again. What motivates him? His love for the game. In spite of the spectacle, Jordan and his fellow players remain pure at heart in their love of the game. Here at the center of sports, lies something which cannot be commodified, our love of the game. The commercial also permits us backstage among a fraternity of men who play the game, and who share a sense of camaraderie, respect, and shared purpose. *Nike* constructs the relationship of these athletes to their work in a way that reproduces C. Wright Mills' ideals of craftsmanship – internal motivation, a unity of work and leisure, and work as play.[18]

Like the Michael Jordan retirement commercial, the "Play ball" commercial uses a similar structural form to celebrate the sociability of an athletic community held together by the shared culture of the game. Sociability is expressed by the cut up dialogue in which players complete each other's sentences and finish jokes, suggesting a shared intertextual culture (knowledge of the game's history as well as contemporary events linked to athletes) organized around baseball.

Cal Ripken: *I believe that hitting a round ball with a round bat*
Kirby Puckett: *is the hardest thing to do in all sports.*
Raul Mondesi: *I believe that Roberto Clemente is the patron saint of baseball ...*
Kurt Gibson: *I believe in the designated hitter.*
Don Mattingly: *I believe that Lou Gehrig's birthday should be a national holiday ...*
Ken Griffey: *I believe walls are hard.*
Don Mattingly: *I believe that no one is bigger than the game*
Matt Williams: *except maybe Boog Powell.*
Don Mattingly: *I believe somebody,*
Kirby Puckett: *somewhere,*
Kurt Gibson: *understands the infield fly rule.*
Ken Griffey: *I believe it's time to sing.*
Don Mattingly: *Take me out to the ball game (he sings)*
Matt Williams: *I believe that even I sing better than Don Mattingly.*
Mike Piazza: *I believe that.*
Kirby Puckett: *And I believe that every player should have a day off after 2160 games.*
Matt Williams: *I believe that dome stadiums are great*
Ken Griffey: *for tractor pulls.*
Kurt Gibson: *I believe that the two greatest words*
Don Mattingly: *in the English language*
Matt Williams: *are play ball ...*
Don Mattingly: *I believe if Shoeless Joe Jackson were playing today he'd have a shoe contract.*

This culture has a history (references to Lou Gehrig, Boog Powell, Shoeless Joe Jackson) and a sense of the sacred with its patron saint Roberto Clemente. Players joke about one another (Don Mattingly "can't sing," Tony Gwynn "sleeps with his bat") and make self-referential jokes about themselves and the game (Ken Griffey's comment about playing in the Seattle Kingdome plagued by falling tiles), while also speaking with admiration about each other (Kirby Puckett's bow to Cal Ripken's record of consecutive games played). Insider jokes signify a shared culture. Any game or team that has continuity develops a comparable culture. This shared culture and bonding mechanism parallels that constructed in everyday life by those who have played on a softball team (*Nike's* other commercial about the octogenarian Kubs), noon-time basketball, or playground basketball. In a social world that has become, by and large, privatized, this *Nike* ad invites viewers to share in this sports community through knowledge of the game, or more importantly, through knowledge of the ad itself – being able to identify the players and knowing the background to the joking references. Recognizing players and their intertextual banter serves as the criterion for admission to the baseball fraternity.

After the screen has gone to the *Nike* logo, the camera returns to Don Mattingly saying, "I believe if Shoeless Joe Jackson were playing today he'd have a shoe contract." Mattingly's banter has now turned on our host as he jokes about *Nike's* habit of signing the stars of the game. The reference to Shoeless Joe Jackson demands some minimal knowledge of baseball legend and lore. To fully appreciate the insider's joke shared by Mattingly with *Nike* we need to know that Shoeless Joe was an old-time ballplayer. Legend has it that Shoeless Joe was just a good ol' country boy who purely loved to play baseball. But he got caught up in the Chicago Blacksox scandal in the 1919 World Series and betrayed the integrity of the game. Shoeless Joe thus became a fallen celebrity of some interest because he represented the cultural tension between playing for the love of sport and the immorality of money. The story has been revived and romanticized by the baseball film *Field of Dreams*, and more recently has been a subject of attention in Ken Burn's epic history of baseball and in John Sayles' cinematic rendering of the Blacksox scandal. At any rate, with the last barb flung back at itself, *Nike* pokes fun at itself, thus including itself into the community of *Nike* athletes.

Ads like this celebrate the community organized around the game itself. The All-Star Game is the perfect venue not just because it has celebrity athletes but because the game celebrates the sport itself. References to the love of the game abound in commercials. *Reebok* depicted its celebrity athletes playing pick-up ball in gyms to demonstrate that "you gotta have the love" and, of course, *NBA* promos use the slogan "I love this game." Though the latter is but a hollow tagline that celebrates the commercialization of basketball when it is positioned adjacent to a series of spectacular images of players and fans displaying intense emotion, the simple reference to "the

Vulgar commercialization: the NBA *transforms its own tagline I LOVE THIS GAME into I LOVE THIS STUFF to hype* NBA *branded clothing.*

game" legitimizes *NBA* practices. In a society inundated by commercialism, references to a mythical essence of sport provide an imaginary core of meaning. The litany of "I believe" in *Nike's* All-Star Game "Play ball" commercial resembles a religious service. Ironically, the commercial has two endings: love for the game and a *Nike* shoe contract. After all, are the two greatest words in the English language "play ball" or "shoe contract"?

Joining the Nike community

The meanings of sports have anchored male public culture for much of the twentieth century. During the previous century, male culture revolved more around tools and making things, or politics. *Nike* and *Wieden & Kennedy* recognize that sport has slowly replaced work, religion and community as the glue of collective consciousness in latter twentieth century America. To be sure, *Nike's* advertising is not unique in extolling the therapeutic merits of ministering to body and spirit through athletic activity. Such ads have become so prolific that a 1995 public service style ad for a religious organization mimics the look and feel of *Soloflex* ads as a lure to enjoining viewers to attend that other "temple" this weekend. As secular religion, few ads have more explicitly caught the metaphor of your body as a temple than the *Nike* "Don't rush" ad campaign for their women's fitness products. *Nike's* men's ads have been less likely to express this blend of therapeutic narcissism, stressing instead sociability. Male sports banter lies at the heart of this advertising – banter similar to that which once shaped, for both better and worse, a proletarian public sphere; and banter that we today associate, thanks to the media, with trash-talking in black urban culture.

Nike ads create a community of athletes who share the *Nike* philosophy: they play intensely because they love the game. While the Jordan retirement ad emphasizes that philosophy, it also constructs a *Nike* community based on sports talk. This includes media hype, advertising discourse, shop talk – strategies, evaluation of players, statistics, and predictions. Media discourse and informal conversation intermix. These stars have become part of the sports fan's family and he/she part of theirs – at least within the spectacle. But there is also an informal discourse that defines the community – trash-talking, jiving, and teasing. For example, when Webber suggests that Jordan quit because he is scared of playing against him, Mullins shares with us a look of humorous disbelief. Viewers are positioned as part of this camaraderie. We are included in the playful exchanges. We are invited into the conversation, and into the community.

Wieden & Kennedy does not just offer the privatized inspiration of body worship, but also a sense of community that can be articulated around sports. Notice, for example, how often *Nike* has returned to old-style barbershops as a stage for their men's ads. Considered as an iconic index of small town and neighborhood **communitas**, in recent decades the barbershop has been supplanted by franchised haircutters and hair boutiques. But *Nike* has resurrected the barbershop as a site for the social activity of male banter, recalling a time when the local barbershop was a slow-moving place for local organic intellectuals to dispense their commentary on the world.

The barbershop has served as the site for banter among *Nike's* basketball stars. David Robinson, Dennis Rodman, Tim Hardaway, George Gervin, Chris Webber, and others have appeared in these barbershop ads. One such *Nike* commercial resurrects George "Iceman" Gervin, a professional scoring sensation two decades back. Tim Hardaway comments about a now-dated picture of Gervin in a white jump suit with ICE inscribed on it. "Walk outside with that on in San Antonio now. You'll burn up." This elicits howls of laughter. "Tell us about that finger roll from the free throw line." Gervin responds to Hardaway's friendly encouragement. "You know that was my patented, that was my patented shot. One thing I could do was finger roll." Everyone laughs as Gervin holds an old red, white, and blue *ABA* ball to demonstrate. The players are seated in a semi-circle. The camera (the audience) occupies the empty side to complete the circle. The sound quality of the commercial makes the jesting particularly difficult to follow. Stacy Wall of *Wieden & Kennedy* says this was intentional. "If you are a fan, you would love to be part of this community. Straining to understand the banter makes you lean in to listen." It literally draws the listener into this mini-community of athletes. You feel as if you were sitting in that barbershop waiting for your haircut. The cinematography and editing mimic a *cinéma vérité* style of swish pans and jump cuts. Even when highlights of Gervin doing his finger roll are edited into the commercial, we see them on a TV monitor within the frame as if the highlights were part of the flow of events in the barbershop. Here, the spectacle of basketball is the spectacle of community signified by the pleasure of spontaneous banter. It is spectacle as pure sociability. The commercial appellates us as part of this community – jiving, teasing, and participating in the verbal play of shared communal experience.

Nike *apropriates* Superfly *style for its logo.*

Just like you and me

While its advertising connects elite athletes to the *Nike* brand, it also creates space for the rest of us. *Nike* advertising celebrates transcendent values in ordinary people. Indeed, if all *Nike* did was to extol great athletes, it would probably find itself in a neck and neck race with the *Reebok*s of the industry. Instead, the *Nike swoosh* has come to stand for the athlete in all of us. This takes us back to what we have called *Nike's* **motivational discourses**. In the late 1980s, *Nike* ran a series of ads that spoke to "our" human spirit. The most engaging piece in this series featured an 80-year-old named Walt Stack jogging across the Golden Gate Bridge. His voice-over deadpans, "I run 17 miles every morning. People ask me how I keep my teeth from chattering in

"It's gotta be the shoes. Well, maybe it's the oysters."

the winter time. I leave them in my locker." Another low-key ad in this series followed a woman running up a steep hill as she speaks to us, "A few years ago I would have had trouble walking up this hill. I smoked. I drank. I was fat. I didn't do a lick of exercise in my life. So I started jogging. Who says you can't run away from your problems." Title cards on the screen identify her as "Priscilla Welch. Winner, New York Marathon at age 42." There is no razzle-dazzle here, only the mundane linked quietly to an extraordinary accomplishment. *Nike* celebrates the heroic potential in all of us. During the 1995 All-Star Game *Nike* also ran a commercial titled "Kids and Kubs" about a softball team composed of players over 75 years old. George Bakewell, a 101-year-old, gets a base hit and then quips, " It's gotta be the shoes. Well, maybe it's the oysters." No one seems to be excluded from participating. Every athletic accomplishment is worthy of note. *Nike* positions sport as a non-exclusionary space where achievement, satisfaction and sociability can flower. Individual achievement, however, is not merely a signified but a sig- nifier. It stands for the human spirit, for universal humanism, for partici- pating in the human community in general. Perhaps this is only an overused sports cliché, but it is a very powerful one. With its "Just do it" tagline and its representations *Nike* has fostered increased participation in sport as well as increased self-esteem and self-confidence.

Ads such as these are why *Nike* is so often praised for messages of empowerment. When *Wieden & Kennedy* chose to use John Lennon's song "Instant Karma" to frame one of its everyone-plays TV ads, the agency did so because the stirring lyric "We all shine on" perfectly framed the ethos of sport *Nike* wanted to convey. In ads like this, and the "Time of Hope" ad discussed below, *Nike* locates itself as the Human Spirit that infuses and inspires a community of play and satisfaction. In these ads, sport is pre- sented as an end in itself, and not as a means to other ends (like money, fame, and privilege). It is no accident that *Nike's* competitors have begun to copy this approach. *Reebok's* 1995 woman's campaign offers an explicit pan- humanist valuation of persons: "There is an athlete within all of us." This represents a partial return to the middle class ideals of amateur sport circa 1900 when the Greek value of sport was seen as offering an arena in which individual human character could be shaped to its highest ends in contrast to commercialized and professionalized sports.

TRANSCENDENCE IN THE HUMAN COMMUNITY

An aesthetic referent for classic humanism is *The Family of Man*, an exhibi- tion created by Edward Steichen for the Museum of Modern Art in 1955.[19] Composed of 503 photographs from 68 countries covering approximately a 100 year period, it was organized around universals – death, gestures (smiles, tears), family relations, play, work, war. *The Family of Man* constructed human essence based on participation in these experiences. We are born, we work, we play, we cry, we laugh, and we die. Ergo we are human.

As corporations like *Nike* participate in the global order they search for both new markets and new resources of production (cheaper labor). In this context, advertising cannot just sell products, it must also legitimate the corporate sponsor as a source of meaning. Classical humanism modeled after *The Family of Man* exhibition offers **a stylistic look** which positions the corporation as global, as pan-human, as multicultural. *Wieden & Kennedy* has embellished the *Nike* philosophy around this look and the philosophy of classical humanism. In the P.L.A.Y. and "Time of Hope" ad campaigns, differences between people in *Nike*'s world are reduced to representations of the common ability in all of us to prevail over our circumstances. *Nike* enjoins viewers not to capitulate to the injustices of circumstance and difference (being poor, black, a woman, or confined to a wheelchair).

The "Time of Hope" ad compiled images drawn from *Nike*'s stock of commercials that mix age, gender, race, amateur and professional athletes. A medley of sports activities compose the ad – baseball, track, volleyball, soccer, basketball, wheelchair marathon, and bicycling. The ad's first sequence of images is kinetic, each scene an action waiting to be completed — a boy preparing to swing a bat, a playground basketball player about to dunk, runners starting a race. The concluding sequence of cuts offers corresponding finishing actions – a dunk, Ken Griffey hitting a baseball, a wheelchair athlete crossing the finish line. Children tend to be shown in less organized play activities, while adults are involved in organized games. "A Time of Hope" celebrates a social democracy where there exists no apparent hierarchy of importance. Parity is created between the amateur and the professional, the child and the adult – each represented as equally important. For example, the match cut shown here pairs Barkley pulling down a rebound with a young girl trying to momentarily balance a basketball on her head.

Amid the flow of images shown in this inspirational sequence, a *Nike* shoe appears but once, approximately 20 seconds into the ad. Hence, this does not register as a product ad, but as *Nike*'s celebration of the true meanings of sports etched across faces and bodies – meanings of intensity and determination, of awe and enjoyment. Using a telephoto lens to blur the background heightens the expressivity of the human face and eyes with their expressions of pleasure, determination, and intensity. Because the ad represents a celebration of the human will, the background doesn't matter; it disappears, whether it is a stadium or the street or a ghetto. The black and white ad uses hyperreal techniques including jump cuts, swish pans, and staccato editing to intermix these poignant images with frames of heavily scratched high contrast film that momentarily burst between the images. As noted earlier, these scratches were intended to signify the opposite of soft drink ads that imply the acquisition of traits magically through the product image. The scratches signify a "rawer, edgier" tone and visually provoke

and amplify the ad's feeling of intensity. The music, cobbled together from several cuts by a band called Buffalo Tom, supports this feeling and builds throughout. The copy that appears across the screen celebrates these moments:

When all that is BETTER
is before us.
A time of HOPE.
HOPE fastened to a GAME.
HOPE not so much to be
the Best to ever play the Game,
But simply to stay in the game.
And RIDE it
WHEREVER it goes.
JUST DO IT.

Throughout, *Nike* celebrates participation over success. Yet make no mistake, this ad continues to build *Nike*'s sign value, by maintaining a tension between the *Nike* stable of star athletes (Barkley, Griffey, Jordan) and the everyday player. Just as the screen reads "Hope not so much to be the Best to ever play the game, But simply to stay in the game," "the Best" appears across a closeup of Michael Jordan.

The emotional texture of *Nike*'s inspirational ads separates them from competitors. This ad overflows with a sense of genuine humanity. *Nike* hails each viewer personally through the mix of images, music, and technique that inspires the viewer to feel as if he or she can "just do it." Although *Nike* commercials encourage viewers to identify with its celebrity athletes, they also hail viewers as potentially sharing the same heroic traits of determination, hard work, and desire to go beyond one's personal limits. *Nike* advertising hails us to be part of the universal community of athletes. They include anyone who perceives her/himself as an athlete or a potential athlete. The *Nike* community is for everyone who demonstrates athletic determination. It is not the athlete that *Nike* so well signifies but the athletic spirit. In this sense *Nike* has tapped into the mythology of sport in ways which its competitors have at best occasionally imitated. This appellation method is populist and inclusive. Depicting HOPE fastened to a GAME suggests a better future when we allow people to realize themselves through sport. While *Nike* preaches an anti-elitist humanism, it also appeals to an almost-Nietzschean will to power as a route to an emergent self – is this everyman a superman or is this superman in everyman?

It's nice to be addressed this way, particularly in an advertising and celebrity culture which continually positions viewers in terms of "abuse value, cynical seduction and chronic humiliation."[20] Throughout the ad, the faces of children register the joys of sport. Images such as a small boy wearing

a miniature Detroit Tigers uniform or a Dominican child with his arm around a pal's shoulder connote a classic humanism or *Nike*'s version of *The Family of Man*. This ad provides viewers with the space in which to feel good about one another without actually having to socialize with others. The mixture of realism and romance in this video album tugs at deeply frustrated desires to realize our species being – our essence realized socially. The ad closes on this utopian desire.

A recurrent theme in *Nike* ads is this decontextualized humanism – the stress placed on an abstract, but universal right of men, women, and children to sports and play. This resonates with Phil Knight's view that "Access to play should be a kid's inalienable right." If celebration of this utopian moment is *Nike*'s primary ideological achievement, so also then, its central tendency to abstract rather than contextualize highlights the greatest weakness of *Nike*'s social and cultural philosophy of sports. For what good is a guarantee of an abstract right in a society governed by the full commodification of resources?

To universalize an experience it must be decontextualized – removed from time and place, disconnected from socio-historical context – and then recontextualized around "chosen" universals. *The Family of Man* removed dates. The activity in each frame was given meaning by its shared similarity with adjacent photographs. Biblical, Native American, and literary quotes, also decontextualized, helped construct the overall themes of the exhibit. Universality was reduced to a maxim. The photographic traces of historical detail were made to signify the universal existential qualities of being human.

How easily the logic of advertising parallels this process: (1) select signifieds; (2) decontextualize them from their historical moments; (3) recontextualize each as a signifier in relation to other decontextualized signifiers; (4) frame these with a slogan. As Berger and Mohr note: "All photographs are ambiguous. All photographs have been taken out of a continuity … Discontinuity always produces ambiguity."[21] Decontextualization is the nature of the medium. When this is understood, we must ask: how are images framed? what motivates their assemblage? what surplus meanings do these encodings give rise to?

Nike uses a photographic style which idealizes individuals. It mixes realism with classicism – ghetto landscapes with low angle shots of soaring basketball players, wheelchair athletes racing down a curved hill, impoverished children smiling to the pleasure of play. Alienation and affliction are the background for the celebration of the human spirit. Subjectivity is removed from existential conditions (time and place) and reframed in relation to a human essence – signifiers of alienation plus signifiers of determination equals transcendence. And it is sport (play) which is the activity which provides the space for transcendence. As long as one stays in the game, life has meaning. One participates in the human community defined by the characteristic that makes us human, the ability to transcend.

The blurred backgrounds in ads like "A Time of Hope" obscure the specificity of time and place. This ad highlighted the conventions of abstraction that underlie classical humanism, erasing contextual features in the interest of stressing a universal human essence. Barthes criticized the classic humanist perspective for removing the realm of experience from the flow of history.

> Everything here, the content and appeal of the pictures, the discourse which justifies them, aims to suppress the determining weight of History: we are held back at the surface of an identity, prevented precisely by sentimentality from penetrating into this ulterior zone of human behavior where historical alienation introduces some "differences" which we shall here quite simply call "injustices".[22]

This kind of abstraction is also a defining mark of modern consumer-goods advertising premised on an assumption of abstract consumption that poses relationships between products and product-mediated characteristics as potentially uniform, rather than as contingent on the biographical positions of individual consumers.

NOTES AND REFERENCES

1. Donald R. Katz, *Just Do It: the Nike Spirit in the Corporate World* (Random House, New York, 1994), p. 466.
2. Christopher Lasch, *The Culture of Narcissism: American Life in the Age of Diminishing Expectations* (Warner, New York, 1979).
3. Philip Martin, "Sport's mostly just entertainment, despite the earnest ad campaigns," *Arkansas Democrat-Gazette,* November 5 1995, p. 1E.
4. Gene Yasuda, "Making Penny a Shoe-Biz Star," *The Orlando Sentinel,* October 29 1995, p. A1.
5. Ibid.
6. David L. Andrews, "The facts of Michael Jordan's blackness: excavating a floating racial signifier," *Sociology of Sports Journal*, 13 (1996), p. 140.
7. Nelson George, "Rare Jordan," *Essence*, 27, 7 (November 1 1995), p. 106.
8. Ibid., p. 106.
9. Michael Dyson, *Between God and Gangsta Rap* (Oxford University Press, New York, 1996), p. 58.
10. Ibid.
11. Katz, *Just Do It*, p. 6.
12. Judith Williamson, *Decoding Advertisements* (Marion Boyars, London, 1978), p. 24.
13. Yasuda, "Making Penny a shoe-biz star," p. A1.
14. Kenneth Labich, "Nike vs. Reebok: a battle for hearts, minds, and feet," *Fortune,* September 18 1995, pp. 90ff.
15. Williamson, *Decoding Advertisements*, p. 71.
16. Ibid.
17. Robert Bellah, Richard Madsen, William M. Sullivan, Ann Swidler, and Steven M. Tipton, *Habits of the Heart: Individualism and Commitment in American Life* (Harper, New York, 1985).

18. C. Wright Mills, *White Collar: The American Middle Class* (Oxford University Press, New York, 1956).

19. Edward Steichen, *The Family of Man* (The Museum of Modern Art, New York, 1955).

20. Arthur Kroker and Michael Weinstein, *Data Trash: The Theory of the Virtual Class* (St Martin's Press, New York, 1994).

21. John Berger and Jean Mohr, *Another Way of Looking* (Pantheon, New York, 1982), p. 91.

22. Roland Barthes, *Mythologies*, translated by Annette Lavers (Hill and Wang, New York, 1972), p. 101.

4.
REFLEXIVITY AND IRREVERENCE

CONSTRUCTING IRREVERENCE AND SIGN VALUE

Nike's public image and corporate persona has been shaped by its ability to distance itself from the "dirty" side of commercialization. This distance has been achieved, in part, via an advertising style that engages in ironic winking, humor, irreverence, and even cynicism. *Nike* advertising characterized by these elements is heavily media referential. This chapter explores *Nike*'s use of self-conscious irreverence to construct both its viewers and itself as savvy media-literate subjects.

From 1972 to 1987, *Nike* grew with only modest reliance on advertising. Towards the end of this first major growth swing, *Nike* fell into a period of disarray and stagnation. Then, the company shifted its advertising to *Wieden & Kennedy.* From 1987 to 1993 *Nike* rose to dominance within the booming athletic footwear industry. Reputedly, on his first meeting with Dan Wieden, Phil Knight introduced himself by saying, "I'm Phil Knight and I hate advertising."[1] This perhaps apocryphal story gets at the key to *Nike*'s construction of their commodity sign. Wieden understood the imperative behind this statement, because his agency was based precisely in opposition to the tradition of American broadcast advertising that predominated from the 1950s through the mid 1980s. In his full-length organizational biography of the *Wieden & Kennedy* agency, Randall Rothenberg has documented how it evolved as a

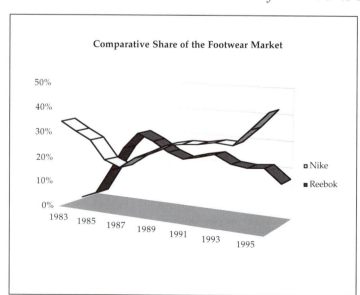

Comparative Share of the Footwear Market

West Coast advertising agency in opposition to the metropolitan domination of the industry by large New York and Chicago agencies.[2] This distaste for advertising formulas would emerge as one axis of the *Nike* advertising aesthetic. In addition to its inspirational and motivational themes, *Nike* cultivated an ironic and reflexive awareness about the role of ads in daily life. One analyst sums up *Nike*'s advertising appeal:

> … its success in tapping and communicating a consistent set of values that many people in the 1970s and 1980s identified with: hipness, irreverence, individualism, narcissism, self-improvement, gender equality, racial equality, competitiveness, and health.[3]

Campaigns starring Michael Jordan and Spike Lee, and Bo Jackson (the "Bo knows" series of commercials) in the late 1980s and early 1990s established *Nike*'s *swoosh* logo as the premiere sign in the consumer marketplace. And the corresponding *Nike* slogan, "Just do it," became a part of the language of everyday life. These campaigns relied heavily on a self-reflexive and media-referential attitude that projected a sense of humor about themselves and about advertising in general. They were irreverent and self-effacing. As *Nike* officials like to point out, they want to communicate with their audience in ways that say "we don't take ourselves or our ads too seriously." *Nike* ads distinguished themselves from the crowd by raising criticisms of over-commercialized celebrities and the role of advertising in promoting the fetish of commodities where, like Barbie and Ken, objects seem to acquire a life of their own.

Nike's profile of self-awareness has developed over time through a range of ads that address the relationship between brand identity and consumer identity. In consumer advertising, the most familiar formula positions viewers to step into an imaginary mirror where they can look to find an imaginary self, a self made better by having this product and its image. Shoe ads, like fashion advertising, tended to appeal to viewers in terms of a desire to identify with athletic heroes, and every once in a while, a superhero like Michael Jordan. Hero identification figured large in *Nike*'s success during the late 1980s and early 1990s, when it not only had Jordan and Bo, but also Charles Barkley, David Robinson, and Andre Agassi. Jordan is the much-publicized king of advertising endorsements measured in dollars. In the over-rationalized calculations that scale the value of athletes as commodities for boosting the value of brands, Jordan scored an "athlete influence rating" of 4.46.[4] We treat such statistical constructs, no matter how absurd, of Jordan's endorsement value to advertisers as a measure of his capacity to generate sign value. Summaries of competitive sign values are reported annually in top ten lists such as the "Most Wanted Sports Spokespersons" and Michael Jordan has topped these lists since 1988.[4] *Nike* and its ad agency, *Wieden & Kennedy*, adroitly exploited Jordan's sign value, while balancing it against a growing indifference, and even resistance, toward advertising's general stress on wearing badges of popularity and finding identity in the commodities the consumer chooses.

As we have noted, *Nike*'s pairing of Spike Lee and Michael Jordan created a playful buffer zone to distance *Nike* from its own marketing agenda. As played by Spike Lee, Mars is the consummate fan, who in the movie *She's Gotta Have It* is so tight with his sneakers that he wears them during lovemaking.[6] Mars appreciates Jordan's greatness (whom he refers to as "Money" because Jordan is like money in the bank when it comes to making clutch shots with the game on the line). But the key to these ads was the knowing attitude that Mars brought about the nature of the advertisement itself: in one ad, he self-consciously interrupts what he is saying and yells out the window behind him, "Hey, shut up! I'm doing a commercial here." Mars also disrupts the usual assumptions about the relationship between celebrity endorsement and commodity fetishism. In one spot he repeatedly constructs an opposition between the shoes and Jordan's talents.

"This you can buy."

"You cannot do this."

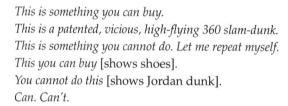

This is something you can buy.
This is a patented, vicious, high-flying 360 slam-dunk.
This is something you cannot do. Let me repeat myself.
This you can buy [shows shoes].
You cannot do this [shows Jordan dunk].
Can. Can't.

Not surprisingly, this ad has been widely mimicked in the last few years: today, *Starter* (branded athletic wear) and *Sprite* (soft drink) have built campaigns that humorously show how consuming their product will, big surprise, not actually give you the ability to dunk, even symbolically. The failed, but humorous, effort at dunking has become nearly as common in today's advertising as was the effortless dunk five years ago.

In advertising today there is a tension between the need for an image that stands out and the impulse to copy the most popular styles and strategies. *Nike*'s willingness to engage in self-conscious criticism of consumerism is no longer a novel advertising strategy, when *Sprite* routinely spoofs brands that promote image fetishism in their "Image is Nothing" campaign. This style of advertising can be called "anti-advertising," insofar as it calls attention to the generic practices of advertising itself. *Sprite*'s parody of conventional soft-drink ads is illustrative. The ad begins with a beach party scene and a jingle, "Just open up a Jooky, it's a party in a can. It's so fun and fruity you'll be dancin' in the sand … Jooky, Jooky, it's a party in a can." As the camera pulls back to reveal two stoned teens watching this commercial on TV, they pop open a couple of cans and when nothing happens, one observes, "Oh man, mine's busted."

While *Nike*'s critical, winking ads self-consciously express the tension between *Nike*'s entertainment persona and *Nike*'s authenticity persona, they also illustrate how advertisers learned to cater to viewers finding pleasure in the act of deciphering the ad itself. *Nike* shares jokes with its viewers based on familiarity with pop culture, and crucially, with its own previous ads. Viewers who appreciate *Nike* commercials usually refer to the pleasure of "getting the joke." *Nike*'s ads flatter these viewers, hailing them as part of a select group who can decipher the wry meta-media humor embedded in the ad.

Obvious exaggeration and self-parody are joined to a sense of playful irreverence in such *Nike* ads. In one ad featuring Deion Sanders and Jerry Jones (owner of the Dallas Cowboys), two of the most blatantly mercenary figures in contemporary sports, Jones yells into a phone, "I don't care what it takes. You get me Deion." Switzer, the Dallas Cowboys coach, asks, "Deion are you ready?" As he grabs his helmet and enters the game, Sanders declares, "I was born ready." When Sanders intercepts the ball and runs past cheerleaders for a touchdown, Jones exclaims, "Hot dang! If I had 11 men like that I could rule the world." He looks out over a crowd holding a banner with a *swoosh* on it. This commercial parodies the spectacle and its formulas. Each character is introduced with titles – Jerry Jones as J.J. THE OWNER, Barry Switzer as THE COACH, Deion Sanders as DEION, and Kevin Smith as THE GIPPER (a reference to Notre Dame football folklore when the only thing that mattered was the game). The dialogue is overstated, while the background score is the triumphant Muzac associated with sports highlight films. Likewise, the shots signify the spectacle, not the game – cheerleaders, the electronic scoreboard, the owner, Deion the Star, and even the *Nike* *swoosh* as a Fascist banner. *Nike* does not disguise the spectacle, but presents it in the form of intentional parody.

Nike advertising is marked by a unity of opposites: tensions between irreverence and inspiration, between humble, self-deprecating celebrity superstars and everyperson athletes. But in the ads discussed above there is no sense of a *Nike* community constructed on the screen; here the only *Nike* community that *Nike* seeks to construct is a community of viewers who identify with *Nike* because of the pleasure of its texts. *Nike* ads consistently joke about its logo and its slogan, **as if to say (metacommunicate)**, "our primary message is still that the capacity to change and develop as a person must come from you. Hey we just sell good shoes with a hip attitude and a sense of humor."

The ironic winking encourages reflexivity about the relationship between advertising and *Nike*, a self-effacing company with a sense of humor that doesn't take itself too seriously. *Nike* ads are willing to poke fun at *Nike* and its participation in the spectacle. In this regard, a recurring feature of *Nike* advertising is its willingness to construct cartoon-like caricatures of its own advertising. *Wieden & Kennedy* revisited this technique in 1996 campaigns

In another commercial Nike *satirizes owner/player relationships. This commercial appropriates both the style and ideology of the Coen brothers' film* The Hudsucker Proxy *to poke fun at the way in which crude capitalistic relationships dominate baseball and other professional sports.*

for both Penny Hardaway and Ken Griffey. When *Wieden & Kennedy* briefly brought the two campaigns together in an ad that features Little Penny commenting on the tongue-in-cheek "Griffey for President" campaign, *Nike* once again metacommunicated to its audience that it does not take itself too seriously. The ad opens with a TV screen and an overlay image of Ken Griffey against the red and white stripes of the flag. Snippets of the solemn reverential announcer's voice frequently used in political campaign ads can be heard, "Ken Griffey Jr, athlete ..." The voice of Little Penny cuts in, "Hey, Nick, Penny, this is a Griffey for President commercial." Little Penny, Nick Anderson, and Penny Hardaway are seated on a couch as the ventriloquist dummy yaks it up about the "Griffey for President" campaign. Nick and Penny appear indifferent to both the ad and Little Penny's commentary. Nick fidgets uncomfortably on the couch as he tries to shield himself from Little Penny's monologue with the *Slam* magazine he's holding. Penny looks away in an obviously pained look of irritation by Little Penny's rant, "You know there's more to life than sports. Man, there's politics."

The ad cuts back to the television set and a scene from the "Griffey for President" commercial features the iconography of red and white stripes overlaying a map of America with yet another overlay of Ken Griffey Jr. swinging the bat. A campaign slogan on the screen reads "CARRY a 31 oz. BAT" while the voice-over is thick with hero worship, "... is a fabulous American hero." Little Penny interrupts again, "He's got some interestin' ideas about that flat tax. Check it out." Back to the TV, Griffey is shown standing alongside the Mariner Moose mascot as the reportorial voice continues, "... picked Mariner Moose as a running mate ..." (the sound volume trails off) "... in consideration of animal rights ..." The camera cuts back to Little Penny's face as his jaw drops open and eyes widen in a look of astonished dismay. Little Penny: "Now that Moose could be a liability. Hey, hey, I tell you what. I should be his running mate. I mean that's a good job. You don't gotta do squat!" Finally, Nick Anderson has had enough. He gets up in disgust, tossing down his magazine and walking away. But Little Penny never stops: "Come on Nick. Power to the people! Stick it to the man! No nukes! Save the whales!" The ad closes with Penny at one end of couch gesturing in embarrassment and disbelief at Little Penny spouting politically correct slogans minus any sense of conviction. Across the scene, centered between the two of them, appears the *swoosh*.

We are not suggesting this ad offers a serious critique of mainstream politics, though it does offer elements of criticism in which **politics** has been reduced to an empty signifier, figuratively encompassing nothing more than hot air. The ad caricatures the spectacle of media politics in such an exaggerated way that viewers are unlikely to take the critique seriously. Though the ad aims at skewering the hollowness of political sloganeering and campaigning, it also reveals its own athletes as passively disinterested in public issues. When the *swoosh* appears at the end, it does not attach itself to the athletes or to shoes, but to the overall attitude of cynical irreverence that *Nike* has constructed. We are back to the knowing wink, which has been of crucial importance in elevating the overall sign value of the *swoosh*.

THE ABSENCE OF THE COMMODITY

Nike has established its sign, its slogan, its style, and its attitude to the degree that the shoe as either a material object or a commodity is absent. The featured item in *Nike* ads is the sign, the logo – the *swoosh*. The *swoosh*, which began as an arbitrary drawing which possessed no intrinsic meaning whatsoever, has grown to the point that it now expresses a philosophy, and is viewed as projecting a multidimensional personality.

The liberation *Nike* offers often appears as if it is available to all who believe and act in the *Nike* spirit. In the late 1980s, when the "Just do it" slogan was starting to hum along, a poster, modeled after a print ad, went up in health clubs and many workplaces. It spoke to the experience and feeling of the pure moment of freedom in a class-based society. "There are clubs you can't belong to. Neighborhoods you can't live in. Schools you can't get into," reads the text above a runner on a deserted country road. "But the roads are always open. JUST DO IT."

Even as the inequalities of social class are acknowledged, both the economic relations of work and the money aspects of consumption disappear from view; like the hours spent working at someone else's discretion to make enough money to buy some stylin' *Nikes*. Absent is the price tag for *Nike*'s "Just do it." To be sure, many *Nike* ads aim at something more than "just buy our shoes." The injunction to run, to work out the body, is also an injunction against giving in to the unfairness of inequality.

Nike ads often hail viewers at a metacommunicative level about questions of authenticity and sincerity. The overt sell, the hard sell, compromises each of these meanings. When the commodity itself is removed from view, trust goes up. *Nike* offers viewers the appearance of something to believe in, something that lies deeper than a commodity surface. This is why irreverence and inspiration go together in *Nike* ads: the inspirational appeal works best when it seems less motivated by crass commercialism, and the irreverent

Where's the swoosh?

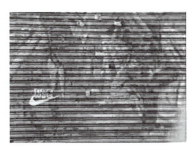

self-reflexivity diminishes culpability for participating in the parade of commodities.

In a 1994 *Nike* series of spots run in New York City the only clue indicating that one was watching a *Nike* ad was the minimalist presence of their logo somewhere in the physical environment. One ad surveyed an open manhole with the "logo placed as graffiti on a barrier," while the logo appeared in other ads on a chain link fence and on an anti-theft security gate that denoted a "neighborhood bodega."[7] *Nike* has so thoroughly established its sign, the *swoosh*, with its audience, that viewers need only see the *swoosh* in the background to recognize these as *Nike* commercials. In one commercial entitled "Joe Regular," the foreground consists of the anonymous voice-over of a young "brother" describing the pleasure and the satisfaction he gets from playing playground hoops. This is *Nike*'s imagery of unalienated and uncommodified activity where competition has only to do with a personal sense of self-confidence and worth. In fact, these hardly seem to be commercials. What are they selling? By shedding the usual formulas of selling a commodity self, these ads offer an impression of *Nike* as sharing and supporting the love of the game expressed in the authentic voices of those who play.

Nike raises concerns about the "pollution" of sporting activity in the wake of the commodity form. *Nike* has established itself as the pre-eminent commodity sign because of the way it handles this contradiction between the commodification of sport that has made *Nike* very wealthy, and the *Nike* moral vision of sport as an anchor for moral individualism today. Routinely, media-literate consumers are exposed to stories and headlines such as, "Hot Athletes and Cold Cash; Image Matters as Much as Winning in the Celebrity Endorsement Game."[8] It is hard to ignore this persistent theme in contemporary sports. *Nike* succeeds because compared to the advertising of its chief rival, *Reebok*, *Nike* invariably comes out with a higher authenticity quotient. John Boulter, *Reebok*'s vice president for global marketing, inadvertently confirms that *Reebok* walks the more obvious commodity route: "We look for top performance, but also good people with pleasant personalities who appeal in all walks of life." It thus seems implausible that *Reebok* could successfully contest *Nike*'s goal-oriented slogan "Just do it" even when it mimics *Nike*'s appeal with a slogan such as "Pure Athletics Plus Humanity."

Most recently, the absence of the commodity has been visible in the *Nike* P.L.A.Y. campaign. The P.L.A.Y. campaign leveraged *Nike*'s powerful symbolic presence built up by years of playful advertising to create ads that do not refer to their shoe products. Jeff Jensen of *Advertising Age* observed that:

> ... the P.L.A.Y. campaign underscores the ubiquity of *Nike*, a name that has become virtually synonymous with the category it continues to dominate. The position allows *Nike* to execute ads that entertain, preach and do

anything else but sell product. "*Nike* has reached such a comfortable and powerful position that they don't have to use their advertising to define their products, and that's a position an agency wants to be in. That's when they do their best work," said Richard Silverstein, co-chairman and co-creative director at *Goodby, Berlin, and Silverstein*, San Francisco.[9]

Indeed, with the P.L.A.Y. campaign, *Wieden & Kennedy* devoted themselves entirely to building up the broader symbolic associations of the *Nike swoosh*: its sign value!

MEDIA-REFERENTIAL IRREVERENCE

While *Wieden & Kennedy* and *Nike* may specialize in "authenticity," their work also epitomizes an emerging media-referential knowingness. On the one hand, *Nike*'s success with its sign, the *swoosh*, has been rooted in its ability to stake itself better than any other marketer to themes of authenticity. And yet, *Nike* is even, as we shall see, willing to desecrate its own logo. This has given its voice credibility, and makes it likable because nothing seems sacred to *Nike*, not even its most precious commodity – the *swoosh* sign. This might explain why *Wieden & Kennedy* would experiment with William Burroughs in the style of the disembodied Max Headroom as a television-based talking head in *Nike* ads for the Air Max shoe line – the same William Burroughs whose biography included the anti-bourgeois novel, *Naked Lunch*, heroin use, mental illness, and manslaughter. So much advertising offers a saccharine and moralizing account of our social world that it makes sense to offer a cynical option: express your alienation by wearing badges endorsed by "cult figures" who signify an anti-authoritarian rebelliousness. To avoid the imagery of prepackaged individuality that comes with most commodities, "rebel advertising" offers signifiers of alienation. This is the tendency that Herbert Marcuse most feared about transforming culture into commodities in his 1964 classic *One-Dimensional Man*: the ability to incorporate, and thereby silence, all forms of criticism.[10] Leslie Savan observes that "the rebellion we have known is usually ground to the fine powder of irony and added ..." back into our images of consumption.

> Consumer culture has always suborned its critics; Lou Reed and Devo have done commercials for *Honda*, as Laurie Anderson has for *Reebok* and Norman Mailer has for the *Trump Shuttle*. But now the realization that nothing threatens the system has freed advertising to exploit even the most marginal elements of society ...Which explains why William Burroughs, everybody's favorite beat poet/heroin addict/crazed gun freak, is on TV flacking product for a major corp. OK, the corporation is *Nike*, and that makes it sound ... cooler. But then, that's what they pay people like Burroughs to encourage you to think. The author appears, of course, with "distance" – his face flashes on various TV

Nike's high tech guru, William Burroughs. "The purpose of technology is not to confuse the brain but to serve the body."

monitors that bounce around in scenes of *Nike* athletes pumping up. From somewhere within his trademark rumpled gray suit, gray fedora, and gaunt gray face, Burroughs's gravel-gray bark of a voice is saying words that sound like his own: "Hey, I'm talking to you," he starts right in. "The purpose of technology is not to confuse the brain but to serve the body. To make life easier. To make anything, anything possible … It's the opening of the door. It's the coming of new technology. Holy Cow!" Burroughs croaks, as a baseball player slides in to spike him on another monitor. "Serve the body. New and weird."[11]

Hopper plays a crazed ref who sniffs Bruce Smith's shoe.

In Charles Barkley *Nike* found an intelligent "bad boy," a celebrity who refused to play according to the constraints of dominant social ideologies. *Nike* also has constructed Dennis Hopper and Dennis Rodman as Bad Boys who refuse to play strictly by the rules. Each campaign focuses on a deviant media character as a way of differentiating itself. Consider the Dennis Hopper campaign in which Hopper plays a whacked-out former football referee obsessed with the game and with a fetish for sniffing the shoes of professional football players. The Hopper character draws on his film persona (*Blue Velvet, River's Edge, Easy Rider, Red Rock West*), although Hopper's subsequent characterization of madness in the film *Speed* included a reference to his *Nike* campaign role, sending the arrow of referential appropriation in the opposite direction. Borrowing on Hopper's film characters also invites a disruption of the usual "gaze" in advertising. In the *Nike* ads Hopper stares directly at the camera. Because his gaze is held inappropriately long, it becomes the "insane gaze" based on the belief that the eyes convey our mental state. In a Superbowl ad that mimicked *Patton* (the movie), Hopper's eyeballs shift back and forth almost as self-parody. The intertextual playfulness of these ads, along with the comic moments of the intense gaze played to maximum affect, drew viewers into these advertising texts, demanding that they become active interpreters of the ads' meanings. The Dennis Hopper ads were media-irreverent in how they positioned viewers on initial viewings to ask "what the hell is this?" When *Nike* ads feature Dennis Hopper and William Burroughs, they engage viewers in a tongue-in-cheek form of hero worship for a media-literate audience.

In Speed *Hopper is a mad bomber who watches football games as he toys with a bus load of hostages.*

Return for a moment to Hopper taking such fetish pleasure in the shoe – caressing it, smelling it. While ads encourage us to love commodities, they rarely want to signify idealized consumers as obsessively neurotic in their relationship to that object. The image of a wild-eyed Dennis Hopper getting pleasure from smelling pro football stars' *Nike* shoes is, at the very least, an ambivalent image open to many interpretations. *Nike* drew on Hopper to signify what they termed "weird intensity" as the sign correlative of their new football shoe. The manner chosen to signify this carried with it, perhaps inadvertently, a stress on anti-value as a new source of sign value.

In fact, *Nike* appears to re-mark its own *swoosh* sign at the end of the Hopper ads by making the background appear to be a rippling piece of raw meat. Now whether the makers of this ad sought to signify raw meat we do not know. What we do know is that the rippling looks that way to us, and that this has the effect of distorting the shape and look of the *swoosh*. The question we are asking is, does this have any impact on how viewers might interpret this momentary distortion of the *swoosh*. We earlier spoke of *Nike*'s use of the *swoosh* to both punctuate and sign their work. Those who work at *Nike* believe that *Nike* stands for excellent products attuned to the needs of athletes. And yet, in their advertising, these new leaders in the political economy of sign value seem to recognize that they must **appear to profane** their own sign value if they are to reproduce and maintain the value of that sign.

The postmodern twist to advertising sports blurs the boundaries between advertising and entertainment. *Nike*'s brand of media-referential irreverence usually blends a "sliver of pop culture" with athletics and "puts in the *Nike swoosh* to make it hip."[12] This is most often accomplished by setting up tongue-in-cheek encounters between athletes and the iconography of pop culture (Godzilla, Bugs Bunny, Santa Claus, TV talk shows, and Vegas reviews). Another dimension of the ads featuring Hopper, Spike and Mike, Bo, Barkley, and Rodman is that they are written to be comic. Some are elaborate one-liners. Others wryly play on the personality of the star in question. The crazed ref character is meant to be no more than a humorous depiction of the "fanatical and passionate fan's love of the game" said a *Nike* spokesperson. But, push too far and someone is bound to find it morally offensive. Hopper's portrayal as the sleepless and obsessive football fanatic offended advocates of the mentally ill.

The sight of Dennis Rodman, the pierced and tattooed basketball tough-guy, bullying Santa Claus played even more poorly with the public, offending both the black bourgeoisie and the suburban middle class.[13] Such are the perils involved with mixing concoctions of athletics and pop culture that try too hard to be irreverent. Trying too hard to be hip is decidedly unhip in this culture. Those who are caught trying to be hip are labeled *poseurs*. Both the Rodman Santa Claus ad (not a *Wieden & Kennedy* ad) and the William Burroughs ad (which was a *Wieden & Kennedy* ad) presented overly-contrived efforts to be clever and hip. Such failures reveal the aesthetic and economic grain of *Wieden & Kennedy*'s success with the *Nike* advertising account. The agency provides broad space for its creative people to fail. Unlike most contemporary advertising agencies, *Wieden & Kennedy* does not over-rationalize their ads. Most *Nike* ads are not based on survey research, or pretest audience analyses, or focus groups. Amazingly, the *Wieden & Kennedy* writers we spoke to all indicated that they do not try to write for a specific audience. One writer responded to our question by asking, "How would I know what a 14-year-old kid is thinking?" *Wieden & Kennedy* is an agency steeped in a distaste for the stale advertising conventions that dominated American advertising from the 1960s through the 1990s. While you can never try too hard at sports and athletics in the world of *Nike*, trying too hard in the

The swoosh *appears in many forms. Here,* Nike *profanes its own sign. Multiple uses of the* swoosh *allow consumers to choose the* swoosh *that best represents their identities.*

advertising industry is, Dan Wieden believes, the kiss of death. In the world of advertising today, if a sponsor appears to chase after authenticity then it will likely be perceived as inauthentic.

THE POLITICS OF IRREVERENCE

A few years ago *Nike* ran the famous Charles Barkley ad in which he issued a cautionary edict about expecting professional athletes to function effectively as role models. In his frank, curmudgeonly way, Barkley pointedly directs his thoughts at the camera. Though he is paid as a basketball mercenary "to wreak havoc" on the court and dunk with authority, dunking and parenting have nothing to do with one another.

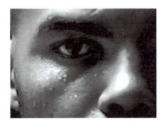

I am not a role model
I am not paid to be a role model.
I am paid to wreak havoc on the basketball court.
Parents should be role models.
Just because I can dunk a basketball
doesn't mean I should raise your kids.

In challenging the idea that professional athletes have a public obligation to perform as role models for children, *Nike* touched too close to a core myth of media hegemony and controversy ensued. The newspaper and TV media were quick to take umbrage in their self-appointed role as defenders of the public moral well-being. This excerpt from the *San Francisco Chronicle* is illustrative of the moralizing that followed.

> … One day recently, Nate Ford, a 24-year-old athletic director at the San Francisco Boys and Girls Club, encouraged one of his teenage basketball players to be more of a leader, especially with the younger children.
> … The boy wanted no part of it.
> … "I don't need to be a role model," he said. "Charles Barkley said parents are role models. I don't have to be a role model until I have kids."
> … Barkley had made the statement on a *Nike* commercial.
> … Athletic footwear ads, particularly those from *Nike*, have become so popular and so sophisticated that their debuts on Super Bowl Sunday are sometimes the highlight of the telecast. Kids, especially, pay attention to the spots because the country's hippest sports heroes play the starring roles.[14]

Recounting the reception of Barkley's ad in the theater of the mainstream media hardly exhausts the possible political interpretations of the ad, though it does point to the most visible ideological response. Houston Baker imagines a very different response from what he conceptualizes as a black minority "counterpublic."

> Even when Charles Barkley says "I'm not a role model," black publicity responds with: "You are intended as a role model of media/consumer culture, Sir Charles. You are meant to convince us that you are not role-modeling, so that we, who have thoroughly discredited the notion of role models, will buy the products that you, Sir Charles, are being paid to hustle." The commercial may be regarded as dope on the street, but nobody black is buying the product simply because of Sir Charles' slickness in relationship to role-modeling. This shortlived commercial is simply one result. The actual wish for real forms of power can be thought of as a desire for counterauthority. Reading through the commercial is a form of rational and emotional resistance by marginal groups.[15]

While we have sociological doubts about just how widely shared this popular critique of advertising "dope" might be, neither are we particularly persuaded that *Nike* abused the public trust of sports spectatorship. But it is unimportant whether or not we find these reactions to Barkley's engagement of a "moral question" particularly persuasive. What is significant is that *Nike* placed a "morality" issue in the foreground rather than keeping it tacit in the background. Once the ad hit the videowaves, it elicited interpretations arranged around the politics of societal morality. Though questions concerning societal morality are routinely raised by politicians, religious leaders, the news media, and even talk shows designed to get ratings by offending moral sensibilities, such big serious questions are infrequently the subject of consumer-brand advertising

The ad's creators relished the letters of protest that it generated, delighted that they had stirred people to thought. It is easy to exaggerate this point, but in a sense *Nike* acted as a *provocateur* in sparking a public forum of debate. Of course, *Nike* is not the only such advertising *provocateur*. *Benetton* and *Calvin Klein* have been notable for their provocations, as they attempt to violate bourgeois taboos, with *Calvin Klein* focused on the erotic and *Benetton* on the moral/political. It is interesting that each of these lifestyle industry companies has pursued a path of moral and ideological provocation in pursuit of expanding their market shares and profits.

The "I am not a role model" ad illustrates a looming tension in the maturation of a consumer society. In the past, advertisers seldom strayed from the straight and narrow of middle class morality, wary of the price paid for too much negative publicity. Today, to get and hold the interest of their audiences, advertisers like those mentioned above feel compelled to transgress middle class moral shibboleths, while also acknowledging as self-consciously as possible the nature of the advertising agenda in which they are engaged. In this light, what if we read the Barkley ad as a *Nike* acknowledgment that its own advertising has unleashed a monster of hero worship? In a rare television advertising moment, it directly confronts a question that is otherwise repressed from advertising discourse because it is a Pandora's box. *Nike* did not apologize for its own role in the commodification process that shaped the problem to begin with, but instead pointed at parents for not taking responsibility for their children's values. Of course, an argument can also be made that *Nike* neatly skirted accepting responsibility for the ways in which it, like other prominent corporate advertisers, has the power to shape the frameworks that define how the public conceptualizes the relationship of hero worship to personal identity. Yet, if the masses are as savvy and distrustful as Baker's critique suggests, able to see through advertising's efforts at self-consciously using moral issues as a device to advance the amoral goals of commerce, then public cynicism will reign.

IN YOUR FACE CYNICISM

Most accounts of Phil Knight's leadership of *Nike* stress the delight he has taken in the "maverick" ways of *Nike* culture. *Wieden & Kennedy* gave voice to a public image of that "maverick" quality that Knight wanted to project. In *Wieden & Kennedy's* hands, "maverick" became "irreverence," a willingness to share ironic knowing winks. Theirs was an advertising sensibility that resonated with savvy, media-literate viewers. The Reagan era was a time during which audiences grew more and more distrustful of television, and for good reason because people had now experienced the use of television as a tool of the pure sell. And of course, Reagan's victories, achieved by way of media excess, epitomized the use of the alienated form of the television spectacle. *Wieden & Kennedy* found a way to talk to their audiences that acknowledged the false side of television commercialism. In this way, *Wieden & Kennedy* could say to the viewer in a metacommunicative way, "we share your distaste for advertising done the usual way; so as long as we have to do it, we'll do it in a way that doesn't insult you and you can have some fun with."

The *Nike* TV ad that best epitomizes the *Nike* genre of irreverent cynicism about sport as a spectacle teamed Bo Jackson with Denis Leary. After Bo Jackson suffered a career-threatening hip injury most observers speculated that *Nike* would abandon him as one of its celebrity athletes. Instead, *Nike* drew attention to Bo's injury and how diligent he was about rehabilitating his hip. The key to this ad was how *Nike* used Denis Leary to aggressively challenge the viewer's position as a spectator. Denis Leary has been described as "the fidgety, *Marlboro*-smoking, profanity-spewing, red-meat-eating, angry Everyman of the Apocalypse."[16] Leary opens the ad by aggressively snarling and barking at the viewer through a chain link fence.

Hey! No more questions about Bo's hip.
OK?
No more questions about football, baseball or advertising.
Shaddup!! You thought it was over. Wrong!

It ain't over till the hip socket sinks. OK?

So Bo's got a bum hip. So what? Look what he's doin' with it. He's hittin' the bike,
he's hittin' the weights. He's wearin' the shoes. As a matter of fact, he's in
the pool wearin' the shoes, ridin' the bike with a hundred and twenty pounds
of weights strapped to his neck.

OK?

And what are you and your good hip doing right now?

WATCHING COMMERCIALS!

I think you hear me knocking. And I think I'm coming in.

And I'm bringing Bo and his big bad hip with me.

Matching Leary's rapid-fire delivery is a swiftly moving sequence of
quick cuts of Bo-related images that look to be taken from one TV ad or
another. Obviously distorted scan lines traced across these images call attention to the media construction of Bo's TV character: TV images of Bo playing
football, baseball, hawking shoes, pumping iron, and working out. Once
again, the passivity of television advertising emerges as a central focus. In
one critical scene that corresponds to "No more questions about … advertising," Bo stands posed as a product shill, holding up the shoe with the caption on the screen beside him. Here, *Nike* mocks television advertising and
their own role in such advertising with a self-mocking cartoon that remarkably encapsulates what we call the "commodity sign." The image of Bo presenting the shoe is flanked on one side by the words "Bo knows" and on the
other side by "*Nike* is neat" to emphasize that most shoe advertising is about
joining the meaning of a celebrity sign with the endorsement of the brand.

In the world of television advertising circa 1993, this was an unexpected
diatribe that put viewers on their heels. Most of the time advertisers hail us
by flattering us. Not here. Leary derisively hails the viewer as a passive
derelict: "And what are you and your good hip doin' right now? WATCH-
ING COMMERCIALS!!!!!" When Leary berates the viewer for "watching
commercials!" he is attacking couch potatoes who are willing to dumbly
watch flashy, but empty, entertainment ads like *Nike*'s own Superbowl extravaganza featuring Michael Jordan and Bugs Bunny in Outer Space. But the
biggest jolt comes at the end when, glaring at us, Leary sharply raps his
knuckles against the glass screen that invisibly separates us. The sharp
knocks punctuate and focus Leary's diatribe, an aggressive and threatening
attitude that intends to intrude into our ordinarily protected, private
voyeuristic space. The last part of the ad is a caustic assault on the couch
potato who consumes commercials. In this way, *Nike* gets across a message
consistent with its long running tagline and sign: "Just do it." The negative
form of address actually provides *Nike* with another method of reinforcing
the overall meaning of its overarching commodity sign – the *swoosh* sign.
But a stark contrast is constructed here between the cartoon of shameless
hucksterism and the "reality" of Bo's unremitting workout regimen.

As Bo Jackson looks on, Leary
abuses the audience. Which do you
prefer? Cynical comic form of
address or formulaic flattery?

IRREVERENCE FEEDING CYNICISM

Judged by viewer enthusiasm, *Nike*'s more effective ads are also marked by a different tone of irreverence – a tone of playfulness. Viewers remark that this playfulness registers in how *Nike* presents its athletes. We have found that viewers still remember the playful, almost quirky, quality of the "Bo knows" ads, full of admittedly bad puns, and unexpected turns, such as pairing Bo Jackson with Bo Diddley and Sonny Bono. *Nike*'s playfulness is most evident in ads structured as media-referential jokes.

JAMES CARVILLE
Political Strategist

Griffey to run for President
Chooses Mariner Moose
as running mate

One senses an air of mischief along one axis of *Nike* advertising. Yet this playful irreverence on *Nike*'s part also hails a strain of cynicism in our culture today. Yeah, its ads tend to be irreverent, but they also call forth our most cynical and rebellious sentiments. In late 1995, *Nike* introduced its "Ken Griffey Jr for President" ad campaign, based on the far-fetched premise of baseball superstar Ken Griffey Jr as a presidential candidate. This campaign combined elements of playfulness, media-referentiality, and cynicism. One ad featured James Carville, political campaign strategist for Bill Clinton in 1992, intermixed with funk musician George Clinton, Phil Knight, and the rap artist Ice-T. Another of the *Nike* commercials had Carville analyzing how he might "spin" Griffey's home run trot for public relations purposes. Carville walks us through alternative political interpretations of Griffey's baseball trot, winking at the viewer all the way.

GEORGE CLINTON
Campaign Manager

ICE-T
Musician/Concerned Citizen

Why would *Nike* introduce a political campaign strategist into their advertising? We might also ask what is being advertised? Our answer is that the object being advertised is *Nike* as **an abstract entity**, or more precisely, the *swoosh* sign along with the slogan "Just do it." Perhaps this is why *Nike* would risk building an ad around the figure of James Carville: because the ad sells an attitude; a sensibility that doesn't take too seriously the times in which we live. The dialogue cleverly plays on double meanings that join together the subjects of politics and sports. The ad opens with Carville identified on screen as a "political strategist," observing that Griffey is the perfect candidate for the times, "people don't want someone coming out of left field. And they sure don't want someone who plays too far right. Griffey's in the center [field], perfectly positioned." Then it's George Clinton, identified on screen as "campaign manager," who applies the baseball metaphor to civic life: "In this country it's the bottom of the ninth, two outs, we're behind. We need Junior. We need a hit." The ad continues with Carville and Clinton drawing parallels between athletics and politics. Says Carville, "If you can hit an Orel Hershheiser slider, you can hit [*pause*] welfare reform."

PHIL KNIGHT
Nike Chairman

This *Nike* ad fashions a parody of the politics of soundbites, a commentary on the soundbites of politics. They playfully tweak the media codes and formulas of political advertising. Like so many other *Nike* ads, this one also has a penchant for including moments of self-reflexivity. Following the campaign promotions of Carville and Clinton, the camera cuts to Ice-T, the high-profile rap artist, identified on screen as a "Concerned citizen," who declares: "Man that Ken Griffey for President thing is a straight-up sell-out. Nothin' but a big marketing scheme." This is immediately followed by a scene of Phil Knight wearing dark sunglasses, and banging a *Nike* shoe on the table as he speaks. "This is not, I repeat NOT, a marketing scheme." In the midst of banging the shoe on the table he catches himself and carefully straightens the shoe so it can be seen as if on display. Though this scene lacks the subtlety and grace of *Nike*'s usual self-reflexive asides, it none the less points to the intentionality of *Nike*'s "knowing wink." While having Knight bang his shoe on the table in mock anger *à la* Nikita Khrushchev sets up a playful moment of intertextuality, the ensuing sequence of him self-consciously straightening out the shoe draws viewer awareness to *Nike*'s presence as a global sports marketer. Knight's denial of the "Griffey for President" campaign as a *Nike* marketing scam is set up by the pseudo-critique voiced by Ice-T. We might call this reflexivity-lite or sugar-coated reflexivity because it consists of a moment of reflexivity that does not yield a deeper critique, but is there solely for the purpose of poking fun at *Nike*.

So how does this kind of irreverent chuckle translate into a culture of cynicism? In the field of cultural studies a distinction is made between encoding and decoding. In this case the advertiser is doing the encoding and viewers may, or may not, be doing the decoding. Given the mass audience of the ad, there probably are multiple decodings or interpretations available in these ads. We are not suggesting that *Nike* intends to make its audience cynics. Rather, we believe the background understandings necessary to setting up this elaborate joke involve heavy doses of political irony, or as Leslie Savan put it, "irony ground into a fine powder and added to our feed." For example, the viewer who recognizes that Carville is President Clinton's campaign director will not likely miss the fact that Carville's voice drips with irony and cynicism in the final lines of the ad. After an interviewer asks from off camera, "Don't you have to be 35 to be President?" Carville grins and drawls in reply, "Well that's what the Constitution says. [*ironic pause*] I mean if you're gone pay attention to that kind of stuff." The ad simply offers a quick laugh, one premised on a broad sense of politicians as slick weasels and politics as the art of spectacle and opportunism. The ad is further premised on the **display** of acting on the part of Ice-T and Phil Knight. The viewer is invited **to see through** their performances, to recognize that these are make-believe moments of reflexivity. Viewers can both laugh at these scenes, while also recognizing just how cynically motivated they appear. Ice-T has been commissioned to offer a hollow critical protest of the make-believe *Nike* marketing and political sell-out while Knight's overly-zealous shoe-pounding defense of *Nike* is equally vacuous. Everything is for show.

This series of ads, which came to an end because Junior Griffey detested being associated with politics, even as a joke, is an excellent example of *Nike*'s penchant for having "fun" with the excesses and absurdities of contemporary popular culture. They not only needle the politics of image-making, they also needle the media commentators who love to apply sports metaphors to politics. Why dwell on the subject of spin control, the practice professional politicians use to pitch issues for media consumption and public interpretation to their own advantage? Certainly, when Carville talks about the political art of spin control as it might be applied to Griffey's homer-run trot, he draws attention to the practice of spin control as much as to Griffey's hitting ability. In this way, *Nike* constructs the impression of a populist rhetoric that aligns them with viewers, and against the powers that be.

YOU SUCK!

In Chapter 2, we discussed the process of appellation in advertising: the practice of hailing and engaging viewers in terms of identity and belief. Typically, the hailing process is located at the opening of an ad, as in *Nike*'s William Burroughs ad where his disembodied television-head barks, "Hey, I'm talking to you." But in recent years advertisers have sometimes shifted the weight of the hailing process to the closing moments of the ad, in part, as a measure intended to hold onto the fragile attention span of viewers who are prone to using their remote control devices to jump around from channel to channel when they spot an ad formula coming their way. Gone too is the guarantee of a cordial tone and a superficially flattering image. In *Nike*'s 1997 youth-oriented "Virtual Andre" ad, the setting is an upscale department store where a self-absorbed teen demands the "coolest virtual game you've got." The game turns out to be virtual tennis played against Virtual Andre Agassi. Virtual Andre's game overpowers the teen, sending the kid careening wildly about the store, shattering objects right and left while swinging vainly to return Agassi's shots. At ad's end the *Nike* logo fills the screen and the virtual Andre voice-over is heard signing off, "Nice game. You suck." In the twinkle of an eye, the attentive viewer will have noticed that Virtual Andre's reflection appeared on the silvery "virtual" surface of the *swoosh*.

At first glance this seems to defy the rationale of advertising. Why would an advertiser whose goal is the sale of a sponsor's product risk closing the ad with the declaration, "You suck"? In the context of addressing those who see themselves as oriented towards alternative youth culture, one of creators of the "Virtual Andre" ad stated, "I'm not going far enough if I haven't offended somebody." Indeed, it might be that instead of flattering the viewer with the lure of an identity or a look located in having the product, that this represents a new form of flattery. Savvy, knowing viewers have learned to see through the superficiality of slick style and empty flattery. In fact, the new generation of flattery hails viewers for their knowledge of the codes of winking irreverence; namely, "You suck." It inverts the codes of civility. It is rude. It is cocky and arrogant and unsportsmanlike. "You suck" also **metacommunicates** a shared awareness of the conventions that govern polite (though manipulative and deceitful) ways of hailing consumers. "You suck" hails the oversaturated, resistant viewer, who is unwilling to participate in the conventional hailing process.

The producers of the *Nike* ads routinely use the term "irreverence" to describe their intent. They prefer an attitude of "irreverence" because they don't care for – and they believe their audiences don't care for – advertising that takes itself too seriously. But they also speak in the voice of "irreverence" because they understand that this is an era when treating anything as sacred may be seen as sappy and undesirable. Because the concept of "irreverence" has its origins in the struggle against the authoritarian dictates of formal religions, its meaning is linked to terms such as "impiety," "sacrilege," "heresy," and "profanity." Today the struggle is no longer against the restrictive codes of Judeo-Christian institutions, but against the dominion and ascendancy of consumerism.

Nike recognizes that the value of its imagery goes up to the extent that it is willing to treat its own logo in a "playful" and "irreverent" way. Hence we get Virtual Andre and "You suck" or even more to the point, the playful profanation of the *swoosh* on a field of raw red meat in the Dennis Hopper ads discussed above. What intrigues us here is that in order to preserve its investment in the *swoosh*, *Nike* is willing to periodically "profane" it. This willingness to engage in self-desecration establishes *Nike* as one of the 1990s leaders in the economy of signs. Just as importantly, the willingness to engage in playful irreverence regarding its own sacred symbol, the *swoosh*, functions to preserve *Nike*'s legitimacy by deflating the image of *Nike* as a giant corporation that might have lost its human touch.

Some see this age of cynicism as a long-term historical product of cultural relativism. That is, if all values are socially constructed and culturally fluctuating, then why would people really commit themselves to any set of values? Another argument views cynicism as a reaction against the pervasiveness of public relations discourse in both the corporate and governmental worlds. After decades of disinformation and spin control, people have become suspicious of the motives behind almost any claim. A third argument holds that the push toward universal commodification has made people wary of how their own value commitments have been appropriated and used against themselves. As economy and culture have wound their way together, the apparatus of a digital culture accelerates the diminishing half-life of cultural images, with a collapse of meaning following in its wake. Rapid transitions from one set of images and values to another confirm the relativist absence of deep commitment to any set of values, and prompts a pervasive suspicion that any value will be put to use as a sales tool. Ironically, compounding this rush to cynicism, the antidote to this, media-literacy (and its intellectual counterpart, deconstruction), contributes to a yet-more refined, detached and apolitical cynicism, since most people are so far removed from the levers of institutional power that all they can do is debunk.

Advertising cynicism is a form of address based on the cultural capital of media experience. As a form of address it flatters the viewer that "you have an attitude" and are "able to recognize irony" and thus able to engage in cynical distance. Irreverent cynicism now amounts to a defensive posture that may be worn much as a blinking sign that announces to others that the wearer is not gullible – in a maturing media society it amounts to a reworking of the old urban saying, "What do you think, I just got off the turnip truck?" Similarly, the attitude of irreverence offers the reassurance of prophylactic protection against the intrusions of other people's morality into our homes and our consciousness. Postures of cynical distance offer a way of seeming to escape a society saturated in public relations discourses; a way of talking back to the banality of canned political discourse; a way of acting out against the practices of emotional labor that require people to sell their personalities. Speaking with cynical distance creates a buffered position in a world where all positions can be suspect, where no posture can be trusted, and no one really "believes" in anything anymore. It is a punk voice softened for TV audiences. Long gone are the days when political legitimacy was calculated in terms of ideological compliance; gone are the days when ideological criticism was threatening because today's "cynical subject is quite aware that ideology is a lie meant to conceal a very different reality; he or she does not believe the "official" view. But, feeling superior to the lie, the cynical subject continues to live by it."[17] While cynicism offers a voice without emotion to express the ironic, the pop mix of media irreverence offers a momentarily more satisfying pleasure of "thumbing one's nose" at some vague, but distant, powers that be.

NOTES AND REFERENCES

1. Donald Katz, *Just Do It: the Nike Spirit in the Corporate World* (Random House, New York, 1994), p. 137.
2. Randall Rothenberg, *Where the Suckers Moon: an Advertising Story* (Knopf, New York, 1994).
3. Miguel Korzeniewicz, "Commodity chains and marketing strategies: Nike and the global athletic footwear industry," in Gary Gereffi and Miguel Korzeniewicz (eds), *Commodity Chains and Global Capitalism* (Greenwood Press, Westport, Conn., 1994), p. 258.
4. Donald Katz, *Just Do It*, p. 145.
5. The 1995 rankings published by the *Sports Marketing Letter* were based on "money earned, diversity of corporate relationships and a subjective evaluation of demand" (*The Oregonian*, July 29 1995, p. D11).
6. In fact, it was this scene in the film that inspired Jim Riswold and Bill Davenport of *Wieden & Kennedy* to pair Mars with Jordan. Katz, *Just Do It*, p. 147; Spike Lee and Ralph Wiley, *Best Seat in the House – A Basketball Memoir* (Crown Publishers, New York, 1997), p. 135.

7. Kevin Goldman, "Nike, H-P gamble on news sales pitches," *Wall Street Journal*, April 8 1994.

8. William Drozdiak, "Hot athletes and cold cash; image matters as much as winning in the celebrity endorsement game," *The Washington Post*, February 2 1994.

9. Jeff Jensen, "Nike comes out to PLAY; public-spirited spots accent shift away from selling," *Advertising Age*, March 28 1994, p. 3.

10. Herbert Marcuse, *One-Dimensional Man* (Beacon, Boston MA, 1964).

11. Leslie Savan "Naked lunch: ads from the underground," *The Village Voice,* September 6 1994, 50 OP AD.

12. Donny Deutsch cited in Jensen, "Nike comes out to PLAY," p. 3.

13. General Manager Wayne Embry of the Cleveland Cavaliers reacted vigorously to the commercial. "What kind of message is that?" Embry rhetorically fumed to the *Akron Beacon Journal.* "That it doesn't matter what you do? That the rules don't apply? That you don't need discipline? Everything is fine if you get enough rebounds? I was offended by this, both as a basketball man and an African-American" (Thomas Boswell, "Selling kids a bill of goods," *The Washington Post,* December 7 1994, p. B1).

14. Joan Ryan, "An odd message in Nike's Santa ad," *The San Francisco Chronicle*, December 15 1994, p. A1.

15. Houston Baker, "Critical memory and the black public sphere," in Black Public Sphere Collective (ed.), *The Black Public Sphere* (University of Chicago Press, Chicago, 1995), p. 15.

16. Peter Howell, "We've got two words for you: Denis Leary blows smoke rings at pop culture," *The Toronto Star*, March 4 1993, p. G3.

17. Joe Sartelle, "Cynicism and the election," *Bad Subjects*, Issue no. 2, October 1992, http://eserver.org/bs/02/sartelle.html.

5.

ALIENATION, HOPE AND TRANSCENDENCE: DETERMINISM OR DETERMINATION?

This chapter looks at how *Nike* translates the relationships of race and class into visual pop culture. Since most advertising represses questions regarding class and race divisions, that *Nike* deals with these relationships at all is in itself unusual in the world of American pop culture. *Nike* assembles generic images of alienation to serve as a semiotic backdrop for *Nike*'s idealism mixed with determination. While some *Nike* ads recognize, and acknowledge, that a world of inequality and alienation exists "out there," its images never reveal – or name – the social, economic, and political forces underlying this alienation. By calling attention to a ghostly aura of class and race injustice, *Nike* both establishes itself as a "realist" voice while at the same time representing sport as a vehicle for spiritually transcending race and class divides. *Nike* simultaneously acknowledges and denies the unequal **social and economic** realities that influence probabilities for both success and suffering. In so doing, *Nike* retells a mythology of sport that has grown dear to our society.

POVERTY, HOPE AND TRANSCENDENCE

Around 1992, a series of *Nike* ads drew attention to the social underside of contemporary life and the condition of youth living in poverty. These ads joined distinctive music with a heavily realist visual tone. Like the photographic tone in the *Nike* P.L.A.Y. campaign, this photography dwelt on the demoralization of youth in poverty. By drawing on the conventions of documentary and art photography these ads focused attention on the idea of their "realness."

A 1993 *Nike* ad constructs a correspondence between a soulful, traditional miners' lament, "Hardrock Miner," with scenes panning slowly across a landscape of ghetto hoops. The ad's narrative is ambiguous, in part, because the ad draws even more on codes than content. "Hardrock Miner" seems to speak from the position of the oppressed about the drudgery of wage work that never ends. By combining video techniques of slow motion with fade-ins and fade-outs, the ad simulates the texture of a journalistic photo essay so that each image can be imagined as a portrait of a day-in-the-life in the ghetto. The camera pulls against the flow of movement on screen, thus seeming to retard the progress of black male figures which trudge past. Scenes in TV ads rarely linger on the screen, but here they pass deliberately to record a poetics of daily life. Mixing the emotional color of the singer's voice with the flat, affectless black and white of the video suggests a feeling of painfully slow, and futile movement towards a goal.

We are miners, hardrock miners
to the shafthouse we must go.
With our bottles on our shoulders
we are marching to the slope.
O'er the land boys, o'er the land boys
Catch the cage and drill your holes.
Till the shift boss comes to tell you
Put it all on the line for this mining
for gold.
Put it all on the line for this mining
for gold.

While the scenes convey a sense of exhaustion and fatigue, the music evokes a tone of persistence. Born of working class pain and despair, this song conveys sadness and hope, simple eloquence and sincerity. As hopeless and barren as each moment seems, the music summons up resilience and possibility. Though melancholy, the ad connotes a solemn and unbending quality – every day may be like the day before, but these guys keep working at their game.

In the context of a bleak and desolate ghetto wasteland, the music strikes a transcendent chord. The miners' song has been modified by a gospel style; coupled with the visual setting it is easy to conjure up an image of a slave spiritual. The soulful lament framing slow-motion video conveys an ethereal quality as well. The text connotes a legacy of spiritual resistance, an unwillingness to allow the yoke of oppression to completely dehumanize them. Yet, the alienation represented here is strangely de-materialized – almost Hegelian – in our heads.

The hardrock miners' lot grew desperate as the gold industry expanded and became more corporate in the late nineteenth century; hardrock miners were "wage slaves," selling their labor for the dream of gold. Still, the miner's dream of striking it rich kept him going. But why use the miner analogy with ghetto basketball? Theirs is not wage work, though we might easily infer this to be the daily labor of black male youth – working to develop their skills to play professional ball, knowing full well the odds against their success. Still they persist. The ghetto kid's dream of making it big as a basketball player is the modern equivalent of mining for gold.

Whether intentional or not, one subtext of this ad is that the photography of black inner city basketball players has been mined for *Nike*'s benefit. What is the relationship of the mine and the ghetto? The lyrics speak of entrapment. They are both prisons, the one a work-prison, the latter a labor-market prison. But why would *Nike* risk the rhetoric of class relations to position black youth? Though athletic shoe advertisers often present basketball as a form of transcendence, this ad permits *Nike* to differentiate itself by politicizing the clichéd construction of the relationship between the black ghetto and basketball.

Athletic shoe ads usually address moments of personal transcendence, hailing viewers with the inference that these moments might also be theirs. However, this ad's lyrics do not hail viewers **as individual consumers, but as members of a political community**. Strictly speaking, this ad is a luxury few firms could afford. It does not speak about any act of consumption, but rather about relationships of race, class, sport, and hope. When, at ad's end, the familiar black logo appears, it is without the "Just do it" slogan. Punctuating this video about race and ghetto life with the "just do it" slogan as a moral commandment might make it seem glib and invite a variety of negative interpretations. Furthermore, by 1993, there was no need to state the slogan aloud, because the *swoosh* implied it.

Perhaps the authenticity of this ad has nothing to do with any relationship between the ghetto blacktop and the ordeal of exploitation, but with the video codes *Nike* uses. After all, the correspondence between the music and the visual frame takes place at the aesthetic level. *Nike* has joined the codes of art photography (as opposed to the codes of commercial photography) with a piece of music that carries no prior commercial connotations whatsoever. In this sense, *Nike* transforms both the meanings of alienation and authenticity into an aesthetic sensibility. A crucial separation takes place here between the referent system of everyday existence in an urban ghetto and the referent system of the advertisement itself as a cultural text. Our interpretation of this is that the meaning of authenticity resides in the relationship between the ad and the viewer, built on top of the *Wieden & Kennedy* aesthetic of alienation that seems grounded in the everydayness of ghetto life.

Viewers might interpret this ad's photographic look and style as a statement about *Nike*'s commitment to authenticity. At the same time, the soulful song to narrate images of young black men trudging through the heavy gravity of the ghetto basketball court, might be heard as romanticizing spiritual resistance. At end of the ad, the *Nike swoosh* is joined to whatever meanings and emotions are evoked by watching the commercial: to us it conjures up meanings of authenticity and the majesty of the human spirit.

Nike's first Spanish-speaking ad was aired during the 1993 Baseball All-Star Game. Titled *"La Tierra de Mediocampistas"* (The Land of Shortstops), and shot in the grainy codes of realist color, it too touched on the transcendence of the human spirit made possible by sport and play in a world of poverty. The story, told in Spanish with English subtitles, is about a poor people who take pride in the excellence of their shortstops.

70 shortstops in organized baseball are from the Dominican Republic.
So when you see a great Dominican shortstop
go for the ball, and you hear,
[Radio announcer voice] "boy, he had to go far in the hole to get that one …"
you'll know, how far, is far.
Just do it.

The narrator's pacing and delivery of the words "you'll know, how far, is far" guides viewers to consider the accomplishment of playing big league baseball for boys who come from the grinding poverty of a semi-rural village in the Dominican Republic. The photography offers a glimpse of the texture of daily life, framed by lively Latin American music. Among the images included as signifiers of this third world place are scenes of: (1) a road where motorbikes mix with burros carrying goods; (2) a squatting peasant tending a cooking pot while a rooster wanders past; (3) boys playing on a crude sandlot surrounded by a junkyard of buses and vans; (4) a woman hitting a ball with a long stick substituted for a bat; (5) a background row of shanty-like shacks; and (6) a barefoot and shirtless boy catching and throwing a baseball. Intermixed with these scenes are those of boys playing baseball in rag-tag surroundings. And of course, the young boy playing shortstop is shown making a remarkable stop of a bad bounce on the rocky infield, and throwing out the runner. The last scene prior to the *Nike swoosh* is a closeup of his big grin.

Just as *Nike* ads do not attempt to conceal completely the alienated side of spectatorship, neither do they entirely deny the alienated side of the "Other" (blacks and Hispanics) who frequently give meaning to styles which eventually "trickle up" to be consumed by the middle class, but who are rarely allowed their own voice. Though these *Nike* ads invite viewers to notice their realism, in the end the material disadvantages of race and class seem to be no match for the cinematic moments of transcendence and inspiration.

THE "WORK" ETHIC: CULTURAL CAPITAL MADE THE OLD-FASHIONED WAY

In 1995, *Nike* presented several first-person narratives of black athletes. The most frequently played commercial entitled "Work" is narrated by Penny Hardaway, the young basketball all-star who plays for the Orlando Magic.

The signified of rural poverty: warmth, community and family.

Nah! I wasn't born with a basketball in my cradle.
For some believe we come out dunking once we are conceived.
Superstar? I got it made, right?
I went from nothing to something overnight.
Well, don't believe the hype.
I had to work to get to where I'm at and that's a fact.
Mom and Grandma raised me to be proud
and they instilled their philosophy in me
knowing that no one could take that from me.
Nah! I had to work to get here.
At the Boys and Girls club. At Memphis State.
I had to work to be great.
Just do it.

Another spot, originally constructed as part of a Street-ball Legends series aired in NYC, eventually went nationwide because the interview footage was so compelling.

The signified of urban poverty: coldness, emptiness, and anonymity.

My name is Peewee Kirkland.
I'm the guy who could have made it, but walked away.
I'm the guy who got drafted by the Chicago Bulls.
I'm the guy who scored 135 points in one game.
In the beginning I lived every kid's biggest dream.
In the end I lived every kid's worst nightmare.
The streets, the life of crime, takes lives and that needs to be remembered.

Unlike most *Nike* ads around 1995, the *swoosh* sign appears on screen to identify this as a *Nike* ad, but minus the "just do it" slogan at the end because the point is not to identify with Peewee, but to think about what went wrong

– a sobering reminder that basketball talent alone won't realize one's dreams. And so it ends, with Peewee's picture inserted inside a boxframe that has been superimposed over an action-highlight scene of an unidentified young, athletic and black ballplayer leaping to block a shot. For Peewee the success story collapsed. On the verge of realizing his dreams, Peewee lost to the streets. Few viewers know Peewee Kirkland because he never made it to the *NBA*.[1] We can only imagine how many Peewees are out there. While few remember Peewee, *Nike* urges viewers not to forget the conditions that tragically turn the lives of so many young black men toward prison, addiction, or an endless succession of dead-end low-paying jobs. Well, actually, *Nike* doesn't encourage us to remember the conditions, but what they can do to a person. Like most anti-drug testimonials by former users who have seen the light, when Peewee speaks of demons, the inference is that others might learn from his experience.

In Penny Hardaway's 30-second autobiographical statement titled "Work," *Nike* offers a formula for success – hard work, a philosophy of self-confidence and pride, a loving matriarchy and the presence of Boys and Girls Clubs. Framing Penny's story of growing up, from the cradle to the *NBA*, are quiet images of Southern poverty shot on slow summer evenings – a wooden front porch and the yellow glow of a porch light, concrete playgrounds, a frog jumping out of a jar – intermixed with closeups of Penny. "For some believe we come out dunking once we are conceived." Written by a black copywriter, this ad immediately acknowledges the condition of race stereotypes in order to emphasize that nothing comes easy, but must be earned through diligent hard work. A fleeting image of an infant is followed by scenes of a young boy in cutoffs and t-shirt (presumably Penny) practicing his dribbling and ball-handling skills wherever he goes. Though the ad acknowledges the conditions of growing up black, in poverty and in a female-centered household, there is no "culture of poverty" present here. Instead, his video family album includes scenes of the adult Penny posed with his Mom and Grandma, the women in his life who supported him and helped build his character. In an ad marked by a tight correspondence between the spoken words and the visuals, the only product shot in this ad is matched exactly to the spot where Penny speaks about how his Mom and Grandma "instilled their philosophy in me." Their philosophy matches *Nike*'s.

Though these advertisements seem directed at disabusing youth of "the hype" surrounding success in athletics, both narratives reduce questions of success to the exercise of discipline and will-power. Very few players will make it to the *NBA*. The chances of being successful if one grows up poor and black are limited not simply by will or dreams but by material conditions and opportunities as well. Peewee narrates from a black and white mortise at the center of the screen against a backdrop of the cityscape, an everyday world of sights and sounds that blur past as if filmed from a moving automobile. "The streets" offer a generic gloss for all that is wrong with urban America – drugs, violence and crime. It is a vivid metaphor, especially in light of Peewee's tragic story, that connotes both symptom and cause of the problem. By focusing attention on "the streets," *Nike* alludes to the social conditions that claim so many lives, but without actually address-ing their material dimensions. This ad has the sober feel of a public service spot, a reminder to young black athletes who believe their "hoop dreams" and fortunes in the *NBA* will be secured simply by showcasing their dunk-ing and scoring talents, that there are obstacles and hazards blocking the way.

Television constructs a binary opposition between the social menace of poor blacks and black middle class success "by privileging individual attributes and middle class values, and by displacing social and structural factors."[2] Though presumably targeted at urban youth, the Penny and Peewee stories privilege middle class values by endorsing Penny's account of the work ethic ("I had to work to be great"). These autobiographical vignettes keep success in sports in perspective by humanizing these play-ers' lives. Though these ads allude to questions of social structure, *Nike* prefers to highlight an individualism that privileges the role of proper values, personal choices, and the will-power not to give in to the lure of easy plea-sures. Lose your discipline and you can lose everything. Such morality sto-ries are redolent of traditional middle class accounts of individual success in a capitalist society.

APPROPRIATING AFRICAN AMERICAN CULTURE

During the heyday of Michael Jordan and Bo Jackson, *Nike* ads drew their value from black celebrity athletes. Yet, the subject of race frequently seemed to disappear in these ads, even though the camera's focus was on the grace and power of their muscled black bodies. *Nike*'s advertising during this period appeared to be race blind, rendering the subject of race absent, or apparently neutral. A celebrity athlete – so long as he had a personality, or appeared to have a personality – proved to be a commodity that seemed unconnected to race as a category. However, this commodity-driven eclipse of race did not impress black civic leaders who charged that this apparent absence of race concealed *Nike*'s exploitation of the black community – both in terms of the appropriation of its cultural capital and its youth as con-sumers of expensive non-durable consumer-goods.

But with ads like "Hardrock Miner," and a series of ads featuring Spike Lee's candid assessment of racial taunts and insults on the playground, as well as the more recent P.L.A.Y. campaign, *Nike* ads began to openly address and acknowledge questions of race as a proxy signifier for class.[3] Advertisers have normalized the subject of race in recent years, often by incorporating black models into the commodity formulas already used with middle class white representations. Herman Gray observed that the 1980s' media constructed black stars as "confirming the middle class utopian imagination of racial pluralism" and hence as different from blacks in general.[4] Jimmie Reeves and Richard Campbell point to Spike Lee's film *Do the Right Thing* where Lee's character confronts the white racist Pino about his hostility to "niggers," even though all his favorite performers are blacks. Pino responds that they aren't black: "I mean they're black, but they're not really black ... there's a difference."[5] Michael Jordan is frequently perceived as not "black" in *Nike* ads and has even been criticized as not being "black" enough.[6] This might be interpreted as suggesting that Michael Jordan is not presented as sufficiently embodying the exoticized Other. This criticism confuses the symptomatic observation with the deeper forces that construct it. Cultural studies theorists point out that "whiteness" is ordinarily so taken-for-granted because its dominant status renders it invisible. Whiteness is thus not "marked" as a category, or put another way, it appears natural rather than constructed. Because television tends to go along with this ideological dominance of whiteness as the natural order of things, it reinforces the invisibility of whiteness that "marks off the Other (the pathologized, the disempowered, the dehumanized) as all too visible – 'coloured'."[7]

Paul Gilroy touches on a related dimension of media representations of blacks in a critique of Spike Lee's *Nike* ads. Gilroy perceives Lee's characters

> revealed as emissaries in a process of cultural colonization, and Mars Blackmon's afterlife as a *Nike* advertisement is the most insidious result. Through that character above all, Lee set the power of street style and speech to work not just in the service of an imagined racial community but an imaginary blackness which exists exclusively to further the interests of corporate America.[8]

Gilroy's point is well taken, and yet we must be careful not to exaggerate. Spike Lee did bring the power of ghetto speech ("Yo, Holmes, yo, Holmes, these sneakers be housin'") into the heart of the commodification machine. However, measured by styles of commercial signification, the *Nike* appropriation of inner city black subcultural codes pales in comparison with *Reebok*'s "Blacktop Slam-Dunk Fest" or *British Knights'* rendering of Derrick Coleman as home-boy video auteur for home-boy wannabes everywhere.[9] The point, as stated by *British Knights'* ad agency, was to convey "an attitude."[10] Ad campaigns such as the latter set the standard for appropriating the "power of street style and speech" for the benefit of corporate America. The appropriation of ghetto speech and hip-hop signifiers has become rampant in consumer-goods advertising, as has the borrowing of dreadlocks and other markers of "blackness." Excessiveness, however, is not measured simply by appropriation, but by how ads transform social relations into a glamorous look or style. The act of appropriating decontextualized pieces of culture is filtered through questions of what motivates the act of appropriation. Erving Goffman's theory of social interaction stressed what he called "sincerity of performance."[11] Ordinarily, others will not trust us if we seem to behave insincerely. When individuals have instrumental motives (i.e., when we want something) we usually try to act in ways that don't permit others to "see through" our performance. So too in the world of advertising, where "seeing through" the act of appropriation renders its motivation suspect. The best example is still the 1993 *Reebok* "Slam-Dunk Fest" commercial which appropriated signifiers of the ghetto – the lingo, the gestures, the chain link fences, the fat boys, and the graffiti – and then glamorized them in an effort to link the cultural desirability of wild, exotic Otherness to the *Reebok* symbol. By isolating and focusing on the exaggerated signifiers, advertisers like *Reebok* construct a fantastic fiction. This tendency quickly contradicts claims to authenticity.

This is what happens on MTV where ritual mimicry of black street jargon combines postures of cool defiance with a disengaged, nihilistic attitude. It is a strange paradox that the "realer" the "talk" that is appropriated, the more the act of appropriation ends up romanticizing resistance and turning it into a style. *Nike* ads steer clear of this appropriation of blackness for appropriation's sake. *Nike* ads avoid the appropriation of Gangsta rap images, which form the axis on which imaginary blackness turns these days, especially on television. Beginning with their social responsibility ads (such as the P.L.A.Y. campaign), *Nike* ads self-consciously introduced the subject of "the ghetto" by photographically stressing its "realness." Conversely, when the question of blackness as a cultural and linguistic distinction is brought into *Nike* ads, it is not the star athletes who engage it, but rather the characters of Mars or Little Penny.

We speculate that *Nike* generally resists directly appropriating the language and the imagery of ghetto speech because such obvious forms of appropriation tend to be transparent. Appropriating ghetto-speak for the purpose of boosting the badge-value of one's logo is a practice that calls attention to itself, and may then become suspect as inauthentic. Furthermore, this kind of usage can make the advertiser susceptible to charges of "encouraging undisciplined acquisitiveness" that "instigates kids to envy and thievery."[12] There can be no doubt that branded consumer items are highly visible in inner city spaces just as they play a prominent role in the materialist imagery of rap culture. As one of the most visible and most desirable brand images, *Nike* – and in particular, Michael Jordan and Spike Lee – has received an exaggerated share of sensationalist finger-pointing for the acquisitiveness inspired by consumerism among the poor. Sadly, the phenomenon of inner-city youth robbing one another for branded clothing and shoes makes for sensationalistic press coverage that displaces attention from the mundane sociological forces at work in our inner cities.[13]

HYPERAUTHENTICITY AND "STREET" VERNACULAR

> The role of the "popular" in popular culture is to fix the authenticity of popular forms, rooting them in the experiences of popular communities from which they draw their strength, allowing us to see them as expressive of a particular subordinate social life that resists its being constantly made over as low and outside ... However, as popular culture has historically become the dominant form of global culture, so it is at the same time the scene, par excellence, of commodification, of the industries where culture enters directly into the circuits of a dominant technology – the circuits of power and capital.[14]

For *Nike*, the symbolic value of the *swoosh* is rooted in its connection to authenticity – first in the authenticity of athletic performance, and second in the authenticity of cultural expression. *Nike*'s approach to the ghetto is to confront its "authenticity," both positive and negative. The ghetto basketball court, like the barbershop and the street corner, are public spaces in which cultural and political matters are socially expressed and bandied about. These are spaces that comprise what is known as a "black public sphere."[15] It is no accident that these are spaces which *Nike* ads adopt as settings. Given its interest in selling sports culture, it is not unreasonable that *Nike* would depict a starkly structuralist view of the differences between the street corner defined as negative social space, space where inactivity and an absence of structure and discipline give rise to delinquency and crime, and the basketball court, a social space represented in terms of spiritual salvation and personal character building. A 1997 *Nike* ad set in Chicago's inner city invokes both sides of this to make a "stop the violence" plea.

*About [one out of] every five black men
die before they reach the age of 25.
That was Benjy's number.
Benjy was good, the first in Chicago history
to ever be named top high school player in the nation,
right before he was gunned down.
But you know what?
Benjy's not dead.
Benjy's spirit lives on in every jump shot.
Remember, shoot over brothers
Not at them.*

Juxtaposed between frames of basketball played against the background of signifiers of poverty are images of Ben Wilson, now a signifier of the tragic consequences of urban violence and also a signifier of Nike's concern.

In a determined effort to keep the focus on the "real" world, this ad presents a sober visual realism that testifies to the horrific statistical toll exacted on black youth by the decaying material conditions of the inner city. Yet, amidst this rubble and death toll, there is a strength of spirit that "lives on in every jump shot."

Behind the relationship between scenes of authenticity and the space of the ghetto is a wider historical moment. Beneath the widespread media imagery of "the street" with its connotations of drug violence, unemployment, hustling, and generalized culture of poverty are the deeper relations of capital flight and deindustrialization that drained away productive resources and semi-skilled jobs to newly industrializing nations. The cultural imagery of inner city basketball as a source of vitality and authenticity is directly linked to the forces of economic abandonment that have turned both buildings and people into discarded debris. The very same forces that have demoralized the inner-city black community have also "produced the black basketball star as a commodity and an object of desire for mass consumption."[16]

Exploring the imagery of authenticity in ads can permit the recovery of these deeper relationships between social class, race, work and consumption. Though not directly visible in the ads, the crucial missing link that joins questions of authenticity to the ghetto is the middle class. Middle-class culture defines authenticity as a state of individual, social, and cultural integrity originating from the conditions of existence in everyday life. Questions of authenticity revolve around what is deemed to be "real," "honest," "pure" or "immediate." Alternatively, the inauthentic has come to be associated with that which is "plastic," "preprocessed," and "packaged." The desire for authenticity has become tied to the quest to occupy (if only psychologically) a social space that has not been taken over by the commodity form, because commercialization (putting things into commodity form) corrupts the authentic.

> Paradoxically, when advertising appropriates a signifier, the content of the signifier is ripped from its context, the source of the authentic. The appropriated signifier reduces the authentic to an empty sign. Almost invariably, commodification hollows out the once-authentic signifier, and a new sign must be located and appropriated. Signifiers of authenticity are thus continually circulated and burnt out only to be replaced by new signifiers. Searching for authenticity within commodity culture results in an endless sign chase. The more that authenticity is signified and attached to products, the more those sources of authenticity become calculated as appearances. Consumers search for authenticity to escape the logic of commodities – always pre-planned and pre-constituted – but usually return disappointed because the signs of authenticity turn out to be no less calculated and pre-constituted.[17]

There is, of course, at least one decisive difference between the black public space of ballyard basketball and the *Nike* **representations** of that space. No matter how beautifully *Nike* represents that space, the very nature of the ad means that it takes decontextualized images and re-presents them to tell a story. In ads, where the representation is always at least one photographic step removed from its referent, the question of authenticity tends to be measured by how it is signified.[18] That is, authenticity becomes gauged by the codes used to signify it. Hence, when it comes to signifying authenticity in ads, the ante keeps going up. This is why advertisers have evolved a style we call "hyperauthenticity."

An exemplar of what we mean by "hyperauthenticity" appears in a 1997 series of *Nike* ads anchored around the African American vernacular associated with the everyday world of the inner-city basketball court. The "hyperauthenticity" in these ads is signified by a photographic style that heavily overexposes and washes out the already exaggerated codes of black and white video realism; along with the vernacular speech given voice by Arkansas Red, an older African American man. This street vernacular is a language of the dispossessed that carries with it connotations of resistance to social domination, and a sense of shared solidarity. Arkansas Red performs the role of "organic intellectual," an indigenous character, who though not schooled intellectually in the institutions of higher learning, has the capacity for philosophically expressing local wisdom. In each ad, he stands adjacent to the scenes, observing, narrating, and providing commentary about this or that **essential** "truth" or "morality" related to either life or basketball. His role as organic intellectual also makes him an oral historian and folklorist, a storyteller who knows, appreciates, and conserves the memory of a community. Linguistically, these ads highlight a sense of unrepressed expressivity in urban African American basketball vernacular. His voice offers a near-lyrical ode to the "love and devotion" of playing basketball.

Oh lord, did ya see that shot, man?
Did ya see, I'm talkin',
that, that was love and devotion, man.
I'm talkin' about that ball, man.
The pill, the rock,
whatever you want to call her.
That's Kevin G's old lady.
Look at his face, man.
it's written all over his face, man.
He not playin' for the money,
he's playin' for his woman
That's his wuh-man.

The vernacular of the African American community has long been associated with a capacity for earthy expressivity, whether that vernacular takes the form of the blues, or

Urban vernacular provided by Arkansas Red and high contrast expressionistic photography transform Kevin Garnett's body into an aesthetic object.

jazz, or rap. While our written reconstruction of Red's spoken words can indicate the expressive vitality of his colloquial dialect ("the pill, the rock"), the written word does not permit us to capture the richness of meaning and the authenticity of purpose signified by Red's pauses, his rhythmic vocal inflections, or the emotion of his voice. The *Nike* ads featuring Arkansas Red illuminate a "poetic topography of race and place centred on the basketball court."[19] In contrast to the calculated excesses of advertising language, the apparent genuineness in Red's voice conveys a sense of linguistic authenticity that permits viewers to surrender to the pleasure of the moment and to the desire for authenticity apparently experienced by the **native**.

Of critical importance in these ads is the fact that the meaning of blackness serves as an intermediary term. The point of the ads is not to signify "blackness" per se, but rather to use cultural codes associated with an urban black subculture to signify authenticity. So far as we can tell, the point of this ad is to express an experiential essence – the sensual pleasure of playing basketball. Arkansas Red speaks about a love of basketball that is its own reward ("he not playin' for the money"). This imagery presents basketball as a place where one can explore the freedom of artistic expression. Red's comments communicate a powerful love of the game as it is played by ordinary players at countless parks and gyms. This ad doesn't simply speak "black," it speaks "basketball" to those who think of themselves as sharing a community and who treat basketball as a meaningful part of their lives.

Still, this ad draws heavily on the flavor of a native culture. It pushes the authenticity of the native culture to include what might seem an impolitic reference to gender. Tapping the authentic vitality and eloquence of black masculinity also carries with it the baggage of unequal power relations between black men and women.[20] Whether viewers hear phrases like his "old lady" and "wuh-man" as a legacy of sexist domination, or as a culturally marked expression of unalienated activity in a native culture, we cannot say. What we can say is that Red's account privileges the motivation of "playin' for his woman" over the motivation of "playin' for money." "Wuh-man" and "old lady" are presented as metaphors connoting an object of pure desire untainted by external motivations like money. Such expressions draw on an uneasy primitivism that equates "woman" with "pleasure" and opposes "woman" against the impurities of a commodity world. The ad turns on a combination of ambivalent meanings evoked by Arkansas Red's manner of expression. His performance opens the possibility of expressing the joys and pleasures of playing basketball in richly sensual ways – from his description of the sensual relationship between the player and the ball, to the soundtrack's resonant attention to the soundings of the ball on the gym floor, to the glistening, sweating musculature of Kevin Garnett's ebony body. At the same time, such primitivist associations with race and gender may also prompt an echo of ideologies of oppression which drew on underlying notions that gender and race are natural and biological (essential) categories rather than historically constructed categories.[21]

Once excluded from advertising's social tableaus by the politics of racism, people of color have historically been relegated in advertising to perform either as "the exotic" or as "what we do not want to be." All that has changed in recent years. Not that racism is dead, but racial and ethnic images have enjoyed a symbolic resurgence in the quest for images of difference, authenticity, and purity of experience.

> Encounters with Otherness are clearly marked as more exciting, more intense, and more threatening. The lure is the combination of pleasure and danger. In the cultural marketplace the Other is coded as having the capacity to be more alive, as holding the secret that will allow those who venture and dare to break with the cultural ahedonia (defined in Sam Keen's *The Passionate Life* as the "insensitivity to pleasure, the incapacity for experiencing happiness") and experience sensual and spiritual renewal.[22]

In the marketplace of culture, Otherness, in the form of blackness or exotic primitivism, has acquired a frame of meaning that encompasses immediacy and pleasure. Otherness has come to signify the ability to be in touch with one's natural and essential mode of being.

> It is precisely that longing for the pleasure that has led the white West to sustain a romantic fantasy of the "primitive" and the concrete search for a real primitive paradise, whether that location be a country or a body, a dark continent or dark flesh, perceived as the perfect embodiment of that possibility … Within this fantasy of Otherness, the longing for pleasure is projected as a force that can disrupt and subvert the will to dominate.[23]

In a metaphorical way, Arkansas Red's meditations about grassroots basketball may be interpreted as a mapping of this space as a primitive paradise. While on the surface these ads have as their topic an *aficionado's* sense of basketball, their subtext is about an identity that derives from belonging to a totem group of *aficionados*. The ads metacommunicate a higher sensibility, an aesthetic of appreciation framed in terms of an African American vernacular spoken in the colorful rhythms of a basketball philosopher. Arkansas Red stands for an aesthetic appreciation of basketball – an appreciation that signifies an ability to give oneself up completely to the sensual pleasures of play. Listen to Red wax rhapsodic about the indescribable pleasures of sinking jump shots.

I'd play just to, just to have that, that look
that, that, that feeling …
That feeling of the ball goin' in
You know, it's a …
You know, it's a feeling that you just can't describe.

See, only another ball player understand what I'm talkin' about.
Something just feel, it feel like snow,
It feel, feel like that pure white snow.
Ya know, ya understand what I'm sayin'?
Ya see, it's a solid shot
You know like all that noise about it
Shhhhhooo, that's all you hear.
Chains may shake
but when it's goin' in
it say shoooo!
See, you and the basket has to have a relationship,
you know, no matter where you go.
You and the basket got a relationship, man.
A lot of ballplayers say
"Man my arm's so tired"
You know why, cause he's missin' so many of them.
But when it is goin' in I never heard one ballplayer yet,
say my arm is tired.
You see your arm never get tired,
not when it's goin' in.

Red's account bears an aura of authenticity that most advertising language can only manufacture and falsify. And where does this pleasure seem to take place? It takes place in the marginalized spaces which fall outside the domain and control of institutions. It is no accident that when, in another ad in this series, Red delivers a manifesto that "nobody owns this game," all the visual scenes point to the unorganized and spontaneous spaces that lie outside the domain of institutional controls – the barnyard, the playground, the sidewalk. Nor is it accidental that the African-American vernacular becomes the chosen language for expressing a spirit of resistance, since it is precisely the language of the native slave. If Kevin Garnett's "dark flesh" offers a fantasy body where we might project our "longing for pleasure," so too these spaces conjure up muffled echoes of spaces where the cultural and social inventions of the most socially downtrodden express the capacity to rise up and transcend the "will to dominate." This is what cultural studies theorists mean when they speak of recuperating the Other as an object of desire.

Paradoxically, "trash talk," the cultural product of young black men who have been systematically discriminated against in education, housing, and labor markets, emerges here as the language of authenticity, as the preferred vehicle for expressing unmediated desire. In an essay entitled "Talking trash," about an earlier *Nike* campaign focused on New York City, Maharaj argued that "*Nike*'s NYC-Attack campaign enacts the economic and cultural logic of late capitalism which produces 'trash' and recuperates it as a sign of difference and a site of desire."[24] Conventionally, the main currents of middle class culture regard street vernacular with fear and loathing. In schools and in the workplace it is treated as negative cultural capital. Yet, its inclusion in the *Nike* ads as an indicator of authenticity reverses that and turns it into a desirable sign of cultural capital. Here, at least, it reveals **good taste** in basketball.

THE SHADOWS OF RACE AND CLASS

Nike's P.L.A.Y. campaign drew on race as a visual proxy for class relations. The P.L.A.Y. campaign draws on the acronym for Participate in the Lives of American Youth. In March of 1994, *Nike* launched its P.L.A.Y. campaign featuring Michael Jordan, Jackie Joyner-Kersee, and Charles Barkley with ads that had the subdued feel of public service spots. This campaign stressed the social alienation of poverty and its possible transcendence via sports. *Nike* positioned this campaign as motivated by a sense of crisis in our communities and playgrounds.

> "There is a crisis in America right now," said Philip H. Knight, *Nike*'s founder and chief executive officer. "Kids' sports and fitness programs are being axed from schools and the country's playgrounds aren't safe anymore. Access to play should be a kid's inalienable right. *Nike* wants to lead the charge to guarantee these rights to America's children are preserved."[25]

With Michael Jordan or Jackie Joyner-Kersee narrating, somber black and white scenes *speak* of an impoverished landscape where nothing grows. The meaning of poverty is etched across these images. Kids lean out the open window of a darkened inner city apartment; an impoverished girl in a cotton dress faces the camera as if in a depression-era photograph; a child sits motionless in a swing on a barren rock-strewn playground, casting a forlorn and ominous shadow. Socially, these youth occupy a world without hope or a future.

The campaign debuted during the NCAA basketball tournament with Michael Jordan narrating. Jordan poses a series of questions:

Jordan appeals to our concern for children and challenges us to participate in Nike's vision of sports programs as the panacea for social problems.

What if there were no sports?
If you couldn't join a team,
what would you join?
If you couldn't dream of touchdowns,
what would you dream?
What if you did something?
What if you coached a team?
Put up a new rim?
What if there were no sports?
Would I still be your hero?

When Jordan asks, "if you couldn't join a team, what would you join?" the scenes turn to the imagery of gangs. Tough-looking teenage girls expressionlessly confront the camera in a desolate and empty barrio setting. Males clad in stereotypical gang garb – wool caps and hooded sweatshirts – stand starkly against a barbed and razor wire fence while other adolescent males hang out in front of a graffiti-covered brick wall. In a barren wasteland, without the opportunity to participate in sports, they appear condemned to a grim life where they display neither affect nor purpose. Without sport, gangs are depicted as the only alternative groups to belong to, but with no motivating dreams to spur hope, and hence no effective socialization into middle class values. Here, as elsewhere on television, poverty and nihilism are made to appear synonymous.[26]

While these scenes capture a sense of the despair that permeates contemporary urban America, they also gloss over the crucial absence of structuring institutions that shape the lives of poor youth. Viewers are confronted, but only indirectly, by the brute force of inequality, now framed as a collective social psychology. The studied photographic posing of poverty creates a simulacrum of poverty. Nothing explains this inequality, its history and its causes are as scattered and ephemeral as its signifiers. *Nike* mythifies inequality so that it can be expressed in a unitary way across the faces of children, and thus vanquished by the rising musical presence of *Nike*'s spirit in their lives, as passivity is replaced by activity.

In these sequences, *Nike* equates alienation with inactivity and boredom. Alienation is reduced to misdirected leisure time among adolescents. Disconnected from social institutions, this alienation has nothing apparently to do with work or school, but rather becomes a mood associated with the generic landscape of poverty. Though capitalist institutions shaped this world, they recede from view in these documentary-like scenes. There are no images of youth working at minimum wage jobs in fast-food restaurants or convenience stores earning money to buy the latest shoe styles; neither are there images of the working conditions in the South Asian factories that produce *Nike* shoes. While welfare has failed to provide a reasonable quality of life and our educational system has failed to provide sufficient opportunities

Charles Barkley puts aside his "I'm not a role model" role to speak for P.L.A.Y.

to escape ghetto life, sport is mythologized as the institution through which dreams of success, identity and esteem are salvaged and given meaning. Sport is positioned as providing poor youth with meaning and purpose, while socializing them into responsible citizens.

After introducing viewers to the depressing prospects of childhood poverty, the mood subtly shifts when Jordan asks, "What if you did something? What if you coached a team?" A background soundtrack of faintly rising children's chatter and a female singing voice usher in activity and movement as boys play basketball with a makeshift basket made of a plastic box nailed to a telephone pole. In contrast to the privatized representations of middle class transcendence, the P.L.A.Y. campaign positions the transcendence of sport as embracing a higher social good, defined as the public well-being of "our" youth. We earlier noted that many *Nike* ads appear without a visible commodity. The appeal in this ad is precisely to the world of the makeshift (the not-commodity), so that *Nike* can express its ethos of the love of sports in its purest form – in the faces and hearts of children.

The ad concludes with a tight close-up of Michael Jordan, who reiterates his first question, "What if there were no sports?" before following it with a more self-reflexive query, "Would I still be your hero?" Onscreen appears the copy of P.L.A.Y. (Participate in the Lives of America's Youth), followed by 1–800–929–PLAY, *Nike* and the *swoosh*. Is this a mixed message? The P.L.A.Y. campaign designates an effort at remedial organized sport and fitness programs with adult involvement to guide and supervise adolescent recreational desires and drives. The privilege of recreational pleasure through exercise and sports is depicted as both a right and a responsibility. Once it is achieved then one has a responsibility to provide the opportunity to others so that they too might realize it. *Nike* thus wraps itself in the stance of *noblesse oblige*. The ad's writer, Jamie Barrett of *Wieden & Kennedy*, claims the final line, "Would I still be your hero?" was not meant to signify a self-aware narcissism on Jordan's part, but rather aimed at humanizing Michael Jordan as someone who recognizes the kind of opportunities that sport has given him. This reading bears *Nike*'s characteristic mix of humility and celebrity. Jordan, says Barrett, is deeply aware that sport is bigger than he is and that it requires him to give something back. Joyner-Kersee echoes this thinking: "Sport has helped me live my dream. I would have hated to live in a world without sport because it taught me discipline, determination and dedication – qualities that have helped me in my everyday life." In the *Nike* press release for the P.L.A.Y. campaign, Jordan says he became the national co-chair for P.L.A.Y. because,

> *Nike* is making a strong commitment so that kids and adults can take back their communities and playgrounds again. Sports can be a great avenue for kids to stand up to the difficult pressures they deal with and is vital to their development. I wouldn't have wanted to grow up without sports.[27]

The P.L.A.Y. campaign included support of Boys and Girls Clubs of America as well as rebuilding city playgrounds. The P.L.A.Y. campaign thus gave *Nike* a method for addressing persistent critics (such as Jesse Jackson and PUSH) who argued that *Nike* has done less than it should in providing minority opportunities. Others argued that *Nike* (and for that matter, all athletic shoe companies) "exploit" inner city basketball without taking responsibility for the consequences. Alarm arose, for example, circa 1990 when a flurry of reports circulated about inner city youths mugging and killing one another for their most valuable commodity – the hot branded shoe of the moment.

We call campaigns such as the P.L.A.Y. campaign **legitimation advertising** because of how it positions *Nike* as taking the moral high ground, apparently placing community interests above their narrow market interests. If ordinarily *Nike* ads frame transcendence by providing the commodity, the sign, the philosophy, and the heroes, here they can also be seen supporting sport activity at all levels while providing moral leadership. *Nike*'s powerful symbolic presence built up by years of advertising permits them to do ads that only infrequently mention or show their shoe products "because they don't have to use their advertising to define their products." Jeff Jensen of *Advertising Age* correctly observed that

> … the P.L.A.Y. campaign underscores the ubiquity of *Nike*, a name that has become virtually synonymous with the category it continues to dominate. The position allows *Nike* to execute ads that entertain, preach and do anything else but sell product.[28]

Exemplifying this is an ad called "Piggott Street" in which Jackie Joyner-Kersee revisits her childhood neighborhood. Black and white video codes convey a tone of authenticity. Though Jackie Joyner-Kersee is one of the premier track and field athletes in the world, her appearance in the P.L.A.Y. campaign is intentionally low key. The ad treats her as a concerned citizen and not as an athlete. Joyner-Kersee functions here as the voice of *Nike*'s social conscience. The video of an impoverished inner city area recreates a realist simulation of the material and social conditions of the East St. Louis urban ghetto area where she grew up. Jackie's voice-over tells about a coach at a local Boys and Girls Club who was an uplifting force in her life.[29] Joyner-Kersee's biography reveals the motivation for her involvement in the P.L.A.Y. program, her desire to put into place the resources so that her story might be replicated in the lives of others. Though the motivation of the ad may be genuine, and its meaning emotional, this culture of poverty argument is little more than wishful thinking. Jackie Joyner-Kersee is not representative of those who grow up subject to the conditions of race, gender and poverty. Young black women growing up in places like East St Louis will require significantly more resources than better playground facilities to dramatically change their life-chances. In fact, the degree of racial segregation is so pro-

Positioning Nike *as a concerned socially responsible corporation, Jackie Joyner-Kersee offers hope to those without hope.*

nounced in St Louis that it ranks among the most "hypersegregated" metropolitan areas in the US.[30] With racial segregation comes disinvestment, dilapidated housing, the absence of infrastructure, and a general intensification of the material conditions that reproduce poverty. Statistically, black females suffer more than any other demographic category from the consequences of discrimination, subordination, and poverty: poor education, limited employment opportunities, low income, inferior health care, inadequate nutrition, and more likely victims of crime.[31]

SIGNIFIERS OF ALIENATION AND HUMANITY

Race as a category seemed to be a non-issue in *Nike*'s early rounds of advertising, but in the 1990s it has become a significant subject in *Nike*'s advertising. First, *Nike* ran a few ads with Spike Lee using humor to directly address the language of racism on the basketball court, pleading for more ecumenical understanding and respect for diversity. More recently, *Nike* has signed the emerging golf superstar Tiger Woods, and has chosen to foreground race as a category, first in order to draw attention to their association with Tiger Woods, and then doing a 180 degree turn to demonstrate the declining relevance of race as a category.

   Nike's first ad featuring its just-signed superstar suggested that Tiger Woods had been denied access to certain golf courses because of his race. The ad quotes Woods, the nation's top black golfer, as saying, "There are still courses in the United States that I am not allowed to play because of the color of my skin." Defenders of golf immediately challenged the factual claims of the ad. When asked for specifics, *Nike* publicist James Small acknowledged there were no such places; rather, the advertisement was meant "to raise awareness that golf is not an inclusive sport." *Nike*'s public relations director maintained the ad was not intended to be taken literally, but as "a metaphor," with Woods representing other black golfers. While Tiger Woods would be welcome to play anywhere because of his stature, less prominent blacks would be denied playing privileges because of their race.[32] Critics accused *Nike* of **exploiting** the social injustice of racism in order to garner attention for itself. Bob Garfield, an *Advertising Age* columnist, fumed that *Nike* "was phony because Tiger Woods was not a victim of racism. And they're exploiting the race issue to sell golf shoes to black people and I think that's cynical."[33] While *Nike* undoubtedly framed the issue of racism in golf to publicize its entry into golf, Garfield's narrow interpretation of the ad illustrates exactly the difference in thinking about racism with regard to celebrity athletes as opposed to the institutions that operate in everyday life to limit the opportunities of discriminated groups.

   A different approach to race as a category structured *Nike*'s next ad featuring Tiger Woods. The "I am Tiger Woods" ad juxtaposes a montage of black and white photographs and color video clips of a multiracial cohort of children in golf-related scenes (playing golf, carrying clubs, etc.) against an occasional shot of Tiger Woods, thus offering a testimonial to Woods' power as a positive role model for youth. Throughout, the young golfers repeat *Nike*'s new declaration of purpose, "I am Tiger Woods." The ad ends with a slow motion shot of Woods driving a golf ball with perfect form. Across the screen, the copy reads "I am Tiger Woods." The words then dissolve into a *swoosh*.

Tiger Woods rapidly emerged as a sports "legend" in the media. *Sports Illustrated* has already named Woods as a Sportsman of the Year. Media representations of Woods focus on his athletic ability, his personality and his ethnicity. *Newsweek* describes Woods as "An old pro at 20: no tantrums, no bad behavior. Just drive, dedication and a gracious, winning style." An *Advertising Age* article observes that "…as he is only 20, and part African-American, part Native-American, part Chinese and part Thai, Mr. Woods will be used to reach demographic segments most golf marketers don't aggressively pursue."[34] Woods' multiracialism signifies marketable multiculturalism: a multiracial heritage with a bourgeois gentleman's personality. His image has been constructed as "intelligent, abstemious, kind to his parents," tough under pressure, yet soft spoken. No trash-talking. No arrogance. Remember how *Nike* constructed Barkley in its "I'm not a role model" ad. Now, *Nike* positions Woods as the ultimate role model. The ad's children don't chant "I want to be **like** Tiger Woods," rather, they state total identification: "I am Tiger Woods."

Of course, constructing an ego ideal in an impure commercialized sports world is subject to contradiction and criticism. Initially, such criticism was directed at *Nike* rather than Woods. One writer summarized this criticism when he bemoaned that this ideal role model had signed

> … with *Nike*, the most egregiously offensive sports merchandising business in the world, presided over by a messianic fast-buck artist named Phil Knight. This means that Woods, as he ambles across the putting green, wears an oversized cap emblazoned with the ubiquitous *Nike* logo, a kind of stylized boomerang.[35]

Nike countered with public relations. "Tiger wants to be an ambassador of change among minorities and youth, and that's certainly a goal of *Nike*," said Merle Marting, marketing communications manager for *Nike*'s golf division. "In the future, we will use Tiger in our brand communications, not just as a category representative."[36] While *Nike* constructs Tiger as a minority spokesperson who will open up the sport of golf to minority kids, *Nike* also draws on Wood's multiracial background to present Woods as a signifier of universality. While Jordan signified physical transcendence, the ability to fly, to do what no man has done before, the ultimate in physical achievement, Woods emerges as a signifier of Humanity itself. This *Nike* ad melds hero worship of the celebrity athlete with the celebration of the human spirit.

If we retrace the steps of cultural appropriation that contributed to this ad, then this rearrangement of meanings engineered by *Nike* becomes even more apparent. The ad draws on a closing scene from Spike Lee's film *Malcolm X* in which a school teacher tells her class, "And so today, May 19, we celebrate Malcolm X's birthday because he was a great, great Afro-American. Malcolm X is you. All of you. And you are Malcolm X." This is followed by a series of African American school children who stand and solemnly declare "I am Malcolm X." Lee 's film concludes with a short monologue by Nelson Mandela lecturing the children: "… we declare our right on this earth to be a man, to be a human being, to be given the rights of a human being, to be respected as a human being in this society on this earth in this day which we intend to bring into existence …" A clip of Malcolm X himself completes Mandela's statement, "by any means necessary."

What might be meant by the way these boys declare that "I am Tiger Woods?" The mantra-like repetition of "I am Tiger Woods" initiates at least three transformations: first, the ideological significance of Malcolm X is replaced by that of Tiger Woods; second, a transformation of agenda in which political activity is replaced by sport; and third, the utterance itself becomes an action signifying that each child carries within him the spirit of Tiger Woods. Whereas the television medium has generally represented Malcolm X as an ideological radical who spoke for racial separation and the legitimacy of violence (rather than trust in authorities to uphold the law) as a response to racist violence, the *Nike* commercial presented Woods as a multiracial icon – a post-racial icon – who represents the end of race as a historically relevant category. The ritual reiteration of "I am Tiger Woods" transforms both the identity of Tiger Woods and *Nike*. Each is positioned as universal in meaning. In Tiger's case, he has been made to stand for that which is most highly valued in our society – recognition for standing out, recognition for great accomplishment, admiration for possessing a self that is transcendent. Identity and equivalence again become joined when the screen reading "I am Tiger Woods" is stamped by the *swoosh*. What might it mean that children proudly avow that "I am Tiger Woods"? When utopian impulses become channeled by commodity relations the signifieds are open – it could be interpreted to mean that I am a good person, that my future is open, that I have a purpose and a goal in my life, or that, with *Nike* in the golf game, it now becomes a democratic sport.

How does a signifier of alienation get turned into a signifier of the human spirit? Inspirational music joined to slow motion sets the ad's tone as uplifting and celebratory. Hyperreal video and discontinuous editing turn glimpses of young hands holding golf clubs into hypersignifiers of hope and opportunity. Documentary style black and white photographs intermixed into the montage signify realism. Scenes of boys looking down from

"I am Malcolm X"

Identification is established by photographic equivalence and reinforced by the tagline, "I am Tiger Woods."

dilapidated brick buildings with "golf" written across the sides provide an obvious poverty signifier. The montage of multiracial children's faces accentuates multiple ethnicities, particularly multiracial appearances and multiple body types. This commercial is an excellent reminder that imagery of poverty and race can be made **free floating** precisely because of how we have become accustomed to "race as a floating signifier."[37] Place gives way to video space. The *Nike* commercial takes advantage of this in two ways: first, the space of golf becomes unbound by geography, ethnicity, or class; second, detached from its moorings in any real lifeworld, race and ethnicity become markers of *Nike*'s commitment to the greater glory of mankind. *Nike* invokes images of poverty and inner city children in order to turn them into the currency of legitimacy.

NOTES AND REFERENCES

1. Maharaj notes, "Significantly, the *Nike* advertisement fails to say that, when offered a chance to play with the Chicago Bulls in 1980, Peewee decided not to join the *NBA* because street basketball was a more lucrative occupation" (p. 99). For a much lengthier analysis of the Peewee ad as part of the "New York City Attack" campaign see Gitanjali Maharaj "Talking trash: late capitalism, black (re)productivity, and professional basketball," *Social Text* 50, 15, 1, (Spring 1997), pp. 97–110.
2. Herman Gray, "Television, black Americans and the American dream," *Critical Studies in Mass Communication*, 6, (December 1989), p. 376.
3. For a different view on the relationship between race and class see William J. Wilson, *The Truly Disadvantaged* (University of Chicago Press, Chicago, 1986).
4. Gray, "Television," p. 376.
5. See Jimmie Reeves and Richard Campbell, *Cracked Coverage: Television News, the Anti-Cocaine Crusade, and the Reagan Legacy* (Duke University Press, Durham, NC, 1994), pp. 101–102.
6. See Michael Dyson, "Be Like Mike? Michael Jordan and the Pedagogy of Desire," in *Reflecting Black: African-American Cultural Criticism* (University of Minnesota, Minneapolis, 1993), pp. 364–74; David Andrews, "The facts of Michael Jordan's blackness: excavating a floating racial signifier," *Sociology of Sports Journal*, 13 (1996), pp. 125–158.
7. Isaac Julien and Kobena Mercer, "De Margin and De Centre," in David Morley and Chen Kuan-Hsing (eds), *Stuart Hall: Critical Dialogues in Cultural Studies* (Routledge, London, 1996), p. 456.
8. Paul Gilroy, *Small Acts* (Serpent's Tail, London, 1993), p. 189.
9. See Robert Goldman and Stephen Papson, *Sign Wars* (Guilford Publications, New York, 1996).
10. In Rich Wilner, "Anatomy of an ad campaign; *British Knights Inc*," *Footwear News*, October 12 1992, p. FN6.
11. Erving Goffman, *The Presentation of Self in Everyday Life* (Doubleday, Garden City, NY, 1959).
12. See Michael Dyson, *Between God and Gangsta Rap* (Oxford University Press, New York, 1996), p. 58; Nelson George, *Elevating the Game: The History and Aesthetics of Black Men in Basketball* (Harper Collins, New York, 1992), p. 235. See also Cornel West, *Race Matters* (Random House, New York, 1994), pp. 17–31, for an extended discussion of

how nihilism arises out of the structural relationship between "the saturation of market forces and market moralities in black life."

13. Henry Louis Gates Jr criticizes those political interpretations of cultural studies that leave aside the sociological. "The chain of causality begins with Spike, who makes television commercials that promote Air Jordans; it ends with the devastated crack-ridden inner city – and a black youth with a bullet through the brain, murdered for his sneakers. All because Spike Lee said he's gotta have it. You think Mars is funny? Those commercials have a body count" (*Loose Canons: Notes on the Culture Wars*, Oxford University Press, New York, 1992, p. 184).

14. Stuart Hall, "What is this 'black' in black popular culture?" in Morley and Chen, *Stuart Hall: Critical Dialogues in Cultural Studies*, p. 469.

15. See Black Public Sphere Collective (ed.), *The Black Public Sphere* (University of Chicago Press, Chicago, 1995).

16. Maharaj, "Talking trash," p. 98.

17. Goldman and Papson, *Sign Wars*, p. 148.

18. One of things that cultural theorists like Roland Barthes and Michel Foucault accomplished was to unmask the concept of authenticity as a social fiction – as an imaginary social construct.

19. Paul Gilroy, "'After the love has gone': bio-politics and etho-politics in the black public sphere," in The Black Public Sphere (ed.), *The Black Public Sphere*, p. 61.

20. Herman Gray, "Black Masculinity and Visual Culture," *Callaloo* 18 (Spring 1995), pp. 401–405.

21. Hall, "What is this 'black' in black popular culture?"

22. bell hooks, *Black Looks: Race and Representation* (South End Press, Boston, MA, 1992), p. 26.

23. Ibid., p. 27.

24. Maharaj, "Talking trash," p. 104.

25. "*Nike*, Michael Jordan and Jackie Joyner-Kersee launch $10 million kids' sports and fitness initiative,"*Business Wire*, March 23 1994.

26. bell hooks, *Outlaw Culture: Resisting Representations* (Routledge, London, 1994), p. 169.

27. *Business Wire*, March 23 1994.

28. Jeff Jensen, "*Nike* comes out to PLAY; Public-spirited spots accent shift away from selling," *Advertising Age*, March 28 1994, p. 3.

29. Even here, however, there is a major ideological difference between *Nike*'s telling of this story as opposed to *NBC*'s. *NBC* took the same story and schmaltzed it up with music and gauzy video and romantic voice-overs to construct an emotional hook for why viewers would want to watch her compete in the Olympic long jump. If she wins a medal, then *NBC* can glue the meaning of this morality tale about overcoming adversity to "America" as the country that permits such opportunity for anyone to shine and prevail.

30. Douglas Massey and Nancy Denton, *American Apartheid: Segregation and the Making of the Underclass* (Harvard University Press, Cambridge, MA, 1993).

31. Margaret Simms and Julianne Malveaux (eds), *Slipping Through the Cracks: The Status of Black Women* (Transaction Books, New Brunswick, NJ, 1986).

32. David Zink, "Ads tee off on controversy," *Rocky Mountain News*, October 6 1996, p. 2B.

33. Cited in Rowan Scarborough, "Critics hit Nike ads with sneaker suspicion," *The Washington Times*, October 31 1996, p. A2.

34. Jeff Jensen, "Woods hits golf jackpot; agent sees $60 million payday for young phenom," *Advertising Age*, September 2, 1996, p.6.

35. Philip Terzian, "A babe in Nike's Woods," *Journal of Commerce*, November 7 1996, p. 9A.

36. Jensen, "Woods hits golf jackpot," p. 6.

37. Hall, "What is this 'black' in black popular culture?"

6.

TRANSCENDING DIFFERENCE? REPRESENTING WOMEN IN *NIKE'S* WORLD

For over two decades now, a debate has simmered about how women are represented in advertising. Does advertising imagery model or reinforce characteristics of submissiveness, passivity, receptivity, and dependency in women? What about the ways in which feminist morality and ideas have been appropriated and exploited by advertisers? Since the early 1990s *Nike* addressed these questions in the process of tailoring a philosophy for a generally middle class audience of women and girls. *Nike* evolved a new **semiotics of gender** that addresses women about the achievement of non-sexist sports identities in a world less bound by patriarchal definitions.

As men's athletic shoe markets matured and flattened out in their growth curve in the 1990s, the growth in popularity and audience demographics of women's sports attracted corporate America. Women represent the fastest-growing category of sporting-goods consumers. According to 1994 sales figures from the *National Sporting Goods Association*, women consumed nearly 80% of all workout gear sold in the United States, and now participate in greater numbers than men in aerobics, fitness walking, swimming, exercising with equipment, and cycling.[1] Perhaps most significant has been the swelling popularity of women's team sports, primarily in soccer, volleyball, basketball, and softball, spurred on by US team victories at the Atlanta Olympiad. Institutionally, women's sports are on the map. Reflecting these social changes, sales of both *Nike*'s women's sports and fitness categories have surged since 1994. *Nike* reported that sales of its women's fitness line grew 26% while the women's sport shoe market increased 45% over 1994; and in 1995 *Nike*'s women's fitness business grew another 51%.

> With our U.S. women's footwear growing more than 40 percent, *NIKE*'s focus on women's sports rose to new levels in 1997 and will remain an integral part of our growth strategy going forward. We signed on to

support the *WNBA* and developed more sport-specific product for women, such as our first women's soccer cleat.[2]

The women's sports market has emerged as *Nike*'s growth market of the moment. Advertising aimed at this women's market has correspondingly shifted its underlying social assumptions as well as its representations. "It's not idealism driving the shoe companies. It's the bottom line. With sales of men's products flattening, the companies suddenly are relying on women's basketball, soccer, and fitness shoes to carry them."[3]

Changes in the representations of women have been driven by underlying social changes that have taken place since the early 1970s. Statistically, "women are in the workplace in higher numbers, earning more money, marrying later or not at all, and facing tighter time constraints between work and family." As a result,

the consumer-goods world is finally catching on to the fact that women have buying power – they have discretionary income of their own. Steady income growth and strong customer loyalty among women have finally created a market niche attractive enough to lure mass-market manufacturers.[4]

Buying power then, in combination with the long-term impact of Title IX, enacted in 1972 to legally bar athletic departments from discriminating against women's programs, "has opened doors for American female athletes and sparked a new level of excellence in women's sports."[5] As several generations of young women passed through institutionalized sports, expectations about women's participation in sports have become normalized.

Since the late 1980s *Nike*'s path of constructing gender difference gravitated from a stance that inferred fitness as a gender indifferent activity; to a gender-conscious poetics that advocated therapeutic fitness and well-being; to a fiercely competitive participation in winning and team sports; to let-us-now-praise famous women athletes. For at least a decade now, *Nike* print ads for women's products have abstained from the conventional male gaze that normally defines how women are posed in magazines and on television. Around 1987, television ads featuring women such as Stacy Allison (the first woman to climb Mt Everest) and marathoner Priscilla Welch (former smoker, drinker, and couch potato turned into champion long distance runner) were part of broader campaigns that stressed *Nike*'s motivational and inspirational themes, rather than gender-related angles. In 1989, *Nike* unveiled a short-lived in-your-face athletic performance ad featuring a female triathlete who, at ad's end, snapped at viewers to stop "eating like a pig" if they wanted to get in shape.[6] This ill-advised ad sent *Nike* back to the drawing-board and eventually led to *Nike*'s popular 1991 "Empathy" campaign which legitimated the subjective experiences of growing up female in a predominantly male-defined world. *Nike* hailed women in a therapeutic voice that resonated with middle class consumers. These quiet, introspective ads advocated taking care of the self. Reflecting the rise of women's volleyball, soccer and basketball, subsequent campaigns in the 1990s evolved from the therapeutic ethos to a more visceral, aggressive, and competitive sensibility, culminating in a dramatic shift of tone and voice in *Nike*'s presentation of women and their participation as athletes in team sports. The history of *Nike*'s advertising to women can be thought of as a series of progressions that have erased, one by one, many of the early differences from *Nike*'s representations of male athletes.

GENDER DIFFERENCE IN *NIKE* ADS

The construction of gender difference in *Nike* ads has changed dramatically in the 1990s. Throughout the 1980s, the *Nike* organization was routinely referred to as a "men's club." *Nike* lost significant ground to *Reebok* in the mid-1980s when it failed to recognize the importance of the women's fitness market. Critics charged that *Nike* devoted over three-quarters of its annual advertising budget to its men's product lines. Yet despite these biases, the differences between men's and women's representations in *Nike* ads do not fall along the lines of traditional stereotypes that divide the world into macho versus diminutive, masculine versus feminine. As a provider of unisex products oriented toward performance, *Nike* endorses an ethos of one size, one ideology, fits all. The core of *Nike*'s inspirational ethos is revealed in the following text from a *Nike* magazine ad directed at women.

All your life you are told the things you cannot do. All your life they will say you're not good enough or strong enough or talented enough. They'll say you're the wrong height or the wrong weight or the wrong type to play this or be this or achieve this … THEY WILL TELL YOU NO, a thousand times no until all the no's are meaningless. All your life they will tell you no, quite firmly and very quickly. They will tell you no. And you will tell them Yes.

Stand up for yourself. Don't let others tell you what you can and cannot do. It is a motivational theme that echoes throughout *Nike* campaigns, whether they speak to men, women, the elderly, or the handicapped. This push towards universality (everyone treated the same) is driven by the abstraction demanded by the marketplace, where a consumer is a consumer is a consumer. Gender equity has been spurred along by the rising tide of the women's sporting-goods market, political correctness following in the wake of marketability: "'Equal' is understood by the shoe companies to mean simply the same."[7] When *Nike* speaks to a desire to experience individual satisfactions by asserting oneself against societal limits, it hails men and

In the TV version of the "High Plains" ad, a female runner traverses the open frame of a rural landscape marked only by the spiritual allusion of an unadorned church.

women with a similar democratic message. Hence, *Nike* ran identical versions of its 1990 ad called "High Plains," one with a lonesome male runner and one with a solitary female runner, silhouetted against a panoramic shot of a countryside at dusk: "There are clubs you can't belong to ... but the roads are always open."

Still, until 1996–7 there remained clearly gendered differences in *Nike*'s world. It may be useful to briefly enumerate some of these differences as a prelude to our tour through the recent history of *Nike* women's ads. Casting these differences starkly here may help cast light on the considerable changes taking place in *Nike*'s representations of women. In fact, some of the historical differences identified here have been erased in the most recent rounds of *Nike* advertisements.

- A primary message in the women's ads has been that staying in good physical condition is a lifelong activity, while the sports-oriented message for male viewers more often involves mastery, achievement, and being a savvy fan. *Nike* ads tend to maintain a strict separation of men and women. This permits *Nike* to hail men and women differently, while stressing the premise of formal equity of treatment.

- *Nike*'s women's ads tend to be structured by extensive written or oral text, while the men's ads depend more on intertextual media references. Though heavily media-reflexive and ironic, the men's ads are remarkably unreflexive about the meanings of being a male in our culture. The women's ads tend toward the inverse of this. They are reflexive about the meaning of being a woman in our culture, and prefer sincerity as a tone of voice over irony. Women's sports advertising still lags behind the men's market in this regard: to effectively compete, the women's ads concentrate on evoking a sense of authenticity of experience. On the men's side, questions of authenticity have migrated into an acute self-awareness of how authenticity can be manufactured in the age of media glitz.

- The women's ads tend to be constructed as narrative acts of subjective expression, while the men's ads represent opportunities for narrative construction based on interpreting a pastiche of media references. Reading the men's ads can be an exercise in creativity, while reading the women's ads is conditioned by identification with experiences that are represented as art. The women's ads, epitomized by the "Empathy" campaign, presume the possibility of a unified female ego, although they address this through the experience of disunity. The men's ads do not necessarily presume such a unity of self, but neither do they make disunity an issue.

- Whereas men banter and engage in camaraderie off-the-field in *Nike*'s men's ads, *Nike*'s women are rarely shown bantering or engaging in playful acts of camaraderie; they seek bonding on the field of play, not off court. We surmise that because women's sports are still in the process of being legitimated, they remain serious business. As one *NBC* announcer at the 1996 Olympic games commented about the US men's and women's basketball teams: "For the men it is all fun and games. But for the women it is strictly business."

Some studies of men's representations identify an ethos of "hegemonic masculinity" in sports advertising. This is defined as stressing male aggression and control linked to toughness and competitiveness, along with "the subordination of women" and the "marginalization of gay men."[8] This seems to us an inaccurate account of how *Nike* ads represent masculinity. *Nike* represents men as competitive and confident in the superiority of their performances, but we do not see the *Nike* portrayal of masculinity linked to either the subordination of women or the marginalization of gay men. Whether it is Michael Jordan, or the imagery of the anonymous runner training across the nightime cityscape, masculinity in the *Nike* universe is tacit, achieved not at the expense of others, but by dominating something much more abstract – the self.

Nike's advertising, as we have pointed out, draws on a vision of classical humanism that presupposes shared universal human traits. Not surprisingly in American culture, *Nike*'s presentation of men is largely unreflexive. *Nike*'s masculine ethos locates men's individual freedom of accomplishment in the pride and ownership of one's performance. Ultimately, this ethos focuses on the strength and persistence of an individual's will to achieve self-mastery. In this sense, *Nike*'s vision of masculinity is profoundly modernist. In the *Nike* cosmology, "male power" means dominating one's own human nature, willing oneself towards transcendence.

From another angle, *Nike*'s tone of voice about masculinity draws on the cultural postmodernism spawned by the history of commercial television in the United States. *Nike* ads directed at males privilege a viewer who favors a sense of irony and recognizes densely intertwined media constructions. *Nike* ads aimed at males favor a sense of playful mischief and a sense of humor. If one reads an ideal male into the sum of these images, it is someone secure enough in the confidence of their ability to perform that they do not have to take themselves too seriously.

REACTING AGAINST THE MALE GAZE

A majority of advertising directed at women draws on the cultural legacy of the male gaze. John Berger and Laura Mulvey offered analytic accounts of how the "male gaze" customarily positions women as objects of desire for an absent spectator-owner. What's more, women are socialized to adopt the external perspective of the surveyor as well, eyeing themselves, and judging themselves, as they imagine men see them. Women become, as Berger puts it, "both surveyor and surveyed."[9]

Even so, it must be stressed that women's representations in advertising are hardly monolithic. The 1990s world of women's advertising has no unified imagery of woman that might correspond to the 1950s imagery of the docile, stay-at-home housewife. This is partly because marketers are now better able to distinguish and target niche markets within the mass media. Advertisers define audience niches on the basis of research that identifies values and ideological preferences. In the late 1980s and early 1990s, a growing number of advertisers sought to appropriate and refashion feminist sensibilities in an effort to defuse the anger of female consumers.[10] Reaction to the now infamous Swedish Bikini Team in the *Old Milwaukee Beer* ads led to a further reduction of ads presenting women as mere sexual objects. So too, some women's ads adopted self-reflexive stances about the ways in which advertising itself promoted an oppressive ideal of women as perfect-sum-of-their-parts dolls. Around 1992, *Maidenform, Vanity Faire, Liz Claiborne, Reebok*, and *Nike* all presented campaigns that self-consciously addressed women's media images and questions of women's place in American culture.[11] Competition for women's markets demanded that advertisers find new methods of hailing female difference with a variety of gender-definition pegs.

Representations of women in print and television advertising frame women in terms of the "male gaze" as objects of visual scrutiny. We don't have to look far to find this male gaze. When aimed at women it tends to be most exaggerated in fashion, cosmetics, weight-loss, and perfume ads, while the male gaze designed for men is most overstated in motorbike, beer, and cologne ads. The male gaze is not just a pose, but also a narrative device that alerts viewers to a scenario. Consider an obvious example for leg hair removal where the male gaze structures the message. When a *Nair* legs ad features a young women with smooth shiny legs frolicking in the sunshine with a young beau who carries her on his shoulders, young women do not need an announcer to explain the underlying logic: having legs that look smooth, soft and hairless will make a girl attractive to her young prince.

"Who wears short shorts?
She wears short shorts."

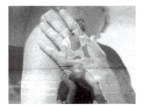   

Legs stay smoother
Days longer than shaving

When you wear short shorts, you've gotta have Nair legs.
Just smooth Nair lotion on, and then rinse hair off.
Nair legs stay smoother, days longer than shaving.

The *Nair* ad coordinates the song and video to invite female viewers to step into the model's place. When the first singer asks, "Who wears short shorts?" the picture corresponds to a pair of female legs in shorts, with the face and head of the model cut off, so the viewer can imagine herself in the scene. In one sense her identity is missing, but in another, her identity is actually located in her legs. The heart and soul of the male gaze arrives centerstage as we see the male model's face, his head turned to give her his full attention and admiration. Now the voice-over turns to its imperative, "you've gotta have Nair legs." Pleasing yourself by being pleasing to him is a story line that is by now thoroughly embedded in the male-gaze scene. And what's more, we no longer need to see a male in the scene to get the point. The male gaze may seem less visible in shampoo commercials for *Revlon* or *Salon Selectives* where no male admirer actually appears, but when the model swings her shiny, full-of-body mane of hair, she is still playing to an absent male admirer whom female viewers have internalized to imagine how her look might play on men. The male gaze continues to define her presence to herself.

However, this kind of advertising not only made women incessantly insecure about the inadequacy of this or that part of themselves, eventually it also prompted resentment and hostility. When women first began expressing anger about being positioned by advertising to occupy a state of perpetual envy of an impossible ideal, one advertiser response was to run ads like *Pantene*'s, "Don't hate me because I'm beautiful" which acknowledged the anger, but then proceeded to repeat the same old mantra that "I wouldn't be beautiful unless I used this product." Between 1990 and 1993, a growing number of ads incorporated the politics of feminism as a way of acknowledging the social history of female subordination and the absence of political or economic equality. In the brassiere industry, *Maidenform* and *Vanity Faire* ran memorable campaigns that played off viewer recognition of the male gaze to appease women weary of being constantly put on duty to perform as an appearance to be surveyed and judged. Suddenly the mirror that women are asked to perform for became an explicit part of the story the ad was telling. These ads attacked advertising's own manipulation of women.

While advertisers like *Nike* and *Reebok* recognized the necessity of contesting the male gaze as an appealing framework, not all efforts to erase it were complete. More often the male gaze remains as a ghostly, yet animating presence. Consider the case of *Reebok*, *Nike*'s chief competitor in the women's athletic shoe market. About the same time that *Nike* ran its "Empathy" campaign, *Reebok*'s "I believe" campaign also sought to appeal to feminist sympathies. Armed with pithy one-liners the *Reebok* campaign explicitly took

This Salon *ad not only constructs the model as a sight but also hails the female viewer to look at herself as an object of the male gaze.*

the side of women while disavowing the patriarchal assumptions that have defined women as objectified appearances who exist to give pleasure to men. For example, *Reebok* hailed feminist rebellion with "I believe that 'babe' is a four-letter word." None the less the *Reebok* campaign continued to visually dwell on a redefined female physique as the goal of working out. Planet *Reebok* offered women a suspect freedom to engage in "the discipline of perfecting the body as an object."[12]

Possessing "buns of steel" is the essential visual correlate of the active women in *Reebok*'s "I believe" ethos; buns of steel are the primary accomplishment of this version of female self-realization,[13] which as *Reebok* puts it, is "the true mark of a healthy individual." Susan Bordo shows how such representations of women in consumer culture also feed the social logic of anorexia: "To feel autonomous and free while harnessing body and soul to an obsessive body-practice is to serve, not transform, a social order that limits female possibilities." Advertisers like *Reebok* take great pains to denounce the male gaze so that "they can pretend to reject the sexualization of women." Turning the female body into both the site and "symbol of resistance in these ads" is "the profoundest of cynical bad-faith."[14]

Where does this leave **empowerment** as a marketing strategy? Flattering women with an image of themselves as independent and in control has become a key axis of advertising and marketing competition, especially in the women's fitness and athletic shoe markets. One advertising strategy has tried to blend conceptions of femininity with feminism, like a recent *Keds* commercial that presents a millennial vision of the community of women. Hailing "you" as someone involved in a circle of gratifying multigenerational social relationships, this ad addresses young middle class women who can identify with nostalgic moments such as "What size *Keds* were you wearing when you learned to take a compliment? And you started to hold your father's hand? What size *Keds* will you be wearing when the first of your friends gets married? What size *Keds* will you be wearing when a woman walks on Mars?" The *Keds* ad weaves together markers of women's traditional socialization with flattery about future accomplishments so that women need not reject a paternalistic past or present in order to achieve a sky's-the-limit-future. Yet another *Reebok* campaign hailed women with its own utopian view of women, athletics, and empowerment. *Reebok*'s "There is an athlete in all of us" called not for universal suffrage, but rather for universal access to the means of athletic play – which was supposedly automatic upon entering the atmosphere of Planet *Reebok*. The aesthetic background of these ads suggests a new space (almost like heaven) where there are no impediments to equality and freedom. In contrast, *Nike*'s representations of empowerment drew on a realist aesthetic in which female actors must assert their own agency. While *Nike* has run its share of subdued glamour shots of lean, muscled female athletes, the *Nike* ads accentuate less the body than the soul as the locus of freedom.

HAILING A NEW MARKET IN A DIFFERENT VOICE

The pivotal 1991 *Nike*'s women campaign drew on research that found women did not respond to "hero worship" as did men. *Nike* decided the ads needed to be "inspirational rather than aspirational."[15] *Nike*'s "Empathy" campaign began with an eight-page magazine insert written by Janet Champ that took the reader on a journey through the meaningful moments of a woman's life ... "You were born a daughter ..." The text remarkably encapsulated the self-contradictory experiences of growing up female in America. Tens of thousands of women wrote to *Nike* in response to these ads, which they read as "heartfelt" and sincere stories of women like themselves who were struggling to learn how to take care of themselves, for themselves.

Nicknamed the "tearjerker" campaign at *Wieden & Kennedy*, the campaign's success was due to its unforced copy, which read like a woman's interior musings – like a woman's own diary entry. Another factor had to do with photographic poses that continued to dispense with the male gaze.[16] *Nike* ads hailed potential women athletes with a gaze that said this look is not about, or for, men. Women in these *Nike* ads confronted the camera straight up, shoulders often squared rather than canted submissively. The campaign addressed women in a different tone of voice. As Charlotte Moore put it, "we realized ... we could talk to women how you would normally talk."[17] Women could read these ads without feeling positioned, and without feeling commanded, because the text addressed them as peers who share cultural experiences.

American consumer culture is marked by an obsessive desire to stand out by virtue of things worn, or looks displayed. If advertisers and marketers had their way, individual consumers would be forever careening from one display of self to another, never quite certain that they have found the right fit, but still convinced that the right fit is out there waiting for them to find it. But advertising is itself schizophrenic about what kind of self is appropriate. The long-standing cultural ideal for males may be referred to as the **autonomous ego** – a self that is resolutely sturdy, confident and once formed, unchanging in its fundamentals. But the ideal that has been installed for female consumers is a far more plastic vision of self, a self cast in terms of fashion. Though few of us would willingly admit that we believe we can find a satisfying self in a package or a box, in a culture geared to finding satisfaction in acts of consumption it is easy to suspend judgment just long enough to buy into the **ready-made identity** associated with the sign of a brandname or a look.

In this cultural context, *Nike* chose to hail female readers with what appeared to be autobiographical narrative excerpts. Hailing women consumers in this way spoke to a recognition that women already have selves, albeit selves that are complex and contradictory, selves that have evolved through existential crises, selves that have survived the assaults of patriarchy and consumerism. *Nike* ads spoke sympathetically to what Judith Williamson calls the "alreadyness" of those existential selves.

> *Nike* was the first sports company to "get" women. A few years ago it published a series of popular print advertisements with sayings like, "You do not have to be your mother." The poetic prose spoke to ordinary women who were lifting weights or doing aerobics for the first time.[18]

This ad from the "Empathy" campaign illustrates how self-conscious these ads were about gender as a socially constructed category. Still the slide from social construction back to the exaggerated mythos of individual self-construction seems a bit too facile. The caption plays on a widespread anxiety and ambivalence about middle class daughters' relationship with their mothers. Here the anxiety is acknowledged for the purpose of declaring the power of the individual woman to resist the forces of traditional socialization. By punctuating the piece with "You Decide," Nike's rhetoric of self-determination and personal choice identifies with women's resistance against ideologies of biological necessity.

The *Nike* "Empathy" ad spoke to the process of developing a self over the course of a lifetime – a self that corresponds neither to the fixed ideal defined by the male gaze nor to the female plasticity that accommodates to other people's vision of you, and of your life. Having established a sense of autobiographical rapport, the ad concludes by raising the female self to a new plateau – "You became significant to yourself." This campaign stressed giving the female consumer permission to fashion her own identity.

And you know when it's time to take care of yourself, for yourself.
To do something that makes you stronger, faster, more complete.
Because you know it's never too late to have a life.
And never too late to change one.
Just do it.

Nike's women's fitness ads celebrate the internal self of everyday women. Like so many other *Nike* campaigns this one metacommunicates a sense of no-hype, no spectacle. Hailing the viewer as "you" invites her to try on these autobiographical musings as if they might be her own. *Nike*'s prose poetry invited subjective introspection and reflection, but more importantly it invited women to join in a philosophy of life. By punctuating this eight-page narrative of a life's journey with the *Nike swoosh* and the familiar "Just do it" slogan, *Nike* positions itself as a philosophy and a way of life.

Nike's first women's TV advertising campaign was aired in February 1993. These ads constructed the appearance of soothing, therapeutic spaces within a world that otherwise seems to be rushing past. One ad followed a woman on a fitness walk through an urban setting. Shot in an artsy, black and white photographic style, Sigourney Weaver's voice-over narration counseled the viewing subject, "Go slow." "Don't rush," she cautioned, "the world will wait for you. The world wouldn't spin nearly as well if you weren't in it." Speaking like a therapist, her voice-over invites women to activate a true inner self and overcome the internalized social forces that block a deep self, the "I," from realizing itself, and perhaps as importantly, taking care of itself. Judging by the volume of letters *Nike* received about this campaign – one report claimed 100,000 letters – it touched a cultural nerve with its messages of "self-actualization" and "empowerment." In contrast to most ads that come across as phony when they try empowerment as a theme, "only the ads that really speak to women with authenticity – the way *Nike* does – are going to be successful at this."[19] *Nike*'s women's ads present the authentic as anti-spectacle by locating its imagery as discourses about everyday life.

Unified by its style of photography and tone of voice, this campaign offered existential meditations. A second ad featured a quiet, soothing voice and a soundtrack of new age folk music, while the prose poetry of Janet Champ again embraced a therapeutic ethos. Expressing awe and wonder about the physiology of the female body, the ad turns into the performance of a secular theology of self in relation to the modern world.

The setting and look celebrates
contentful introspection.

The next time you walk by a mirror, look at your shoulders, how they rise, how they fall. Look at the way your neck holds up your head … It is a miracle. This body. And every move you make is another celebration. Or a prayer.

While the mirror as a prop usually positions women as objects of the male gaze, here the combination of text and image frames the absence of the male gaze. The way the model admires herself does not speak to an imagined male, but to her own pleasure in her body and its movement. The advertisement presents a justification for being-in-yourself. It offers none of the usual enticements that physical workouts are worth it so you can appear more attractive to others – the kind of imagery that dominates the covers of magazines like *Self* and *Shape*.

The last of the three ads, called "Running," follows a woman emerging from a triangular space of water, then running in slow motion along vaguely surreal corridors, even though her expression indicates that she runs with purpose and direction.

You were born. And oh how you wailed. Your first breath is a scream. Not timid or low but selfish and shattering. With all the force of waiting nine months under water. The rest of your life should be like that. An announcement.

Juxtaposing metaphors of biology against those of culture, this ad offered another cautionary tale urging women not to be timid or submissive because of their female socialization, but to be assertive, indeed, even "selfish and shattering."

Turning the marriage vow on its head

Nike boosted its profile in women's sports in the following years, creating Air Swoopes, its first basketball shoe named for a woman, and sponsoring the US women's soccer team, the high school girls' All-America basketball game, as well as a "huge volleyball festival in Davis, Calif., for 7,500 high school girls."[20] *Nike* ads reflected the emergence of women's team sports in volleyball, soccer, and basketball. Unlike the previous round of therapeutic narratives, these ads focused less on the individual woman who has accepted the *Nike* ethos into her life, than on the experience of women's team sports. One *Nike* ad for women's soccer turned the language of traditional marriage vows against patriarchy in favor of female bonding. The contrast between the intensity of women's team sports and the traditional language of marriage vows reveals what is at stake. For these women, shown leaping and diving to achieve a team victory, the meaning of team (female bonding) has taken on the supportive covenant of the marriage vow while leaving behind those passages that deal with "obeying" a patriarchal order.

The voice-over, viewers are led to believe, is that of Mia Hamm, a premire American soccer player under contract with *Nike*. She is, however, neither named nor identified.

We are flesh and we are blood and we are bound together
for better, or worse,

Female sports are serious business signified by flashing glimpses of athleticism and voices of grim determination.

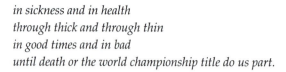

in sickness and in health
through thick and through thin
in good times and in bad
until death or the world championship title do us part.

An ear-piercing scream calls the others to order. These vows are then repeated by the collective voices of the United States women's soccer team set against a compendium of spectacular action shots. Their marriage vow now refers to their commitment to one another in their desire to win the world championship. This goal requires a total commitment shared by all the team members. Celebratory images, a montage of soccer highlights – kicks, headers, saves – dissolve into focused and determined facial expressions. An acoustic guitar builds in intensity, lending the images a sense of emotional consequence. The commercial aims to show empowered women through athletics.

Their bodies fly through the air, collide, and skid through the mud. The ad celebrates a toughness of both body and spirit. Their goal and their qualities of determination, concentration, and toughness become the basis for female bonding. While *Nike* often constructs male bonding around the activity of humorous banter (see Chapter 3), *Nike*'s representation of female bonding takes the form of passionate sincerity. Apparently, for the female athlete to be taken seriously, intensity is necessary. In the mid 1990s, *Nike* represented sport as empowering to women by constructing its female athletes as resolute, determined, committed, and humorless. *Nike* women played sport with serious resolve, rather than for fun.

They are a pack of wolves: beware your sheep

Themes of toughness, dedication and determination to accomplish the goals of being the best and winning are also played out in a *Nike* women's volleyball ad that draws an analogy between the women's volleyball team and a pack of wolves. Matching the athletes' looks of unwavering firmness of purpose is a background soundtrack that consists of team chatter along with the ambient gym sounds of players engaged in intense practice. The video is punctuated by a guttural, bloodthirsty scream of effort and intensity as a young woman strikes the ball in a put-away attempt. An older female voice-over narrates as these lines appear across the screen.

[They are] *not SISTERS*
[They are] *not CLASSMATES*
[They are] *NOT FRIENDS*
[They are] *not even the GIRLS TEAM.*
[They are a pack of] *WOLVES.*
Tend to your SHEEP.

JUST DO IT
[*SWOOSH* symbol]

The ad purges all traces of femininity. These volleyball players are depicted minus the construct of the feminine. They don't necessarily even care for one another. What they do is work as a team to achieve domination and the kill. Just as the voice-over pronounces them a pack of "wolves," we see a young woman going up in slow-motion to spike the ball. Her teeth are clenched and bared in fierce determination as she prepares to execute the kill. Women can come together with seriousness of purpose and not be deterred from goals of mastery. We have observed women who read this ad as empowering, as well as those who read it as an intimidating and overly aggressive construction of the female athlete.

This ad takes explicit aim at all conventional imagery of women's athletic teams. Forget everything you've ever assumed about females, the ad cautions, because these women are hungry to win. Does membership in the women's team provide the collective focus necessary to overcome the restrictions of traditional social relations? How does the symbolism of wolves and sheep play out in terms of gender relations? Paired together, the symbols of wolves and sheep, function as a semiotic opposition. Wolves connote wild, aggressive animals that roam and kill in packs. Sheep represent the opposite: domestic and meek, they follow passively in herds and are the prey of wolves.

Hood river women: reading the open text

Earlier we noted that *Nike* has tended to picture women engaged in sport as humorless and intensely serious. A notable exception to this tendency was a *Nike* ad titled "Jodi" about young women living and playing in the woods above Hood River, Oregon. Shot as an excursion into the everyday life of several young women who live in this wilderness area, "Jodi" spoke to the *joie de vivre* of the physically active life.

This is where you can mountain bike, you can sail, you can climb, you can bike.
I just get, like bruises and things. See my bruise.
You know I'd hate to just die, being old and not have had any fun.
Wow, I live here.
Balancing your play, your work, your social life.
I'm happy here.
But we both need [pause] *really cool men.* [Laughter]

Unlike the soccer and volleyball ads where female bonding is based on strong affectional behavior of teammates focused on winning, here there is a convivial attitude. In "Jodi" the young women ham for the camera which

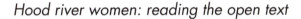

Do these women really need "cool men?"

opens up the possibility of multiple interpretations because the viewer has more difficulty gauging how distant the speaker is from the words she utters.

Though on first glance we might suppose that depicting women as bloodthirsty and aggressive animals in the volleyball ad would place them closer to male representations, "Jodi" actually comes the closest to portraying women in the same way *Nike* portrays men. These women enjoy a bond based on the banter and shared jokes of a common lifestyle. And yet, it is precisely here in their banter that interpretative ambiguity arises. Just how adventurous is this ad in challenging conventional hegemonic encodings? Perhaps quite inadvertently, the ad yields different interpretations by opening up the question of whether we rely on heterosexual or non-heterosexual assumptions. Read on the basis of cultural assumptions about heterosexuality, the joke at the end of the ad goes something like this: "yeah, we love it here cause it gives us a chance to stretch and experience ourselves while we are young, and yeah we love being self-sufficient, but ha-ha, in the end we still need and want guys." But the joke reads quite differently if the reader suspends presuppositions of heterosexual relations. This second reading draws on visual cues as well as the discursive text, so that as the last line is uttered, the young woman who is speaking clutches the arm of her friend while yet another women, her back turned to the camera, walks past them through the kitchen. Can this be read as women joking about the absence of men because they have found a satisfying paradise based on a community of women?

"If you let me play"

When play is transformed into sport, the physical body is made social.[21]

One of *Nike*'s most talked about TV ads debuted in August 1995. Titled "If you let me play," this ad gave voice to the consequences of denying girls the same opportunities for sports that boys routinely receive. This ad combines quick camera takes and slow-motion shots of preteen and teenage girls on a park playground signified by swing sets, monkey bars, and a simple merry-go-round. The spot features a turn-taking of girls' voices as they recite the long-term advantages in their lives if they play sports. Shown in tight facial close-ups, the young girls solemnly speak in soundbites that sound as if they have been scripted by social scientists and women's health advocates. The encounter with children speaking adult thoughts is initially startling, as they stare into the camera and flatly intone:

If you let me play
If you let me play sports
I will like myself more.
I will have more self-confidence.

If you let me play sports.
If you let me play
If you let me play
I will be 60% less likely to get breast cancer
I will suffer less depression.
If you let me play sports
I will be more likely to leave a man who beats me.
If you let me play
I will be less likely to get pregnant before I want to.
I will learn
I will learn what it means to be strong
To be strong
If you let me play
Play sports
If you let me play sports.

Just do it
[*Swoosh* symbol]

Nike positions sport as the panacea for social problems by linking images of childhood to statistics that will determine their future.

Nike represents a new breed of advertisers who try to make ads serve their own narrow commodity agendas by trying to give the ad a place in the field of **public culture** – a space where public debate is raised. The creators of "If you let me play" – Janet Champ, Rachel Nelson, Jennifer Smieja, and Angelina Vieira – have been explicit about their intentions.

> What we hoped to create with this advertisement was twofold. One, we wanted to help end the discrimination every little girl - and woman - is faced with when it comes to organized sports. And two, to alert fathers, mothers, teachers, friends, family members and girls themselves to the profound, and unsettling, benefits that sports and fitness can give them if they start young enough. (T)he benefits (of sports for women) are astounding.[22]

In another interview, Janet Champ stressed her concern that without realizing it, parents and teachers buy into the ideology that little girls need to be protected. This, Champ observed, results in lower self-esteem and confidence, and precipitates a self-fulfilling gender prophecy.[23]

Indeed, the ad brings together elements that otherwise rarely co-exist in the entertainment world of advertising. Advertising normally tries to avoid serious issues, because such issues are apt to generate controversy on the part of some audiences. But generating controversy is precisely the agenda here. Obviously, *Nike* is not alone in challenging these boundary norms – witness the advertising of *Benetton* in recent years, or the pro-environmental spots put forward by *Esprit*, or the *Liz Claiborne* billboards which focus on violence against women.

"If you let me play" exemplifies *Wieden & Kennedy*'s effort at breaking through the clutter of television advertising. Remember that every other maker of women's athletic shoes and apparel was also fashioning some blend of feminism and consumption. The *Nike* ad broke through the clutter not just because of its message about women's health and well-being, but also because it violated conventions about how ads address or hail us.

This ad startled viewers as an adventurous effort at changing what is acceptable within the field of advertising discourse. It is immediately obvious that the young girls are reading lines given them by others. They have been instructed not to "act" but to recite their lines as if reading them. This rhetorical trope allows them to speak about their future in such a way that the children become both the subjects and objects of their own discourse. Newspaper reviews of the ad called it "chilling" or "eerie." We are not used to little girls looking straight into the camera and reciting "facts" about "adult" subjects in the low-affect tones of social scientists.

Though *Nike* and *Wieden & Kennedy* may have had a specific message they wanted to get across, this ad invites multiple interpretations. It should be quickly noted, however, that multiple interpretations are of no concern to *Nike* because the goal of "If you let me play [sports]" was to "stir the pot." And that is what the ad did: it generated talk.

> The first time I saw the commercial, it stopped me cold in my living room, and I had to sit down for a moment, just to absorb what had been said. Part of me was thrilled by what I was seeing. Part of me was profoundly disturbed. More than 20 viewings later, I am still pulled in two directions.[24]

This ad worked like a Rorschach test, eliciting a range of interpretations and emotional intensities based on what the viewer brought to its interpretation. A survey by sociology–anthropology students at Lewis & Clark College found that wealthier and more educated young women were more likely to negotiate the ad's meaning in a cynical and skeptical way. They tended to question *Nike*'s agenda for running the ad, whether *Nike*'s commitment was to the lives of adolescent girls or to garnering more sales. Typical of this response was a student who wrote on the survey, "Does *Nike* really have a social conscience, or are they just trying to sell shoes?" Of course, these are not necessarily mutually exclusive goals; but in the minds of many young people who have been exposed to thousands and thousands of ads, there does seem to be a distrust of pecuniary motives even when they are accompanied by rhetorics of concern for others. Alternatively, young women from working class families, or whose families do not have a history of college education, or who are from small towns, seemed to embrace the ad more enthusiastically and with fewer qualifications. Young women who self-identified as athletes were most likely to see the ad favorably.

But girls were only one audience for this ad. Liz Dolan, *Nike*'s Vice President of Marketing, stated bluntly that the ad was aimed at parents. "We felt we needed to talk to adults about the benefits if girls get to play." "Our intention was to be provocative; we wanted adults to think" about barriers to girls' participation in sports. *Nike*'s women's sports marketing manager, Sue Levin, added that "Dads with daughters – my greatest allies are dads with daughters. They want their kid to have every opportunity in sports that they did."[25] Indeed, if it has become "socially acceptable for girls to play – and excel – at sports," one major reason is that the current generation of fathers want to share the experience of sports with their daughters. "We finally have the first generation of men who lived through the women's movement," Billie Jean King said. "They may not want to admit it, but they're making a difference with their daughters. These dads want their daughters to have opportunities."[27]

Of course, because the *Nike* ads, men's as well as women's, seek to **stir the pot** and get people buzzing about the ad, they also run the risk of antagonizing some viewers. Many an ad makes truth claims – but this *Nike* ad stood out because it did not make truth claims for the product, but rather about the benefits of sport for girls. The *Nike* ad advanced truth claims about health issues, gender equity, and women's futures. The ad commented on broader social issues. For this it was hailed in many circles. But truth claims also invite people to look for evidence that might counter the truth claims. Is there really evidence that by playing sports "I will be 60% less likely to get breast cancer?" One criticism of the ad questioned whether there was real statistical data to support these claims. *Nike*'s advertising department anticipated this with a fact sheet on women's health and participation in sports activities. Its background research showed that half of all girls who participate in sports have above-average levels of self-esteem; that female athletes have more positive body images than non-athletes; that adolescent girls who participate in sports are less likely to become drug dependent, have lower teen pregnancy rates, and are more likely to graduate from high school. They also gathered claims from studies that showed a lower propensity to heart disease, osteoporosis, diabetes, high blood pressure, obesity, and back pain in sportswomen.

In our own survey of young people's responses to the ad, we found the ad elicited thoughtful and reflective criticisms. Some were put off by the method of having children recite "adult facts" about cancer and abuse, because this violates a sense of childhood innocence.

> I do remember being quite struck by the ad, and unsure how to respond to it. It does have a jarring effect, something like watching ventriloquism – the words seem very disconnected from the girls who speak them. You

don't want them to be saying them, or even to be thinking of things like depression or breast cancer. (Jen W.)

The ad elicited responses that went well beyond the text itself. For example, some questioned the reductive simplicity of asserting that sports would solve the problems confronting women. One such response called into question *Nike*'s implicit "class-ism."

> Women who stay in an abusive relationship are subject to some of the blame themselves, since they could leave, or turn their spouse in to the police. The *Nike* ad plays indirectly on this sort of judgment – "I will be more likely to leave a man who beats me" suggests that at some level it's simply a matter of volition, independent of the fact that she may be pinned by economic advantage, or rather, disadvantage. (Jason H.)

Perhaps the most telling criticism came from women who resented the permission-requesting tone of "If you let me play." Why not, retorted angry women, say "When I play sports …"

> One obvious problem: Why do the girls have to beg? What are their brothers doing while these girls stand passively on the playground? Boys don't have to ask permission to play sports. Like adults, they just do it.[27]

This same author goes on to note, however, that young girls are quite capable of contesting and discarding that aspect of the message.

> Fortunately, girls are laughing, too. A coach reports that the girls on her team are using the phrase "If you let me" jokingly, the way they joke about "I've fallen and I can't get up." It is ironic that in an effort to defeat some of the consequences of a patriarchal system that positions females to, as bell hooks puts it, "do it for daddy," *Nike*'s ad situates the daughter's fate in father's decision to "let" her play sports.

Following the release of the ad, however, there were more reports of positive reactions than negative. *Nike* received calls from viewers who thanked them for "affirming that sports are good for girls." Callers included "coaches, teachers, fathers of young girls, mothers choking back tears while describing their dashed dreams of playing sports as children."[28] The ad played especially well to women 35–55 years old who have children, who work full time, and work out three to five times a week. Women seemed to like the strong, non-whining message.[29]

The ad resonated with Americans' long-held belief that there is something inherently valuable in athletic competition, that "character" is built in locker rooms and on playing fields. This ethos of amateur athletics now extended to include all women. This is ironic, given the fact that *Nike* has become rich and powerful by treating more and more sports as commodity centered. As one journalist observed, "Despite the fiction that sports is designed to teach young people valuable life lessons, the truth is that most of our sports – down to the scholastic level – serve mainly to generate winners and entertain the community."[30]

More broadly, this ad might be seen as directed at the broader adult public as a pitch for public support for athletics and play facilities for female youth. This fits with the agenda of *Nike*'s P.L.A.Y. campaign aimed at a crisis of community recreation facilities. Like the P.L.A.Y campaign, the "If you let me play" ad legitimates the company as having broad social and public concerns and interests. As a corollary to such legitimation claims in these ads, *Nike* did not name itself as such, but rather identified itself solely on the basis of the *swoosh* symbol and the slogan "Just do it."

One year after "If you let me play" was aired, *Nike* released a sister ad, "There's a girl being born in America." Its video style immediately identified the ad as *Nike*'s follow-up to the previous ad.

There's a girl being born in America
And somebody will tell her she is beautiful
And somebody will tell her she is strong
Somebody will tell her she is precious
And somebody will say she is tough.
There's a girl being born in America
And someone will give her a doll
And someone will give her a ball
And then someone will give her a chance.

Unlike the previous ad, this one juxtaposes the socialization of girls into a world defined by the male gaze (for example, this scene of a little girl wearing heart-shaped sunglasses and applying lipstick) against imagery of sports participation. By posing the issue in a binary way between "dolls" and "balls" the *Nike* ad sought to privilege action over appearance. The preferred reading of the ad is consistent with the earlier ad, equating "chances" with leaving behind a life defined by gender stereotypes.

About the same time that *Nike* aired the sequel, *Reebok* released an ad that took dead aim at "If you let me play," using the line several times to mock *Nike* as wimpy. The *Reebok* ad is what we call a "sign war" ad because it doesn't pay much attention to products, but focuses instead on *Nike*'s imagery or sign. *Nike* had hitched its *swoosh* sign to "If you let me play," and now *Reebok* sought to make *Nike* pay for this by trying to ideologically one-up *Nike* in the competition for the hearts and minds of young women. *Reebok*'s professional basketball-playing women won't ask permission because they intend to do it, period: "and we are most definitely not waiting for anyone to let us play."

"We got next" changes of address?

To no one's great surprise, in late 1994 *Nike* researchers found that when asked what came to mind when they heard the name *Nike*, young girls typically mentioned Michael Jordan or Charles Barkley or another male athletic star.[31] This spurred *Nike* to sign up a number of female basketball stars and to develop a new basketball shoe designed for women and named after their young star, Sheryl Swoopes.[32] More generally, *Nike* began to change direction in its women's advertising.

Joan Benoit-Samuelson is revered on the *Nike* campus as one of a select inner circle of sainted athletes. But few outside the *Nike* faithful remember this pioneer women's marathoner. Jackie Joyner-Kersee was *Nike*'s first luminous female star, but her most prominent advertising appearances were in the P.L.A.Y. campaign where she gave autobiographical testimony to the claim that coaches and athletic facilities can make a difference in the lives of impoverished youth.

A booming marketplace for women's sports prompted *Nike* to change direction in 1994 to develop female athletic stars who combine intensity of focus with a desire to win. Today, the *Nike swoosh* brands a stable of female athletes that includes Swoopes, Lisa Leslie, Dawn Staley, Gabriella Reese, Mia Hamm, Monica Seles, and Picabo Street. As *Nike* draws on these established performers, it has begun to mimic the approach that worked for them with their male celebrity athletes which was to play off the athlete's personality and sport. Hence, Monica Seles, a tennis star, is presented in a lighthearted entertainment ad full of intertextual playfulness (she plays at being a female James Bond), while Mia Hamm, the premier American soccer athlete, appears in ads that pay homage to her intense drive and dedication, drenched by the elements and her own sweat.

Nike commercials of Reese and Street end in a photograph signed with a swoosh.

During the buildup to the 1996 Summer Olympics, women's athletics received a higher television profile than ever before. Just prior to the Atlanta Olympics, the *NBA* announced they would leverage the excitement and hype generated by *NBC* during their Olympic coverage into a new professional women's league. Since the enactment of Title IX in 1972, making it illegal for athletic departments to discriminate against women's programs, the quality of women's sports programs has gradually improved. "In the 24 years since Title IX was passed, a generation of women athletes has come of age."[33] It was thus no coincidence that the final *Nike* ad run during the 1996 Olympic games used the simple device of a voice-over reading from Title IX to frame an edited sequence of images of young women playing sports: "No person shall on the basis of sex, be excluded from participation in, be denied the benefits of, be treated differently from another person, or otherwise be discriminated against in any interscholastic, intercollegiate, club or intramural athletics."

The act of reciting of Title IX like it was the Pledge of Allegiance decisively indicates *Nike*'s public commitment to the agenda of women's athletics. We would suggest, however, that the more profound ad in terms of changing how an advertiser hails women about athletics was a 1996 *Nike* ad that told a story about three members of the US Olympic women's basketball team playing a pickup game on the park playground. A Spike Lee voice-over narrates: "Once upon a time, three girls went to Rock Steady for a pickup game." Three young women are seen walking to the park. They approach a playground where five young men are playing basketball. As they near the court, the tallest woman casually calls out "Yo!" One of the young men turns to face her/us and half

Nike stars prepare to take on the boys.

smiles, as she continues, "We got next." The camera returns to her face, as Lee identifies each woman in turn: "Lisa is a center. Sheryl is a forward. Dawn's a point guard." Each of these women play for the US Olympic Team. They are not named as such, but sports fans will recognize Lisa Leslie, Sheryl Swoopes and Dawn Staley as *Nike* endorsers. The camera seems to prefer Lisa Leslie, long and lean, stretching out her legs, before moving to a shot of Swoopes removing her sweatshirt, and Staley in the motion of tying an unseen shoe. A connecting shot of them slapping low fives, gives way to the game itself played against guys on the playground. The first, and most significant, scene shows Staley banging bodies with the opposing point guard who lays a shoulder into her chest as he tries to drive past her on offense. We can hear her grunt with the force of the blow. On the audio track, the collective voice of the gallery reacts with an "ohhh." Perhaps coincidentally, perhaps not, in the background on a school wall appears a repeating sequence of cut-out doll images of little boys and girls holding hands.

Images of performance are linked to gestures of achievement, acceptance and camaraderie.

Swoopes drives to the basket past one of the larger men, her quickness leaving him flat-footed. A closeup shot of a young man watching through a chain link fence represents the primarily male gallery scattered around the court observing and commenting on the quality of play. They seem duly impressed. In the following scenes, Staley is seen playing physical basketball, setting a moving screen so that Leslie can spot up and shoot. Throughout, viewers can hear the women chattering to one another in the background like, "take the jumper Lise." After sinking another running jump shot, Leslie slaps a high five with one of the guys as she says "good game." Another game follows with the only *Nike* sneaker image in the ad, as one of the women makes a cut down the lane. The following camera shot of Swoopes driving successfully to the basket suggests that she made the move. Other scenes show Swoopes acknowledging the assist from Staley, and the women playing defense, getting their hands on the ball defensively and knocking it away. While Swoopes is seen playing defense, Lee chimes in again: "And this isn't a fairy tale. So, they didn't beat every guy." Swoopes tries to block a shot but her opponent scoops the ball over her and into the basket. But, with a dozen or so guys watching from the sidelines, Staley launches a two hand set shot that drops. Lee continues, "But they beat enough to say: 'basketball is basketball. Athletes are athletes.'" The screen cuts to "Just do it" painted across the playground, which is then replaced by a *swoosh* across the shadows cast by a chain link fence across the asphalt. As the video of the *swoosh* becomes overexposed one of the girls can be heard calling out, "our ball," suggesting that the games continue.

Less spectacularized than the "Wolves" ad, which gave a metaphoric turn to participation in women's athletics, this ad takes a superrealist approach. The story narrated by Spike Lee is one of authenticity – it is told as a story that has the ring of truth to it. This authenticity is expressed in the visual details of the ad. The gesture of acknowledging the assist is, for example, a gesture formerly associated with men's play. Its inclusion in the edited flow of the game signals that *Nike* has elevated the women's game to the status of legitimate basketball. The video naturalizes and normalizes the activity of women basketball players going toe to toe with the guys holding court on the playground. "And this isn't a fairy tale" steers us back to the everyday world of hoops in the park, where competitive women athletes will win their share of contests.

Sometimes the most profound shifts in media representations are the unobtrusive and quiet shifts. The 1997 Nike *street basketball campaign hailing ballplayers (featuring the musings of Arkansas Red), made no effort at differentiating the mix of scenes of women playing ball from the scenes of men playing ball. Though they are depicted separately, they are sequenced as equivalent.*

CONSTRUCTING FEMALE CELEBRITY ATHLETES

Since the watershed ads discussed above, *Nike* advertising to young women has raced along, with each new series of ads shifting the ground of representations. While the most apparent change is the move away from self-conscious legitimation of women's sports, it is no less significant that *Nike* has shifted the weight of its women advertising to focusing on star athletes. These revisions are driven by *Nike*'s perception of changes taking place amongst the young women who make up new markets. *Nike* feels that these young women are no longer concerned with justifying sports for themselves, but rather accept women's sports as a natural part of their lives.

Listening only to the male voice-over reciting the words of a *Nike* soccer commercial, someone who had grown up in the male-dominated American sports culture would not likely assume it to be about a woman.

The best football player in America
Will not be seen on television this Sunday.
Not while there's a Pro Bowler's tour.
America did not see the best football player win a gold medal in Atlanta.
America did not see the best football player win our only World Cup.
Because all the networks agree
The best football player in America [pause]
Isn't good for ratings.

This ad is scripted to play off the common expectation that in the context of sports, an unmarked gender statement will be read as male. The European reference to "football" as opposed to the American distinction between soccer and football (the latter, an almost universally male dominated game) renders this uncertain. Still, the opening scenes suggest a deliberate attempt to confuse the identification of a gendered body. Even subtle background codes that mark gender identity are either scrambled or missing: the soundtrack amplifies ambient sounds into metallic, grating, discordant noises, while the deglamourized setting of the opening scenes is an overexposed copper-tinted closeup of water dripping in a corner, framing a closeup shot of the back of a sock-covered calf and cleated shoe. One might guess, based on familiarity with sports, that the scene's referent is the runway from the locker room to the field beneath an older stadium, where players prepare to take the field, nervously kicking the wall to knock debris from around the cleats, while water drips from pipes above.

Like the other three ads from this campaign, this ad hailed soccer fans and players about a shared resentment (note the sarcasm of "not while there's a Pro Bowler's tour") that comes from being ignored by American television networks wed, in equal measure, to the masculine violence of the *NFL*, and to an American ethnocentrism that regards its sports as superior to other cultures' games. However, unlike the other ads, this one is about a female, Mia Hamm, the "best football player in America." Those who know soccer, players and fans, already recognize Mia Hamm in spite of her relative lack of media exposure. Other viewers might not recognize her on the first viewing, unless they alertly catch sight of her surname as it flashes across the screen in a fraction of a second on the back of her jersey as she launches her-

self to head a ball. Alerted to the presence of that flashing identification mark, second and third time viewers may also figure out and join the significance of Mia Hamm to the other meanings of the script. Hamm is identified not as America's best "female" football player, but as *the* best. When the edited video is placed against the soundtrack, it turns out that *Nike* may not just be referring to a network bias against soccer, but against women's sports as well.

The *swoosh* that comes across the scene of the closing frames is the sign of an imaginary totem group. We use the word imaginary not to invalidate this totem group, but to call attention to the way in which the placement of the *swoosh* as a signature refers not to a thing, but to a Desire. That desire might be hero identification, "to be like Mia Hamm." In fact, "I wanna be like Mia" is the subject of another sponsor's ad, where it explicitly plays off viewer familiarity with the oft-cited *Gatorade* ad of some years back with its tagline, "I wanna be like Mike." More broadly, this ad invites young women athletes to join the symbolic totem group signed by the *swoosh*. It invites them to see in *Nike* an entity that understands and supports resentment about biases against women's sports and soccer; an entity that respects and supports excellence in sports, no matter the question of gender.

It is also important to observe what desire is absent from this representation. Markers of femininity have been tossed aside in representing the body. For the purpose of demonstrating how different *Nike* advertising has become from the typical television representations of femininity, compare the *Nike* ad with a commercial for *Pert Plus* shampoo that also features the same Mia Hamm, but constructs her as an athlete who is also/still an attractive woman. The *Pert Plus* ad splits Hamm into two, one the sweaty athlete (the before image) and the other, attractive woman (the after make-over image). The *Pert Plus* ad offers the solution to the desire for an imaginary ego-ideal that unifies the competitive, sweaty athlete and attractive (to the male gaze) young woman. *Nike* does not offer this solution, but rather constructs Mia Hamm, the female athlete, as an ego-ideal that is wholly integrated as an athlete. Concern with appearance constructed as a feminine trait has no place in the *Nike* philosophy. Once upon a time, sports-hero worship had no place in the *Nike* women's philosophy, but all that has changed.

Finally we must report that in August of 1997 *Nike* aired a series of ads promoting the *WNBA* and some of its marquee athletes. Reminiscent of the Dennis Hopper ads for *Nike* football, these ads built on the premise of an obsessive fan who surrounds himself with life-size cardboard cutouts of *WNBA* team members. These strained efforts at quirky humor together with the visual tone associated with the amateur handheld camera indicate another milestone in the development of *Nike*'s advertising to women as it is now sufficiently established that it no longer needs to take itself or women's sports so seriously.

THE NEW WOMAN IN THE NEW CAPITALIST WORLD ORDER

Since the Summer of 1996, the disparity between the ideology of empowerment that *Nike* addresses to female consumers and the employment practices of *Nike* subcontractors in Indonesia and Vietnam became front-page news. Human rights groups charged that Indonesian women workers who assembled *Nike* shoes were not paid a living wage, were subject to unhealthy working conditions, and were denied the most basic of rights, including the right to freedom of association and free speech. In a widely noted *New York Times* editorial, Bob Herbert argued that "the definition of empowerment, for *Nike* officials, depends on whether the woman is buying their shoes or making them."[34] On a tour of the US designed to amplify these charges, a representative of the Indonesian women seeking better working conditions commented that she and her co-workers had always assumed the *Nike* "Just do it" slogan which they saw on posters in the factory, meant "Don't talk, work harder."[35]

As the leader of a new global political economy of sign value, *Nike* has a vested interest in depicting a new pluralism of differences united by its interest in reproducing its capital and the commodity form. Like other advertisers in recent years, *Nike* has been willing to bend away from patriarchal ideologies to a more diffuse, some would say pluralistic, construction of gender frames and definitions. Patriarchy does not deliver profits to *Nike* circa 1996. Because *Nike*'s women's advertising builds on the premise of providing sport to as many individuals as will consume it, *Nike* bears no allegiance to patriarchal conceptions of what is or is not appropriate behavior for women. *Nike* has always positioned itself as the upstart company, always the rebel or maverick, and authentic in an unpretentious way. To back away from these meanings in its advertising and promotions aimed at women would not likely serve its market interests. As the leader in the contemporary shoe industry, *Nike* has an interest in attacking the appearances of domination based on gender, race, class and sexual preference. "Supporting girls in sports yields tremendous marketing benefits for advertisers" in so far as "the women's sports market is currently a $10 billion market and growing."[36]

Nike's successive strategies with regard to its women's ads illustrate an ideological process that sociologists refer to as "the moving equilibrium of hegemony."[37] Questions of hegemony are always about contests over power, including the power to define issues. This is why battles over hegemony are typically fought out in the realm of language and images, where we encounter the frames and the categories that predominate in how people make sense of their world. In contests over how to define relationships, the "moving equilibrium of hegemony" suggests that dominant ways of interpreting the world may be flexible enough to absorb oppositional points of view as a means of deflecting the brunt of criticism. In the case of *Nike* advertising, the engine that drives this moving equilibrium has been market competition to secure wider market niches. *Nike's* success in growing the women's athletic footwear market testifies to the fact that in today's world of consumer advertising, the most successful advertisers assemble ideological representations that both support and oppose dominant social interests.

We are not dismissive of *Nike's* makeover from a men's club to a prominent corporate ideologue in behalf of women's rights and equity just because it has been driven by the pursuit of profits. However, this relationship between cultural imagery of women and the forces of commodification reopens unsettling questions about whether women are empowered or disempowered by the extension of market institutions. The contradictions of capitalism confront us starkly – on the one hand, expansion of the consumer marketplace demands that marketers embrace images of female equity and empowerment, while on the other hand, the profitable production of shoes and apparel press women in developing nations into the grip of disempowering market forces.

NOTES AND REFERENCES

1. Nancy Lieberman-Cline, "Sporting goods companies target women's market," *The Dallas Morning News*, November 2 1995, p. 4B.
2. NIKE, Inc. 1997 Annual Report.
3. Jeff Manning, "Corporate America is finally embracing women's athletics," *The Oregonian*, July 2 1995, p. A15.
4. Michele Mahoney, "Courting Women," *The Denver Post*, April 29 1996, p. F1. See Suzanne Bianchi and Daphne Spain, et al. "Women, work, and family in America," *Population Bulletin* 51, (December, 1996), pp. 1–48.
5. Rita Henley Jensen, "Far from the finish line," *The Oregonian*, July 21 1996, p. C5.
6. Donald Katz, *Just Do It: the Nike Spirit in the Corporate World* (Random House, New York, 1994), p. 152.
7. Michael Lewis, "Just buy it," *New York Times Magazine,* June 23 1996, p. 20.
8. Mark Trujillo, "Hegemonic masculinity on the mound: media representations of Nolan Ryan and American sports culture," *Critical Studies in Mass Communication*, 8, September 1991, pp. 290–308.
9. John Berger, *Ways of Seeing* (Penguin, New York, 1972); Laura Mulvey, "Visual pleasure and narrative cinema," *Screen*, 16 (1975), pp. 6–18.
10. Robert Goldman, Deborah Heath and Sharon Smith, "Commodity feminism," *Critical Studies in Mass Communication*, 8 (September, 1991), pp. 333–51.
11. Cyndee Miller, "Liberation for women in ads," *Marketing News*, August 17 1992, p. 1; Karen Avenoso, "Trapped by self-actualizing ads," *Advertising Age*, November 23 1992, p. 18.
12. Susan Bordo, *Unbearable Weight: Feminism, Western Culture and the Body* (University of California Press, Berkeley, CA, 1993), p. 179.
13. Susan Douglas, "Flex Appeal, buns of steel and the body in question," *In These Times*, September 7–13 1988, p. 19.
14. Bordo, *Unbearable Weight*, pp. 179, 298.
15. Jann Mitchell, "Instinct for inspiration," *The Oregonian*, October 23 1994, p. L4.

16. Robert Goldman, *Reading Ads Socially* (Routledge, New York, 1992).

17. Cited in Warren Berger, "You've come a long way … maybe," *Advertising Age*, February 1 1993, p. 22.

18. Mariah Burton Nelson, "Nike just doesn't get it," *The Buffalo News*, October 18 1995, p. 1D.

19. Berger, "You've come a long way," p. 22.

20. Nelson, "Nike just doesn't get it," p. 1D.

21. John Wilson, *Playing by the Rules: Sport, Society, and the State* (Wayne State University Press, Detroit, 1994), p. 37.

22. pubweb.acns.nwu.edu/~ksa878/wchb/astound.htm.

23. Karen Anderegg, "Women who shape our ideas of fitness: Janet Champ," *Mirabella*, March 1996, p. 33.

24. Jennifer Frey, "Nike puts shoe on other foot; it fits, though perhaps not comfortably," *The Washington Post*, October 15 1995, p. D7.

25. Manning, "Embracing women athletes," p. A15.

26. Tom Zucco, "Giving girls a crack at the bat," *St Petersburg Times*, May 21 1996, p. 1D.

27. Nelson, "Nike just doesn't get it," p. 1D.

28. Mary Schmitt, "Nike commercial makes a long-overdue point; ad extolling benefits of sports for girls elicits grateful reactions," *Austin American-Statesman*, October 19 1995, p. C2; Lieberman-Cline, "Companies target women's market," p. 4B.

29. Mahoney, "Courting women," p. F1.

30. Philip Martin, "Sports mostly just entertainment, despite the earnest ad campaigns," *Arkansas Democrat-Gazette*, November 5 1995, p. 1E.

31. Greg Hassell, "Sold on games that women play," *The Houston Chronicle*, July 17 1996, p. 1.

32. Lewis, "Just buy it," p. 20.

33. Hassell, "Sold on games," p. 1.

34. Bob Herbert, "In America: from sweatshops to aerobics," *The New York Times*, June 24 1996, p. A15.

35. Julie Whipple, "Nike vows to improve monitoring in Asia," *The Business Journal*, July 26 1996, p. 27.

36. A media kit for Girls and Sports Extra cited by Stuart Elliott, "*Sports Illustrated* and *Nike* hope girls just want to read about women's sports and female athletes," *The New York Times*, July 15 1996, p. D11. Appearing on ABC NIGHTLINE, June 24, 1997, Sue Levin of *Nike* acknowledged that by the year 2000 *Nike* seeks to derive 40% of its sales from the women's market: "This is an opportunity where what's good for *Nike*'s business is also the right thing to do because we really believe strongly as a company that sports are good for girls and women."

37. Todd Gitlin, "Prime time ideology: the hegemonic process in television entertainment," *Social Problems* 26, 3, 1979, pp. 251–265.

7.
THERE ARE MANY PATHS TO HEAVEN

A statue of Michael Jordan hovers above the boutiques of NIKE-TOWN.

It has become a truism that sports stadiums have taken on characteristics once associated with places of worship. Each week millions of people enter these temples and shrines of sport to participate in the ritualized competitions they offer. Sports events now chronicle the transition of the seasons. Holidays are big game days, while miracles reprise as the Play of the Day. Religious metaphors fuse with sports lingo in colloquial expressions such as "the Hail Mary pass". We bestow deity-like status onto athletic heroes. We wear the corporate emblems and colors of our chosen teams on our clothes, and even tattoo insignias on our bodies. When you walk down the street or through the mall do you see more *swoosh*es or crosses?

How often have we heard sport described as offering individual redemption through overcoming physical and social adversity? As the power of religious discourse wanes, sports discourse sometimes replaces it as a place for presenting middle class homilies about the meaning of moral life. Sports stories routinely adopt allusions borrowed from religion that blend determination and will power with themes of transcendence over the social world, the limitations of one's own body, and even fate. However, these moralizing platitudes associated with sport stand in stark contrast with the obvious commercialization of sport and the frequent violations of legal and moral codes by big name athletes that get reported in the news (spouse abuse, drunken driving, rape). In response, to relegitimate themselves, sports leagues tout their good works with promotional messages that reveal players supporting a higher calling – e.g., the *United Way* or the *Special Olympics*.

Having hitched its business to the spread of sports culture, *Nike* has tried to distance itself from the sign of corrupted, over-commercialized sports, while maintaining an irreverent, even sacrilegious, attitude. And yet, while *Nike* ads disdain embracing anything that might smack of endorsing the religion of sports, or the excessive moralizing that goes on in its name, they do speak to questions of spirituality.

SPIRITUALITY À LA CARTE

Nike ads address questions of personal spirituality couched in aesthetic representations of athletic activity. Under the sign of ecological enlightenment and reenchantment, *Nike* hails its *ACG* audience with a multimedia ode to finding one's spirit in communion with nature. Elsewhere, under the sign of respect for difference, *Nike* addresses the subject of AIDS, while its 1996 Olympic ads hail the spirit of ascetic self-denial in pursuit of a goal. The idea of a single path to heaven is fundamentally inconsistent with *Nike*'s wide range of niche markets, so *Nike* ads offer a plurality of spiritual ideologies to choose from. *Nike* appeals to what some sociologists now call "religion *à la carte*." In a social world defined by individuation and privatization, the search for spiritual meaning often turns into "a practice of appropriation of symbols, ideas, and meanings into a religion oriented around, and legitimated by, the self." Stewart Hoover sees religious practice in the television era as "a situation of seekers turning to a largely commodified inventory of symbols, values and ideas out of which they appropriate those which fit best into senses of themselves."[1] Like shopping for shoes, pick the pair you like, leave the others behind, and if the clerk gives you any grief over your choices, find another place to shop. Religion *à la carte* as a set of consumption choices clearly fits well with the stress on niche marketing; so well, in fact, that it prompts us to wonder whether the therapeutic ethos of advertising has actually contributed to this preference for customized religion.

In their role as our mass-media public philosophers, *Nike* offers homilies and narratives well suited to consumers who select their religion buffet style. Where better to seek a morality fit for living in a world of commodity relations? They rarely if ever get preachy; they aren't into guilt; and their ads respect the viewer. And the morality comes in all sorts of flavors and styles. While multiple flavors, individually wrapped, make for what some would call a "postmodern fragmentation" of meaning and belief, they also have a decidedly anti-authoritarian overtone. There is no single path to heaven.

Irreverent spirituality and the crisis of meaning

In the 1970s, the US began to experience in an acute fashion what Michel de Certeau calls "the devaluation of belief."[2] This devaluation of belief has been the product of a long historical process in which beliefs were "harnessed" and "captured" so that they could be "transferred" to emerging institutions – for example, beliefs lodged in churches were transferred to secular institutions such as the nation state. We argue that the routine and continuous practice of reassigning cultural and social values to commodities eventually took its toll on the public will to believe. When Belief and

Meaning are routinely put to the service of marketers, consumer wariness builds. Where once Belief and Meaning were thought to be limitless and inexhaustible, there now stands impassive, cynical disbelief. As we noted in the earlier chapter on irreverence, the leading edge of advertisers has reacted to this cynical turn among audiences by adopting a self-reflexive and mocking stance in sympathy with the viewer. Yet, while *Nike* ads preach irreverence, they also seek to project the idea that *Nike* has a spiritual core – that *Nike* has a soul!

An architectural critic recently wrote that *Nike*'s lavish new NIKETOWN in Manhattan turns "shopping into a form of worship" in a "shimmering temple to capitalism."[3] If so, then NIKETOWN might rightly be called a temple of sign value. But if this is the shrine to the "Church of *Nike*," its ministry is located in *Nike* ads which tend to a diversity of spiritual attitudes among a world full of jaded and cynical viewers who still want to believe in something. Wade Clark Roof observes that the religious mood in the United States in the mid 1990s has shifted away from a theology of fixed beliefs toward an experiential and expressive quest "attuned to body, mind, and self."[4] It is precisely this latter experiential and expressive quest that *Nike* addresses.

Saving the self

Might we be stretching too far if we suggest that *Nike* advertising sometimes envisions sport as a form of secular salvation or redemption? If religion is conceptualized in a traditional way, replete with fixed theology, ornate symbolism and clergy as father-figures, then indeed *Nike* ads will be found wanting. As we have already seen, *Nike* keeps its symbolism streamlined, and tightly minimalist at that, while almost always leaning toward anti-authoritarian expressions. And, while we are still debunking the idea of *Nike* coupled to religion, we should add that *Nike* never, ever, proclaims that a wearer will achieve salvation.

Instead, one body of *Nike* ads constructs sport as a conduit to another level of consciousness. If we look carefully, we can still see traces of Protestant traditions underlying these contemporary representations of spirituality. While the bulk of *Nike*'s imagery glorifies the desire to achieve and excel through hard work, *Nike* also uses a therapeutic voice to spiritualize the quest for inner peace and self-satisfaction. But *Nike*'s engagement with questions of spirit does not end there. It offers, as well, an occasional glimpse of a re-enchanted, sometimes magical relationship with the world via our interest in sports.

While the visible appearance of religiosity has been expunged from these ads, we see traces of various Christian conceptions of the soul flavoring *Nike*'s advertising. On the one hand, there was the sober, pious Protestantism that Max Weber saw as demanding that individuals perform their "calling" – the activity they had been destined by the Lord to perform. Individuals were enjoined to work, and ascetically deny themselves all pleasure, to fulfill the Lord's bidding. Over time, this ethic became intertwined with the spirit of capitalism, and the austere connotations of eternal salvation or eternal damnation dropped away while questions of personal transcendence became associated with individual determination – the will to succeed.[5] We now recognize this simply as the "work ethic," the ideal that hard work results in achieving beyond socially defined limits and success is the consequence of one's own initiative and doggedness. The twentieth century motivational discourse surrounding athletics draws heavily from the language of this value system. Clichéd stories – and there are a myriad of them – about athletes who, despite hardship and handicap, achieved beyond expectations because of their inner drive remain a staple of television sports coverage. *NBC*'s 1996 Olympic coverage concentrated on telling stories of athletes who transcended poverty, or a horrid family life, or physical injury to reach the Olympic competition. Corporate legitimation ads (*IBM's* great moments in sports), military recruitment campaigns (the *Army's* "Be all you can be" campaign), and commodity advertising (*Champion*, "It takes a little more to never say never") hammer away at this "tried-and-true" motivational narrative drawn from sports: have a goal, don't be distracted or dissuaded, work harder than anyone else. Achievement is realized through competition. Self is realized through its achievements.

Neither Luther nor Calvin offered the possibility that one could achieve salvation. With Luther one was saved by faith, not by good works, and with Calvin salvation was assigned by God and could not be earned based on human action. Nevertheless, as Weber observed, true believers persisted in seeking signs of their salvation in "good works" – at first, the logic of this was that if you proved yourself worthy, then perhaps you were affirming your predestination to everlasting life. Somewhere along the line, notions of predestination became perceived as archaic, supplanted by a modern ethos of performance and merit as the measure of a man's worth. And yet, an ascetic work ethic resurfaces in *Nike* ads such as the "Search and Destroy" ad that pushes it to the extreme. The 1996 campaign which surrounded this ad presents an inverted Protestant ethic which calls not for suffering in the workplace, but a suffering of one's body in an activity pursued at no one's discretion, a suffering endured willingly without threat of coercion. In this way, the self proves (demonstrates) itself worthy of recognition through suffering.

T. J. Jackson Lears refers to an alternative Christian ethic which "flowed from the Augustinian ethic of piety and which sought to close the gap between heaven and earth through the cultivation of intense inner experience."[6] This ideology stresses finding one's place in the world, being in touch with oneself, and achieving a level of self-realization that emphasizes a state of being. This self is contingent upon being deeply absorbed in experiencing the world, particularly one's inner world.[7] The goal of this ethic is personal immanence, achieving a state of peace with oneself. Robert Bellah calls this ethos "expressive individualism" and pictures it as a therapeutic discourse which served as medicine for a soul crippled by the forces of modernization – urbanization, industrialization, and bureaucratization.[8] A call for self-actualization, personal self-fulfillment, emotional well being, and the value of sensate experience countered the narrow self-fulfillment attained from economic success. This ethic spurs those disenchanted with the spread of urban civilization to search for salvation within themselves or in their relationship to nature. Despite the fact that sport has grown increasingly rationalized, sport is nevertheless positioned in opposition to rationalizing forces as an activity that allows one to achieve a state of personal immanence. Often associated with non-competitive sports, this narrative has traditionally been used in advertising to hail women more than men.

Sports discourse offers several paths to heaven: personal achievement, self-actualization, transcendence or immanence. Each path assumes the possibility of individuals achieving a coherent identity. The path of achievement constructs identity in a state of becoming. There is always potential. Identity and self-esteem are attained in dialectical relationship with the level of competition. One sets goals, overcomes obstacles, achieves those goals, and repeats the process ad infinitum. Or, one can choose the path that constructs identity as a state of being that is already there but disrupted by the modern world. Sport provides a path for rediscovery, a chance to know thyself again. While some sports tend to be associated with one theme over the other, athletics in general provids avenues for both transcendence and immanence. We should hasten to add that these themes are not mutually exclusive. The hypercompetitive and therapeutic themes can be seen blended so that physical exercise mixed with determination provides spiritually rewarding moments.

Spirit and the struggle against decay of the body

It is important to remember that for *Nike* the growth of sports culture means both the growth of participation and spectatorship. In the realm of participation, the religious theater of sports and consumption gives way to the advocacy of a personal philosophy of life.

A 1994 *Nike* ad attacked stereotypes and clichés associated with the senior population. The senior athletes who appear in this *Nike* commercial appear to transcend any presumed physical limits of their bodies while contesting prevailing definitions of old age. Aging itself is framed as a social-psychological construction.

I do not play bingo.
I am not shrinking.
I am not strong for my age, I am strong.
I will retire for the night

I will begin again tomorrow
I will never say I have fallen and I can't get up
I am wrinkled and I am gray
but I am not old.

In *Nike*'s universe, the typical social construction of the elderly as physically winding-down crumbles before the will-power of individuals who persevere at the hard work necessary to offset the diminution of the body.

> Age, like time, was no longer seen as a gift from God over which the individual had little control. Now both time and age were seen as a kind of private property, capital that, when used well and invested correctly, would produce more time and better aging, but when used badly could bring failure and humiliation. In the second half of the nineteenth century, the meaning of old age changed abruptly. A long life was no longer a sign of God's grace but an accomplishment attributable to the virtues of the individual. Hard work and the right habits of consumption were now the source of longevity ...[9]

In the late 1980s, *Nike* ads also featured senior citizens – recall Walt Stack who ran 17 miles every day through the streets of San Francisco and the softball playing octogenarians in the "Kids and Kubs" ad. Whereas those ads relied on a wry, understated sense of humor along with a twinkle of tone in their elderly voices, the anti-stereotypes ad has no cuddle to it. The black and white video conveys a tone of earnestness, and *Nike* constructs a correspondence between these declarations and the visual testimony of senior athletes diligently training in the empty confines of a deserted stadium. Hyperreal techniques mix jump cuts, swish pans, and dissolves with slow pans to create a montage that celebrates power, strength and, most importantly, the human spirit. Amplifying this spiritual dimension, the black and white grainy film with high-key lighting creates a temple-like atmosphere.

In the Nike *philosophy the only limit to physical achievement is one's lack of will .*

This ad presents working out as a solitary and prayerful activity for those committed to their personal existential quest. This is no retirement community. These venerable male and female athletes lift weights, throw the shot put, run the stairs and the track, with one man narcissistically posing his developed upper-body musculature. Juxtaposed to his wrinkled face, his smooth musculature appears even more incongruent and striking. This scene is, however, an exception to the rule in *Nike* ads. Unlike so many other sports fitness ads, *Nike* ads do not often dwell on muscled bodies. *Soloflex* ads, for example, highlight a different notion of transcendence based on the ability to reshape (remake) your body. The narcissism of body sculpting is the reward of working out:

> the workout, as the contradictory synthesis of work and leisure, may well represent the most highly evolved commodity form yet to appear in late-

twentieth century capitalism. The workout isolates the individual for the optimal expenditure of selectively focused effort aimed at the production of the quintessential body object. Nevertheless … the workout, and particularly the nautilus workout, includes utopian dimensions as well.[10]

Soloflex exemplifies this intensely rationalized activity, scientifically organized to yield the greatest results. Unlike *Nike*'s alternately celebrity or play-driven vision, *Soloflex* offers the perfection of a machine-like body. Instead, *Nike* offers a vivid evocation of the therapeutic ethos, an ethos that evolved with the demise of Protestant religions and their influence on the moral life of the middle class soul. In the *Nike* philosophy, advancing age need not be regarded as a barrier. A drum and guitar background intensifies the closeup expressions of determination matched with low angle shots of physically challenging feats. The body is only limited by its own physicality when the human will submits to the aging process itself. Decay is a state of mind for those who allow it to happen. Once again, this ad joins the themes of transcendence and immanence. The identity of these seniors is not dependent on the social definitions that construct their age group, rather it is about an inner sense of purpose expressed by their resolve to push their physical limits. "Just do it."

Hailing inner motivation

Running ads often mix statements of achievement motivation with therapeutic imagery. Running can be constructed as a competitive sport (the race) or as a solitary activity (the euphoria of the run). The physiological, psychological and even spiritual benefits of long distance running are often touted in running magazines. Inner peace, a sense of confidence, and mind–body harmony may be achieved through the repetitive rhythm of running. The spiritual side of running is not about competition but the **being-in-the-world** that the activity itself offers participants.

Nike's first television ads directed at women may have shifted the emphasis from running to fitness walking, but the theme was similar, celebrating the self-realization and inner peace gained through the physical activity of fitness walking. The therapeutic workout resulted in a healthier self. Time spent with self in solitary activity permits self-reflection about one's own spiritual well-being.

The commercial titled "Heritage" captured an ethereal sensibility as a solitary runner was shown running past a collage of familiar *Nike* images and scenes from other ads, projected across the skyline of a darkened city backdrop. The tagline, "There is no finish line" quietly appeared at ad's end. Subsequently, the ad was re-released with the "Just do it" tagline. "Heritage" gave voice to *Wieden & Kennedy*'s recurring vision of athletic activity as nourishment for the soul and as an end in itself. The collage, however, shows

As a lone runner runs past a street cleaner in the pre-dawn hours, a spectacular sports moment is projected on a city building. What is the relationship between these two moments? Equivalence or opposition?

highlights of great sports moments – Jordan dunking, Kurt Gibson's game winning home run, a runner crossing a finish line, sprinting wheel chair athletes, a shot putter, and so on. A soothing piano background accompanies the runner through dark, deserted urban canyons. The images projected on buildings and bridges have an ethereal feel against a harsh urban backdrop. While the music and the rhythm of the commercial are therapeutic, we also sense the internal motivation of a person who needs no prompting and no reward. Despite the cold urban environment, this runner is at peace with himself. While the city sleeps, his commitment to running remains internally motivated.

In a similar fashion, *Nike*'s reference to AIDS in another running commercial pays tribute to the spiritual strength and fortitude that refuses to surrender to this disease. The ad's structure is simple. A male long distance runner runs through a scenic wooded landscape. The tone of the ad is therapeutic, running through a natural setting with a pleasant and uplifting musical background. Situating this solitary workout in this peaceful setting are pithy, straightforward titles in black frames.

RIC MUNOZ, LOS ANGELES.
80 MILES EVERY WEEK.
10 MARATHONS EVERY YEAR.
HIV POSITIVE.
JUST DO IT.

The matter-of-factness of the presentation – 80 miles a week, 10 marathons a year, HIV positive – somewhat masks the therapeutic mode of address. But this ad struck a chord not because of its therapeutic tone of address but because *Nike* ventured into the often repressed political climate surrounding HIV with an attitude of both normalization and transcendence. *Nike*'s sign value is contingent on its willingness to take risks in its representations. The AIDS commercial itself supports this side of *Nike*'s self-image.

SUFFERING TO WIN

At the same time that *Nike* privileges a therapeutic ethos, personal equilibrium, and the concept of domination-free play, there are plenty of *Nike* ads that privilege a model of self grounded in the intensity of aggressive competition and the work ethic gone ballistic. The therapeutic ethos emerged with a consumer society. Twentieth century industrial capitalism produced the goods and services intrinsic to such an ethos, as well as the social conditions such as bureaucratization and urbanization that prompted a search for secular solace. Self-actualization is a philosophy based on abundance. On the other hand, survivalism is a defensive ethos based on insecurity and threat –

a response to the erosion of economic security by corporate outsourcing and downsizing, the increasing gap between rich and poor and the resultant frustration, hostility, tension and violence which has made for a seemingly less safe social world. For males, survivalism may be a coping strategy for slippage in physical prowess as female physicality is defined increasingly in terms of power and performance; for females, it offers an expression of seriousness of purpose and sense of empowerment. As the world becomes increasingly perceived as less civil, the display of physical prowess becomes a survival strategy. The appearance of physical prowess, whether it serves as a form of protection or not, allows one to navigate such a world with a dramaturgical front of confidence.

Citing concerns about over-commercialization, *Nike* declined to participate as a sponsor for the 1996 Atlanta Olympics. Nevertheless, in a tactic akin to "ambush advertising" *Nike* bought air time for a series of TV ads during the Olympics on local and regional feeds. This $35 million *Nike* AIR campaign highlighting *Nike*'s coterie of Olympic athletes debuted on the *X-Games* broadcast on *ESPN*. Moving its image further away from the sentimental look of sport highlights films, this campaign extols intensity of purpose raised to a higher degree of signification. Considering the mawkish, syrupy, and sentimental tone that saturated *NBC*'s broadcast coverage of the Summer Olympiad, as well as the celebratory tone of other Olympic-themed commercials, *Nike*'s campaign constituted a welcome reprieve from the mass appeal schmaltz. *Nike* has always associated itself with dedication and hard work but in this new era of *X-Games* that is not enough. *Nike* chose to move its look to "the dark side of sport" in which the driven inner-will overcomes the physiological limitations of the body depicted as screeching in pain, physically beaten, and oxygen deprived. Intimidation and menace were additional themes of this campaign: deep in the soul of the world-class athlete lies the desire to dominate one's competition. Red, with its associations of heat, blood, and emotional intensity, was the color of choice for this campaign, bathing the frame in its fiery aura.

Several years earlier, *Nike*'s "Instant Karma" ad portrayed a community of humanity who share a love of sport, but in these ads the global sports community fades away, replaced by the raw relationship between spectators and those who compete to be champions. Champions are those who display the hyperintensity and the will to destroy their competitors even at the expense of self-destruction. Of interest in these ads is the fact that the frenzied crowd and the prying eye of the camera are actually included in the scene that the ads construct. If *Nike*'s sports philosophy parallels or reflects, in any way, American cultural change, it speaks to what postmodernists have called the "end of the social" which can be seen in the mounting privatized social separation and fortification of cities.[10] *Nike*'s 1996 campaign was tinged with a Hobbesian aesthetic reflecting a social landscape of "a war of all against all."

Blood, sweat, and vomit

The signature commercial of the AIR campaign was a one-minute montage
that opened with two runners crossing a finish line as a white dove flies
into the air. This symbolism of the white dove serves as a prelude to the
dark side. The commercial arranges quick cuts of elite Olympic athletes
(Lewis, Johnson, Torrance, Agassi, Bubka, Hardaway, Barkley, Pippin) in a
montage of performance shots (pole vaulting, running a marathon, sprinting), expressions of intensity (focused stares, mouths shouting, grimaces),
close-ups of *Nike* shoes, and quick unrecognizable blurs which speed up the
overall flow of the ad. Perhaps the most important aspect of this composition
is the fast-paced music taken from Iggy Pop and the Stooges' 1973 song entitled "Search and Destroy."[12] Combined with the jarring editing and off-center cinematography the violent music establishes a raw, jagged, heart-racing,
adrenaline pumping aesthetic.

Written in the first person, the song's opening vocal defiantly declares
an anti-middle-class, anti-social soul, "I'm a streetwalking cheater with a
heart full of napalm." The lyrics turn the language of American military
technology's deadliest weapons into metaphors of a self incapable of repress-
ing its anger and rage. In the next line, Iggy makes this declaration more
direct: "I'm the runaway son of a nuclear A-bomb." The cultural origins of
American proto-punk and its "rage against the machine" can be seen here as
a reaction against the capitalist excesses of cold-war culture and technology.
And we must not forget the hostility against the white-collar life built on
self-regulation and repression. Years later Pop's recollection of the origins
of this song are framed by his anti-bourgeois images of a drug-snorting punk
in an English garden.

*Sport as transcendence signified
by the white dove gives way to a
vision of sport as physical
destruction.*

> "Search and Destroy" – The name came from a column heading in a *Time*
> magazine article about the Vietnamese War. I was sitting reading it, snort-
> ing big Chinese rocks of heroin under one of those grand English oak
> trees in Kensington Garden outside the Kensington Palace on a summer
> day in Merrie Olde. I used to go out there to sit and write, wearing my
> leather cheetah jacket, leather pants, wraparound shades …

Though the song had "nothing to do with [killing] gooks," the lyrics
do refer to the madness of the Vietnam War, fusing its "search and destroy"
metaphor into a generalized accounting of social life in the early 1970s. If
we try to locate the meaning of these lyrics in the context of this *Nike* ad,
we are bound to be confused. What possible relevance does this have to the
world of *Nike* athletes? Early on, Iggy and the Stooges aimed their music at
"high school drop-outs, troubled drug kids, kids who were so totally into
music that it wasn't just a part of their lifestyle." Rather, *Wieden & Kennedy*
selected the music because of the feel it lends to the text: it is violent and

Sport as war.

Intensity and determination as
violation of bourgeois codes.

fast. Consider again the piercing declaration that opens the song: "I'm a streetwalking cheater with a heart full of napalm. I'm the runaway son …" This would seem to connote everything that a sports morality detests. But punctuate it with the insertion of a gutteral scream of athletic tension release – "Aaaarrrrgggghhhhh" – and let the high velocity music and image-flying context take over, and we have a driven, restless energy – a soul that fits readily with *Nike*'s self-image of rebellious mavericks driven to excel in their own ways ("I am the world's go-gotten boy, the one who searches and destroys"). Iggy Pop's punk imagery conjures up the hostile, and out-of-control results of a civilization obsessed with the technology for destruction. *Nike* redirects that imagery into a battlefield of track and field competitions. Spliced into the music, the sound of a crowd's rising crescendo frames the culture of violence that sometimes surrounds sports in a scene of crowded stands at a European soccer match with flags waving and red smoke bombs going off. Spectacular shots convey moments of pain and intensity – hurdlers and runners fall down, blood splatters from a punch to a boxer's mouth, a runner vomits. A scene of an athlete being stretchered to a medivac helicopter testifies to the risks of competing in the arena before the crowds of frenzied fans. This is no parable about sportsmanship. Indeed, this is no parable about the transcendence of the human soul, or even of its immanence. This is about being driven relentlessly by inner demons – but demons given legitimacy when channeled through sports.

The motivational advertising done by corporate sponsors usually celebrates quiet determination and the social support of family, coaches and the corporate sponsor. Such ads are done by formula: the cute little gymnast whose plucky determination and long hours of practice pay off in beaming moments of shared satisfaction by gymnasts, parents and coaches in *McDonald's* and *Coke* ads. *Nike* moves the signifiers of will, focused intensity, and motivation to another plane altogether. Green vomit, fallen runners screaming in agony, and blood droplets flying across the frame are spectacular images. On first viewing these images stand out because they are out of the ordinary. The image of a runner kneeling on a track vomiting is a clear violation of acceptable commercial imagery. The logic of the spectacle drives advertising to continually find new styles and new signifiers to differentiate one's signs from the competition. The ante always goes up. Carlton Fiske doing sit-ups just doesn't do it any more. In the age of accelerated image flows, memorable signifiers have value when they have the power to shock audiences out of their complacency and make them take notice.[13] Violating bourgeois perceptual codes regarding body fluids gives the ad an aura of authenticity, a meaning upon which *Nike* has built its empire. Further, it differentiates *Nike* from the field: this ain't no *Disney*, this ain't no *McDonald's*. Indeed, the violence of this drama is accentuated by a smashed camera (an intertextual reference and comment on *Canon* commercials?) cut between two frames of Andre Agassi making his way through a mob of photographers. Of course, *Nike* is not alone in pushing the frontiers of what is acceptable in style. *Benetton* is the most infamous player in this field: constructing its sign value by investing it with such code violations as a nun kissing a priest, an infant still attached to the placenta, a deathbed scene of an AIDS patient, or two horses copulating. To appellate youth one must be willing to violate codes. Still it is crucial to remember that while *Nike* uses the visceral to shock, it does so in the service of bourgeois individualism and the belief that success is the consequence of simply trying harder.

Nike presents the old adage "no pain no gain" imagistically. Pain, however, is not the signified; *Nike* doesn't celebrate sado-masochism. Rather, it is a signifier for intensity, focus, and determination. Pain represents the point at which the will takes primacy over the body. Focused intensity becomes a monomaniacal obsession to win; pain marks this obsession while at the same time carrying connotations of the spiritual side of sport contingent on self-sacrifice. Pain indicates the rite of passage into a spiritual dimension in which spiritual rewards only come after disciplining or even punishing the body. This is ascetic Protestantism at its best. Transcendence is no longer a moment of aesthetic grace but the passing through a moment of unbearable pain. Pain is the purification rite where suffering attests to purity of motive.

Blood and sweat signify that one deserves to be an Olympic athlete, a *Nike* athlete. For *Nike*, performance is always about the will, about self-affirmation, about exceeding limits by refusing boundaries. As noted earlier, *Nike* has positioned itself against the boundaries associated with the social construction of race, class, gender, and age. Such ads speak to a specific social condition, to a specific social group or to a set of social definitions that have emerged historically and which operate as artificial barriers to success, achievement, and performance. There is, however, a universality to pain. At some point the body breaks down. It can no longer go any farther or any faster. Certainly anyone who participates in sport knows those limits. *Nike* hails all of us to push beyond that point by sheer tenacity of spirit. Of course, the ultimate athlete is one who dies performing his sport, and not surprisingly, the "Revolution will not be televised" commercial eulogizes Hank Gathers and Fred Wilson. Nor is it surprising that many athletes do break down. What ads usually don't show is the trail of damaged bodies and psyches of those who didn't make it, despite pushing their bodies beyond their physical limits. While the success stories are regularly broadcast, seldom do they dwell on the psychological and physical casualties of such a philosophy. However, in "Search and Destroy" we see the carnage and the casualties of pushing physical competition to its outer limits.

Trial by pain

"If you don't lose consciousness at the end, you could have run faster."

Cumulatively, the *Nike* ads shown during the 1996 Olympics presented a primer of pithy proverbs or maxims. One ad featured a blurred slow motion

"Some people quit when they reach their threshold of pain, some don't."

"There are two sides to a sprinter. The side that wants to crush his opponents and leave them blue and lifeless by the side of the track, [pause] and the other, darker, side." The aesthetic of intensity mixes the standardized codes of modeling with the gestures of the athlete.

"There's a time and a place for mercy. And it isn't here and it isn't now."

close-up of Jackie Joyner-Kersee sprinting. She runs into focus, her head canted back, eyes closed, the hollows of her cheeks rising and falling in slow motion, a grimace of pain covering her face. She is rendered as a portrait of determination. A sober voice-over by actor Willem Defoe frames the scene: "If you don't lose consciousness at the end, you could have run faster." The screen turns bright red with FASTER lettered across it. A close-up of Joyner-Kersee fades into a red frame named by the *swoosh* and a pulsating AIR beneath it. Passing through the threshold of intense pain indicates the level of one's determination. If there is no pain, no adversity, if an athlete doesn't lose consciousness then she hasn't pushed hard enough. The greatest sin an athlete can commit is wasted potential. This commercial suggests we can never be satisfied with less than the ultimate performance. And, since the ultimate is not fixed, one can never be satisfied. This theme of pushing oneself to surpass the experience of pain recurs throughout this series of ads. Another ad juxtaposed a slow-motion scene of a swimmer exploding out of the water, against the soundtrack of a slow motion roar of arctic wind mixed with wind chimes, as the voice-over flatly beheld, "Some people quit when they reach their threshold of pain, some don't." As the swimmer strains for his next breath, he is framed by water droplets filmed like frozen jagged ice pellets that fade to red. The ascetic aesthetic itself signifies the barriers that must be broken to succeed. Here one realizes oneself by overcoming one's own nature, rather than finding oneself by becoming one with nature, as in the *ACG* campaign.

No mercy

A frequently run ad in the series featured the world record-holding sprinter, and star of the 1996 Olympic games, Michael Johnson. The opening shot symmetrically composed Johnson poised on the starting blocks, staring intensely, straight-ahead, into the camera. If this is *Nike*'s aesthetic of concentration and purpose, it is also their aesthetic of intimidation. Johnson's fierce eyes dominate the frame. When joined to the dark and foreboding electronic music, Johnson's intensity and focus appear almost excessively obsessive. The voice-over slowly draws out the meaning of this look. The dramatic pause reinforces the ominous tone of a "darker side." As these last words are spoken, the camera drifts, almost David Lynch-like, into the surface of the track itself before fading to red with the *swoosh* and AIR printed below. Forget the humanist ideologies of sport so freely repeated during the Olympiad – that we are all brothers and sisters bound together by an ethic of sportsmanship – instead, these ads speak to the obsessive dedication to domination. *Nike* does not confine this warrior mentality to male athletes. Another commercial features Mia Hamm, *Nike*'s female soccer celebrity, shown fiercely diving through the air to head the ball. There are no reference points, and no ground, only Hamm soaring in slow motion through a snowstorm signifying the extent of her determination and grittiness. Defoe's voice ominously declares her purpose: "There's a time and a place for mercy. And it isn't here and it isn't now."

Yet another *Nike* ad consisted of extreme close-ups of *Nike*'s Dream Team basketball players – John Stockton, Penny Hardaway, Scottie Pippin, David Robinson, Charles Barkley, Gary Payton, and Reggie Miller. Their expressions mimic the boxer's practice of staring down an opponent, their faces unsmiling masks marked by menacing and unflinching looks. To break eye contact demonstrates weakness. If you can't stare down your opponent, if you blink, you don't have the will necessary to win. Towards the end of this collage of stares the voice-over methodically intones "Anyone, anywhere, anytime." Ironically, the US Olympic basketball team so overmatches their opponents that the last thing one expects is intensity. Olympic basketball is about marketing, not about competition. In the 1992 Barcelona Olympic Games, the real battle took place over whether *Nike* athletes would wear *Reebok* jackets to accept the medals.

"Anyone, anywhere, anytime." Never mind playing for fun or for the love of the game or for a deep sense of comradeship. Nope, in these ads sport is serious business. Even baby-faced Reggie Miller is given a dark side.

Win at all costs

During the Summer Games in Atlanta, *Nike* put up billboards around the city. One of the most notable posters featured the message, "If you're not there to win, you're a tourist." In the television series of ads, Andre Agassi, wearing a black hood, moves in extra-slow motion through a phalanx of photographers, like a boxer preparing to enter the ring. The soundtrack composed of discordant sounds of slashing, static and pounding, framed this as a portrait of intense concentration impervious to any distraction. Images of Agassi playing in a match are edited into this scene; perhaps, they are his mental images which now focus his attention. Finally, the voice-over intones, "If you're not there to win, you're a tourist." The ideology of sport has shifted direction with this derisive insult. Forget that saccharine nonsense about "playing for the love of sport," and hail the tunnel vision obsessed with winning, period.

"If you're not there to win, you're a tourist."

These ads are not simply about winning, they are about **the look of winners**. Interpreting an ad like this is partly dependent on our intertextual knowledge of Agassi as a celebrity athlete. Anyone can be a tourist: a tourist is a spectator, a consumer, while only the especially dedicated will become champions. And yet, by emphasizing the look of winners – of power, success, and focused obsession – these ads create only the illusion of the depth of soul and subjectivity, instead reducing the athlete's look to a caricature of determination. Richard Sennett has written that the Puritan ethic has been translated into a narcissistic ethos in modern times.[14] The look of intensity and the ascetic aura that suffuses and defines these displays of cold desire can be read as making "a statement to oneself, and to others, about what kind of person one is."

Discipline or liberation?

But there is yet another way of making sense of these ads. Michel Foucault offered an approach that reversed standard interpretations of history. Consider the familiar interpretations of the Enlightenment that associate science and reason with progress and human liberation. Foucault, however, argued that science and reason had less to do with freedom than the emergence of a new form of social control, **disciplinary power**. According to

Heavenly Trails

These two Nike *commercials featuring mountain biking offer thoroughly different philosophies. One shows a lone female mountain bike racer pushing the envelope, oblivious to the risk of serious injury to skull, knees, ribs, liver or spleen. All that matters is winning the race. Jarring fast-paced music and a jumpy camera follow the mountain biker down a hill. Mixing off center closeups of the biker's body and face with the jumpy camera's subjective shots of the bike bouncing off the rocky winding trail give the viewer a sense of being on the bike itself. The biker's androgynous face is splashed with mud as she goes through a puddle. Willem Defoe narrates, "You can protect your eyes and your skull and your ribs and your knees and your liver and your spleen. Or you can protect your lead." The word SPLEEN appears on the screen. The trail turns into a fast moving blur as the scene fades to a red background and a* Nike *swoosh.* Nike *hails us to push our bodies to the limit. To win, fear of injury must be overcome. This is an X-Games' mentality put into the* Nike *philosophy. Extreme sports are only now being turned into competitive ones to make them marketable.*

In stark contrast is a 1996 ACG mountain bike commercial that opens with a mortised black and white cartoon character. As he chases an umbrella across the screen he states, "Hey, try this for a mantra. I like the rain. I like the rain. I want it to rain." The camera follows a group of mountain bikers in a heavy downpour. As they slush through puddles one biker goes over his handle bars and lands face first in the mud. His mud-covered grinning face tells us that not only is he not hurt but he takes great pleasure in this moment. To an acoustic guitar background the narrator's upbeat voice completes the mantra, "I want to wallow in the mud and slop with reckless abandon. And when I die, I want to say, 'I did carpe the diem – no matter how cold, how wet, and how nasty the diem was.'" An animated umbrella rolls across the frame leaving behind a script font of "Just do it." Nike *mixes humor with the language of Eastern religion (mantra) with a signifier of philosophy (carpe diem) to hail its perceived ACG market niche.*

Foucault, Western history has been a process of refining the technology of the body to exact greater social control, to produce what he called the "docile body": "a body is docile that may be subjected, used, transformed and improved."[15] Discipline replaced punishment not because it was more humane but because it was more efficient. Viewed this way, these images of athletes struggling through pain represent not simply images of freedom and achievement, but images of social control. Withstanding pain becomes an indicator of discipline. Learning to handle pain takes place within a training regimen. Foucault began his analysis of the political technology of discipline with the soldier, examining how the apparatus of discipline makes him both powerful and obedient. Subsequently, a comparable approach to regimen, technique, and strategy were brought to bear in the rationalized workplace. These same practices have today thoroughly penetrated athletics. What does it mean to be an Olympic caliber athlete? What regimens does one have to give oneself up to – diet, training, sleeping, sexual abstinence? To be an athlete is to give oneself up to social discipline and its morality. The seemingly heroic nature of this moment of transcendence could be a moment of extended social control in which the individual demonstrates he/she is willing to sacrifice his/her body for the good of the society or the corporation that sponsors the team.

"Sandpits assume there is a limit to how far a human being can leap"

RE-ENCHANTING A DISENCHANTED WORLD

Traditionally, religion, the festival, mantras and chants, hallucinatory drug use, and dance have all been used to facilitate entry into socially transcendent states of being. Many of these practices have disappeared as social and economic life became increasingly subject to rationalization. While the mystery of sport is systematically disassembled amid the computerized readings at the US Olympic training centers, *Nike* advertising constructs sports not as a rationalized activity, but as a channel to an altered state of consciousness.

Max Weber spoke of the "disenchantment of the world" as the flip side of the continuous rationalization of social life.[16] Capitalism and science displaced religion, but Weber also observed that the Judeo-Christian tradition itself had contributed to this process by eliminating magic and promoting universal deities. Sociologists like Jacques Ellul and George Ritzer have applied Weber's theory to describe a world in which spontaneity, idiosyncrasy, and superstition have been erased in favor of efficiency, predictability, and replicability. Trained experts supplant the amateur, while mastery and control mean developing consistent techniques, strategies, rules, and procedures. The Enlightenment held out the promise that scientific knowledge could unlock the mysteries of the world, giving humans the means to purposefully control their lifeworld. However, Weber suggested that in the well-rationalized social organization, the freedom promised by the discourses of modernity vanishes, replaced by an "iron cage" of rules, regulations, and bureaucratic codes. We become cogs, automatons, or burnt-out bureaucrats who routinely perform repetitive tasks without a sense of purpose. Ellul viewed the process of rationalization as technique, which, driven by its own imperative, spreads outside the control of human agency. For Ellul, no life sphere is immune. For example, technique in the guise of counseling psychology invades our most intimate moments – child rearing, family relationships, sexuality. Imagination, spontaneity, and even the magical moments of love relationships are all subject to rationalization and packaging. In *The McDonaldization of Society*, Ritzer uses *McDonald's* as an exemplar of rationalization applied to both the workplace and consumption. In showing how *McDonald's* translated its concerns about efficiency, predictability, calculability, and control into routine practices, Ritzer discloses how an extraordinary range of social activities become subject to the means–ends calculus of rationalization.[17]

When pitted against an excessively rationalized world, sports discourse promises an alternative way of being. At times transcendent, at times therapeutic, and at times ascetic, sports narratives have the capacity for reinjecting meaning and enchantment into the modern world. Sport is hyped on the promise of being a site for magical moments in the same way that "human interest" stories are compelling because emotions eclipse technique. There is historical irony in this insofar as sport has been a primary site for the encroachment of rationalization over the last century. Recall, for example, that the early proponent of rationalizing the labor process, Frederick Winslow Taylor, actually began his approach by breaking down golf swings into gridded and mathematicized analyses. And yet, as we approach the millennium we perceive an increased reliance on sports discourses to reinstill not only the spiritual into the social, but meaning and enchantment into what is often constructed as a cynical epoch.

"There are yet places that speak to our souls"

When addressing the middle class, *Nike* strikes a philosophical pose that appears deeply connected to American transcendentalism. Locating freedom, individuality, and transcendence outside the limits of socially organized time and space, *Nike* positions the social as constraining. *Nike*'s *ACG* campaign looks to Nature as a therapeutic space. These ads address a desire to escape bureaucratized and managed spaces. As the textual descendants of American transcendentalism – particularly Emerson and Thoreau – these ads locate self-fulfillment in one's relationship to nature. When the men's basketball shoe market flattened out in 1993, the sporting goods industry discovered the outdoor recreation market. To address this new market, *Nike* boosted its outdoor shoes "to 78 styles, from fewer than two dozen styles" in 1992. *Nike*'s outdoor manager defined the problem that confronted their marketing.

> We're going to have to change the formula of putting shoes on athletes. This is not like basketball, tennis or football where you can use the athlete hero as a spokesman. That just doesn't speak to this category.[18]

What would speak to this category and its audience? *Nike*'s *ACG* shoe campaign chose to evoke a quasi-mystical spiritual sensibility organized around a love of nature. The *ACG* campaign taps into an environmentalist ethic convivial to middle class baby-boomers and post-boomers, drawing loosely on the tradition of American transcendentalism in its construction of the relationship between nature and the bourgeoisie.

A technology and commodity-driven civilization leaves less room for the spiritual dimension. The sacred, Emile Durkheim reminded us, is always rooted in the social, even more so, in a secular world. Spirituality in *Nike*'s world has little to do with formal religion, but with a broadly humanist metaphysics about a universal relationship between the self and a force greater than the self. Hence in their "Instant Karma" ad *Nike* paid homage to what Durkheim called the "cult of the individual" by addressing a spiritual sensibility of universal individual immanence, while the *ACG* campaign locates spirituality in the relationship between Nature and the individual soul.

Given *Nike*'s irreverent style of advertising, it may seem curious that a 1995 *ACG* ad campaign opened with an admonition against the cynical drift that has become the dominant motif in 1990s pop culture.

Do not become a cynic.
That is a sure sign of physical and spiritual atrophy.
For those of you who would seek adventure, take heart.
There are yet places that speak to our souls.
And to the dim-eyed know-it-alls they will say "I have a surprise for you."

In this ACG *campaign Nike rekindles the philosophy of American Transcendentalism. Experience in Nature revitalizes both the body and the soul.*

In an age of nearly universal commodification, cynicism becomes seductive because it buffers disappointment. But the cynical voice and the snide, arrogant identity of been-there, done-that has so saturated the marketplace that a backlash was inevitable. Because the *ACG* line of shoes has nothing to do with the inner city, *Nike* entered the competition in this outdoors market niche by appealing to a transcendent vision of nature and personal identity. Escape the urban media culture dominated by "physical and spiritual atrophy." For those who seek uncooked and unmediated experiences – adventure – "there are yet places that speak to our souls." And that of course, is what many yearn to have – something that speaks to their souls, that reminds them even that they have souls. A second *ACG* ad pursues this theme:

Monuments are a hoax,
a conspiracy designed by bureaucrats and construction companies
to draw you away from the important places,

Using a spectacular image of nature Nike *positions itself and us against the spectacle of Nature.*

*the ones found off the roads, atop the mountains, amidst the rivers
and mostly, by chance.
They are not marked by placards and statues
but by epiphanous moments that give you the sense that no one,
including yourself, may ever find this place again.*

Just do it.

Again the *ACG* campaign hails middle class youth who scorn the beaten path that has been already commodified or organized by the logic of administrative rationality. This is the search for pristine Nature, unpolluted by efforts to commercialize it into pre-constituted photo opportunities and souvenirs. *Nike* depicts a Nature breathtaking in its beauty and serenity, a Nature that still offers you a place in which to discover and realize yourself. Here *Nike* plays to a deep antipathy towards the administered society, offering a critique of national parks as administered spaces. In contrast to the monumentalism of Mt Rushmore or the iconography of Yellowstone geysers, *Nike* beckons viewers to seek out unregulated spaces and deep, unstructured experiences that only pure and wondrous Nature can provide. *Nike* endorses a place where there is no naming of Nature, "no placards and statues" to mark spaces that offer a pre-constituted vacation experience. Rather, *Nike* endorses the "epiphanous moments" that can never be repeated. "Live on your own time and according to your own choices in an unmarked wilderness, deep in the heart of nature and maybe, just maybe, you will experience your true self." The text rouses visions of freedom, as well as the bourgeois conceit of self-importance based on knowing a special, untouched place that others don't know about. But the choice of the word "epiphanous" conveys more than this – it stresses a spiritual connection. Recall that Epiphany originally referred to the Christian festival celebrating the birth of Jesus. Its secularized meaning – the meaning referred to in this *Nike* ad – comes to us via James Joyce who used the concept to grasp moments of sudden revelation and insight in which "the soul of the commonest object … seems to us radiant."

In the tradition of American transcendentalism, *Nike* constructs Nature as an uncorrupted space in which authentic self-fulfillment may be attained. Natural spaces allow for experiences that can never be reproduced nor repeated. *Nike* presents this world as an alternative to the managed, and increasingly rationalized, worlds of tourism. The ad addresses the progressive disenchantment of the world, extended now from our cities and our work back into the world of nature. It speaks to our sense of personal spirituality by endorsing the re-enchantment of nature – so that the charm and magic of unfiltered nature can mix with our souls. Indeed, the nature that is depicted in the *ACG* campaign is nature spiritualized, nature infused by the vital animating force that we think of as spirit.

The *ACG* ads rely on natural, sonorous, melodic, non-amplified music that connotes a space of spiritual simplicity. The prior *ACG* ad semiotically draws on a distinctly Indian musical tonal quality to signify harmonious, ethereal, and non-western, relations between humans and nature. So too, in 1990, *Nike* appropriated John Lennon's song "Instant Karma" for their Air Huarache shoe line in order to signify "self-improvement: making yourself better …"[19] *Nike*'s "Instant Karma" ad constructed a sense of performance as a flow experience that was an end in itself, acting without self-consciousness and without hesitation. *Nike*'s version of 'Instant Karma' appealed to a recognition of the inner self in relation to species-being. But, whereas Marx stressed labor as the fundamental act through which humans are capable of recognizing our selves in our connectedness, *Nike* locates this potential in the activity of athletic play. While the camera work aestheticized and celebrated the inner call to play itself, Lennon's lyrics seem to hitch personal transcendence to a universal spirit that binds us all. Joined to the camera work, the song's refrain, "We all shine on," reframed the playground basketball court as a space where we can experience the immanence of our own soul in relation to the grandeur about us.

The twilight zone of commodity theology

Cynics and critics (have the two become synonymous?) would be quick to point out that any mention of *Nike* in relation to religion must include the way that *Nike* has constructed for itself – at *NIKETOWN* and in its ads – shrines to itself. And to be sure, both *NIKETOWN* and *Nike* ads are prime sites of postmodern culture. A *Nike* ad featuring Michael Jordan that aired during the Christmas shopping season of 1996 provides an excellent textual opportunity for exploring the aesthetics of religion as a signifier. We conclude our exploration of themes of spirituality with this *Nike* ad that reads as a homage to Jordan as the pinnacle of commodity culture.

We have strung together a series of stills lifted from the commercial to provide a flavor of the visual aesthetic style. In this ad, the essential channels of communication are the music and the photographic style. There is no voice-over, neither is there any mention of *Nike*, except one fleeting shot of the *swoosh* on Jordan's shoe. Perhaps, the most important thing to be observed about this commercial is what is absent. There is no *Nike* swoosh at ad's end. Instead, the ad ends with the red "Jumpman" icon representing Jordan in flight towards a dunk. This ad appeared at roughly the same time that a cologne bearing Jordan's likeness and name was being launched with a wave of advertising. In spite of this, and the fact that Jordan's celebrity value has been diluted by *Gatorade*, *Hanes*, and *McDonald's* ads, *Nike* was confident viewers would recognize this as an Air Jordan commercial, as a *Nike* ad, because Jordan and *Nike* **form a single unified logo-refrain**."[20]

Music and style of photography connote an ethereal and liminal space – a kind of twilight zone. The structure of the commercial is disjointed in that it superimposes adjoining frames, leaves afterimages, changes speed within shots (fast to slow motion), and overexposes and tints parts of the frame so that greens, reds, yellows, and blue are exaggerated. The ad visually differentiates itself from other commercials by its foregrounding of style and color, using photographic technique to disturb the ontological landscape. The most jarring violation concerns the flow of time. Jordan's nickname of "Air" refers to his extraordinary ability to jump and hang aloft on his moves to the basket. While in previous commercials this was expressed by having him visually transcend the natural limits of space, this ad depicts the same meaning in terms of the fourth dimension, time. The commercial freezes and unfreezes time, leaving the video apparition of Jordan alternately frozen in time and moving faster than film time so that he leaves image trails, while the spectators appear in still frame or slow motion as if suspended in time.

The ad opens with an eerily tinted shot of the Bulls playing against the Los Angeles Lakers. Jordan moves to receive the ball and upon doing so the ad shifts into another time zone. With Jordan poised to drive past a defender to the basket, the scene cuts to a row of trance-like runners on treadmill machines at an exercise club mesmerized by Jordan's performance on a television monitor. The ad oscillates back and forth between Jordan's drive to the basket and spectators momentarily suspended in time. A man stands in the midst of shaving, transfixed by Jordan on the television screen, while behind him the bathroom sink overflows in slow motion. In the smooth discontinuity of cross-cutting, Jordan's spin move foregrounds the number 23 on his shoe for a split-second, giving way to a scene of a boy and his mother, captivated by Jordan's TV image, while a dog, blurred in the background, shakes water out if its coat. A small boy stares up at a television through a store window, while a slightly older boy stands watching a television in a garage as his bike falls over – in super slow motion – in the driveway. Like the scene of the sink overflowing this scene signifies the suspension of time as Jordan completes his move and elevates for his shot. Two older men in the crowd look on spellbound, their mouths agape, while two young boys look up in awe and wonder. When Jordan finishes his dunk, he is replaced by the red Jordan-in-flight logo on the screen, punctuating the dunk, and the experience.

As we have observed, *Nike* has always toyed with the spectacle by being self-reflexive about the nature of commercialization. On the one hand, *Nike* parodies the spectacle of crass commercialism and false sentimentalism, even attacking the media marketing circus of hype for corrupting the essence of sport (e.g., *Nike*'s criticism of the 1996 Atlanta Olympic games as overcommercialized). Its ads have contrasted the love of the game with the shallowness of the spectacle, drawing an equivalency between ordinary athletes and its stable of superstars. Nevertheless, despite its reflexivity regarding the spectacle and its democratic stance concerning sports, *Nike* has built its sign value on hero worship, or on the gap between the everyday and the spectacular. And, for *Nike*, Jordan has been the heart of the spectacle: in this ad, Jordan has the capacity to suspend time in the lives of spectators engaged in everyday life. The ad illustrates in an eerie way Guy Debord's observation that "the spectacle is not a collection of images, but a social relation among people, mediated by images."[21]

Spiritual overtones in the ad stem entirely from the signifier of the choirboy's voice. Sweet and angelic, the child's voice suggests an aura of reverence and serenity. Along with the photography, the choirboy's voice frames Jordan with an aura that could be described as god-like. Able to transcend time and space, he is on another plane than mere mortals. The viewer's position is clear. All we can do is gaze in awe. The commercial reduces everyday life to the routine and the commonplace. When slow motion is used to show Jordan, it celebrates his physicality, calling attention to how lightning quick he is. When used to portray everyday life, it slows down our routines, emphasizing their mundane character and flow. In the spectacle, we look to supermen to amaze us, to take us out of our daily routines. The ethereal slow motion places us in another dimension where we can, at least momentarily, disappear outside everyday life in the modern world. W.F. Haug coined the phrase "commodity aesthetics" to describe the lure of images associated with commodities. Haug wrote about the "fascination of aesthetic images" in which "the beautiful image becomes completely disembodied and drifts unencumbered like a multicolored spirit of the commodity into every household."[22] The spectator's fascination with such commodity aesthetics has been built largely on the pleasure of the gaze.

The aura of spirituality and the spectator's gaze, nominally opposites, have been fused together. Precisely by means of its aesthetic style, *Nike* has elevated (pun intended) the floating signifier of Jordan (pun intended) into something that appears transcendent. It comes as no surprise to anyone who follows pop culture that, to invert Marx's famous line, "all that is **sacred** melts into Air."[23] And yet, here is Jordan, presented as the commodity deity of the moment, while also confirming Guy Debord's observation that "The spectacle is the existing order's uninterrupted discourse about itself, its laudatory monologue."[24] The higher *Nike* elevates Jordan, the higher it elevates itself. The higher his sign value, the higher the exchange value of commodities branded by *Nike* logos. And, it is indeed worth reminding ourselves that the Jordan Flight icon has signified the top of *Nike's* line. No wonder lines of kids waited on Sunday morning at a local mall for the new Air Jordan shoes to just arrive.

NOTES AND REFERENCES

1. Stewart Hoover, "1996 Gerbner Lecture, 'Media and Religion'," *Annenberg Newslink* (Annenberg School of Communication), 1996, p. 15.

2. Michel de Certeau, *The Practice of Everyday Life* (University of California Press, Berkeley, CA, 1984), p. 178.

3. Randy Gragg, "Bow down at the altar of retail," *The Oregonian*, December 15 1996, pp. T1, T2.

4. Wade Clark Roof, "The baby boom's search for God," *American Demographics*, 14, December 1992, pp. 50–1.

5. Max Weber, *The Protestant Ethic and the Spirit of Capitalism*, translated by Talcott Parsons (Charles Scribner's Sons, New York, 1958).

6. T. J. Jackson Lears, *Fables of Abundance:A Cultural History of Advertising in America* (Basic Books, New York, 1994), p. 47.

7. Colin Campbell maintains that by the early nineteenth century, Puritans had evolved "an intensely personal subjective experience" to gauge the authenticity of their faith," in *The Romantic Ethic and the Spirit of Modern Consumption* (Blackwell, Oxford, 1987).

8. Robert Bellah, Richard Madsen, William M. Sullivan, Ann Swidler, and Steven M. Tipton, *Habits of the Heart: Individualism and Commitment in American Life* (Harper, New York, 1985). See also Richard Fox and Jackson Lears (eds), *The Culture of Consumption: Critical Essays in American History, 1880–1980* (Pantheon, New York, 1983), pp. 3–38.

9. John Gillis, *A World of Their Own Making: Myth, Ritual, and the Quest for Family Values* (Basic Books, New York, 1996), p. 84.

10. Susan Willis, *A Primer for Daily Life* (Routledge, London, 1991), p. 69.

11. See Mike Davis, *City of Quartz* (Verso, New York, 1990).

12. Iggy Pop and the Stooges, *Raw Power*, 1973.

13. Robert Goldman and Stephen Papson, *Sign Wars* (Guilford Publications, New York, 1996), p. 166.

14. Richard Sennett, *The Fall of Public Man: on the Social Psychology of Capitalism* (Vintage, New York, 1978), p. 335.

15. Michel Foucault, *Discipline and Punish: The Birth of the Prison* (Vintage, New York, 1979), p. 136.

16. Max Weber, *The Protestant Ethic*.

17. Jacques Ellul, *The Technological Society* (Vintage, New York, 1964); George Ritzer, *The McDonaldization of Society: An Investigation into the Changing Character of Contemporary Social Life* (Pine Forge, Newbury Park, CA, 1993).

18. Cited in Jerry Schwartz, "In shoes, the great outdoors beckons," *The New York Times*, February 13 1994, section 3, p. 6.

19. Nina Baker, "Nike's ready to go all out to promote latest sneaker," *The Oregonian*, March 14 1992, p. B1.

20. Susan Willis, *A Primer for Daily Life* (Routledge, London, 1991), p. 113; emphasis added.

21. Guy Debord, *Society of the Spectacle* (Red & Black, Detroit, 1977), p. 4.

22. Wolfgang Fritz Haug, *Critique of Commodity Aesthetics: Appearance, Sexuality and Advertising in Capitalist Society* (University of Minnesota Press, Minneapolis, 1986), pp. 45, 50.

23. The original line from the *Manifesto of the Communist Party* is found in a section discussing how capitalism necessitates an end to traditionalism and the inauguration of an era of constant change: "All that is solid melts into air, all that is holy is profaned." (Karl Marx and Friedrich Engels, *The Communist Manifesto* (International Publishers, New York, 1992), p. 35.

24. Debord, *Society of the Spectacle*, p. 24.

8.

"JUST DO IT," BUT NOT ON MY PLANET

FROM CULTURAL ICON TO SYMBOLIC CAPITAL

Think of the *Nike swoosh* like a piggy bank. Every time you watch a *Nike* ad that gives you viewing pleasure, or provides a moment of identification, or that encourages you to think of *Nike* as committed to something broader than its own self-interest, then you deposit a little bit of value (almost like dropping a coin in the piggy bank) into the sign. In our estimation, the *Nike swoosh* has become swollen with this kind of accumulated value to the extent that *Nike* no longer needs to name itself, but can merely show the *swoosh* symbol to brand and set apart the world of *Nike* and its imagery. "*Nike*'s marketing formula: integrate the *swoosh* into the cultural fabric of sports and harness its emotional power. The formula has proven successful, as *Nike*'s growth has coincided with the growth in sports."[1] Relying on the *swoosh* to brand its business has paid off handsomely in an annual growth rate of roughly 40% during the mid 1990s.

We have suggested that there is more than just a passing relationship between the creation of the *swoosh* as a universal cultural icon and the expansion of *Nike*'s economic capital. *Nike* is representative of a new stage of capitalist institutions rooted in the kinds of cultural economies we have been observing. Global and transnational capitalism has brought with it industries where commodities are themselves symbols.[2] No firm better fits this model than *Nike*, whose symbolic capital has acquired a huge global reach.

The primary vehicle through which *Nike* has built its cultural icon and its symbolic capital has been its advertising and sports marketing. What sets *Nike* advertising apart from others at present? In the world of television's rapid fire movement from image to image, consistent, coherent philosophies have eroded or fractured into the scattered cultural debris of images and styles. What separates *Nike* from its competitors is that it has endowed its *swoosh* symbol with the appearance that it stands for a philosophy of life.

Nike has achieved its brand preeminence in several broad stages. First, *Nike* established itself as equivalent to sports and sports culture. *Nike* has long since entrenched itself as being dedicated and committed to athletic excellence. Next *Nike* adopted a self-mocking attitude toward its own advertising. *Nike* then capitalized on the trust built up to raise a broad range of social issues like the crisis of inner-city youth that advertisers normally avoid. With *Nike*'s dominance in US markets, the next push (it has already begun) involves a global advertising strategy, which in the words of Liz Dolan, *Nike*'s former brand manager, will be based both on "a global point of view" along with "a country-by-country plan to make the brand part of the cultural fabric."[3]

In the US, the meaning of the *swoosh* stands out because so many of *Nike*'s ads acknowledge the underlying conditions of commodity relations in an often dehumanized world. Rather than repress these experiences as do the vast majority of ads, *Nike*'s sports marketing rejuvenated a middle class motivational discourse at a time when other such discourses have been discredited by the relentless hype and cynicism of television. *Nike* advertising has engaged the cultural contradictions of contemporary life in such a way that it appears to have a complex corporate personality that possesses greater authenticity than its rivals.

For almost a decade, *Nike* competed with its primary rival, *Reebok*, in what we call **sign wars**.[4] Sign wars take place between marketers as they try to top rival brand images but with relatively little mention of actual product benefits. With *Wieden & Kennedy* at the helm, *Nike* has thus far won its sign war battles with *Reebok*, although *Reebok* continues to counterattack. Indeed, with their "Planet *Reebok*" campaign, *Reebok* sought to counter *Nike* by constructing its own imagery of a life-world space animated by a *Reebok* philosophy. Though this campaign subsequently collapsed, *Reebok* even mimicked *Nike* by dispensing with their name proper and using only their vector icon to sign their ads. The athletic shoe market is no longer a two brand race. *Nike*'s market share has risen to 43%, while *Reebok* has dropped back to 17% and *Adidas* has risen to challenge for significant market share. Given the *swoosh*'s current dominance, *Nike* can anticipate further sign war attacks from rivals who will try to leverage the value of the *swoosh* to their own advantage. *Reebok*'s recent swipe at the successful *Nike* women's ad "If you let me play," is illustrative: "we are not waiting for anyone to *let us play*." Another recent instance of a sign war attack appeared at the end of a Shaquille O'Neal ad for *Reebok* when an imitation of *Nike*'s Little Penny puppet appears, wanting to join "Planet *Reebok*." In the next instant, Shaq "inadvertently" [wink-wink] elbows the puppet out of the picture. This is a sign wars attack pure and simple.

Reebok has not competed well against *Nike* in the area of authenticity. In the summer of 1997, the *New York Times* quoted Ruth Davis, a global product director for *Reebok* who seeks trendy celebrities to wear her shoes "and show

While Nike *appears to set itself above the fray by not mentioning or making references to* Reebok *in its advertising,* Nike *still skillfully undermines* Reebok *sponsored events. According to an article in* Advertising Age, Nike *used ambush advertising to include the* swoosh *in a marathon sponsored by* Reebok *in South Africa:*

"Last year in South Africa, Nike, *a nonsponsor of the Comrades Marathon, captured some of the publicity surrounding the competition by offering to donate $5 to the national team of disabled athletes for each runner who crossed the finish line with the* Nike swoosh *painted on his or her face. The marathon, an annual 89-kilometer race from Durban to Pietermaritzburg, was sponsored by* Reebok. *Before this year's marathon in June,* Nike *tried again, sending the* swoosh *nasal strips (said to enhance athletes' ability to breathe) to all race entrants. A threat of disqualification, however, was enough to discourage any from wearing the strips."*[5]

up in the gossip rags." Her goal at the time was to put the recording sex goddesses of the moment, the Spice Girls, in *Reebok* shoes.[6] When we interviewed a *Nike* executive a few weeks later, we mentioned *Reebok*'s pursuit of the Spice Girls. She responded by pretending to clutch her throat and making a gagging gesture. Her reaction spoke not just about *Reebok*, but about the way that *Nike* envisions its own corporate identity and mission. To the *Nike* executive, the Spice Girls signified pure glamour, not authenticity. *Nike* defines itself, first and foremost, as a company that designs and markets the best products for athletes. *Nike* defines itself as the company able to tap the authenticity of sport. Here is Dan Wieden himself, reflecting upon the matter of authenticity in the body of advertising work his firm has done for *Nike*.

> The people at *Nike* taught my partner, David Kennedy, and me how to advertise — and how not to advertise. Back in 1980, when David and I first started to work on the account, *Nike* made it very clear that they hated advertising. They had developed close relationships with athletes, and they didn't want to talk to them in any phony or manipulative way. They were obsessed with authenticity, in terms of both the product and the communication. And they had a sense of what was cool.
>
> Those attitudes have guided all of *Nike*'s advertising. We try to make honest contact with the consumer, to share something that is very hip and very inside. We don't translate the inside jokes because we figure it's OK if the people who are faddish don't understand. Either you get it or you don't. It's more important for us to be true to the athletes by talking to them in a way that respects their intelligence, time, and knowledge of sports.[7]

THE IMAGE OF PHILOSOPHY OR THE PHILOSOPHY OF IMAGE?

Many sociologists and anthropologists who study commodity culture have observed that it tends to anesthetize civic discourse and impoverish public space. Until recently we would have agreed with this. However, the growing wave of protests against *Nike* starting in 1996 regarding treatment of third world laborers seems to have shifted matters around. Might it be possible, that under shifting cultural circumstances, commercial television, sports, and advertising can actually contribute to a public sphere of discourse? During our interview with Liz Dolan in the summer of 1997, she related a conversation she had with Mark Penn, a national public opinion pollster who also works in behalf of President Clinton. Following months of criticisms in the media about the labor situation in Southeast Asia, *Nike* asked Penn to do an opinion poll for them on the subject. When Penn spoke to Dolan about the preliminary poll results he observed that *Nike* registered

A Land of Lost Children

Remember those "Happy Days" of youth when kids could be kids and didn't have to deal with adult problems, when kids did nothing but play. This mythic vision of childhood still appears in Saturday morning advertising where children are shown enthusiastically playing with advertised toys. More recently, advertising has turned to another view of childhood, the child–adult. A 1994 Fuji film commercial introduced a montage of technologically sophisticated, self-aware children who "don't play kick the can any more." MCI, Microsoft, and American Express commercials replicated this look. Nike has capitalized on the sober

and gray side of childhood. The self-reflexive child–adult debuted in the P.L.A.Y. campaign's look, and was evident in the "If you let me play [sports]" commercial. A comparable look reappears in a 1997 P.L.A.Y. commercial, focused on estranged children who seem to bear the weight of the world on their shoulders as they gaze directly into the camera. "We are your children" was saturated with encodings of cinema reflexivity – including black and white film, off-center framing, the look of being deep-in-serious-thought, and cold background landscapes – to signify children longing for an unalienated childhood.

We are your children
Your boys
Your girls
Your sons and daughters
we are old for our age
we are too fat
can't do a pull up
we smell
we inhale
we drink
we are mothers
we are fathers
we are old for our age
we have no place to play
we have no place to play
we want to be strong
we want you to come out
and play
teach us to hit
teach us to throw
we are your children
we are you

Is this what is meant by a society of lost childhood? Has childhood disappeared? Or is this another instance of a panicky middle class hysterically contemplating a world where so many forces seem out of control? At the very least, this commercial invests the subject with moral drama. Nike's social imagery hints at a world where children learn to be spectators and undisciplined consumers, rather than active players. But the Nike appeal is more pointed as it bemoans the absence of adult guidance and appropriate places to play.

The Nike ad addresses the crisis of childhood but couching social criticism in cinematic codes makes it difficult to pin down the critique. Are today's parents wanting in parenting commitment? Or is it poverty with its wrenching of the family fabric that poses a significant threat to our youth? Or maybe it is tele-

vision with its incessant mantra to consume that leaves youth soft in the head and the belly? Can absent parents be convinced to resume caring for their children? Here then is the crisis of childhood. Children who are unmuscled, soft and overweight, who have become jaded and cynical before their time, yearn for the return of their parents and a place to play – they yearn for a moment of innocence, the innocence of PLAY.

Consider another reading of the ad. The advertising industry has helped turn youth into a lucrative market. Advertising promotes higher levels of consumption, which necessitate higher levels of disposable income to support these purchases. Looked at this way the Nike P.L.A.Y. campaign begins to ring a little hollow, since its prestigious swoosh and its pricing practices tempt less well-to-do youth to make themselves into money-earners as

soon as possible. Does turning children into brand name consumers as early as possible contribute to the erosion of childhood?

    *This commercial invites a variety of interpretations
depending on the assumptions viewers make. Nike's appeal to
parents to get more involved in their children's lives by teaching
them to play might be cynically interpreted as a call to buy kids
high-priced athletic shoes. Or, it might seem as a public-spirited
call to volunteer ourselves and our resources to the future of*

*America's children. As much as any ad, this one reveals the ten-
sions between selling commodities and constructing images of
public legitimacy. Embedding moral issues in the philosophy
of image, no matter how well intentioned, reminds us of the perils of public discourse in the age of television. For all its moral
and emotional intensity, "We are your children" frames the matter as one of choosing between hope and hopelessness, while
avoiding the fundamental matter of market forces and market
moralities.*

high awareness and familiarity scores regarding these issues. Penn added
that he wished the Clinton White House could generate such interest and
awareness on its issues. Dolan replied that if Clinton's concerns were placed
on the sports pages, then he too might achieve this kind of expanded issue
awareness. Moral and political discourse now finds itself daily woven into
sports discourse.

    Nike is one of very few contemporary corporate advertisers that has
successfully constructed a recognizable philosophy. What constitutes a philosophy in the realm of television advertising? Since Western philosophy
has an academic tradition, we tend to think of philosophies as grandiose
encounters with metaphysical questions about Truth, Reality, Morality.
Thinking of philosophy as a system of images supported by slogans and
maxims seems to trivialize our inherited notions of philosophy. In the latter half of the twentieth century, both critical and conservative critiques of
mass culture have decried the invasion of these simplified philosophical
capsules. Writing at mid-century, Max Horkheimer and Theodor Adorno
scorned the preconstituted commodity packaging of experience of any sort.[8]
Imagine what they might say if they encountered the prepackaged philosophy of "Just do it" embedded, and ready for consumption, in the *swoosh*
sign?

    Nike has taken up its position as philosopher in campaigns ranging
from the P.L.A.Y. campaign to the women's campaigns that address the
meaning of everyday life. Beyond articulating a philosophy of empowerment that informs our lives, *Nike* has made its advertising a space in which
to raise social questions and issues of conscience – the HIV epidemic, the
plight of inner city children, the benefits of sports for young girls. These
Nike ads touched an important chord insofar as they signified resilience and
empowerment.

    Perhaps it is difficult to accept that a sneaker company could become so
central to public discourse. Here we must recognize how central the discourse of sport is to supporting a moral order. As commodity-driven sports
aphorisms echo through American culture, they offer a fleeting sense of
coherency and purpose in an otherwise increasingly fragmented social and
cultural formation. Consider how many corporations participate in this

discourse, as they intrusively associate their names with every aspect of sport – player of the game, bowl games, local races, starting lineups, half-time reports, points in the paint, hardest hit of the week, ad nauseam.

Because *Nike* promotes bourgeois values supported by vignettes of achievement, it appears to constitute a moral center in a media culture that otherwise seems to have none. In this sense, *Nike* television ads appear like moments of moral oasis: against the cynicism of the news (the O.J. Simpson trial), against the pornographic realism of media violence (*Top Cops*), against the hypercommercialization of other commodity signs (the *NBA* and "I love this game"), and against exaggerated sexual posturing (*Calvin Klein*). When *Nike* seems to take moral stands as in its HIV runner ad, *Nike* positions itself as standing against flashy, empty image candy in favor of the human spirit. Participation in sport is associated with morality – with learning teamwork and individual discipline, that success is associated with hard work. Still, *Nike* is perceived as having philosophical integrity not merely because it upholds the remains of bourgeois morality, but because it is relentlessly irreverent about image-based posturing.

For much of the twentieth century, sport in America has been depicted as the field within which divisions and distinctions of class and race can be transcended. The ideological argument is simple: in sport, the only thing that matters is performance, achievement and playing within the rules. Today, sport is socially constructed as central to local communities, to parent–child relations, and as a prime activity for socializing youth into occupational achievers and citizens. Sport is thus positioned as an activity through which we construct our identities. When constructed as a moral force, there follows a lot of moralizing about sports with expectations that athletes maintain exemplary moral standards like priests before them. Aware that such an arena is full of hypocrisy in an era of full-contact commodification, *Nike* distinguishes acting out the principle ("Just do it") from mouthing the words. Working on the premise that consumers now seek to wear their motivational commitments and identities on their clothing, a Michael Jordan t-shirt available at *NIKETOWN* sums up this *Nike* worldview:

If you don't back it up with performance and hard work,
talking doesn't mean a thing.

We have argued that *Nike* has both an image of philosophy and a philosophy of image. *Nike*'s best-known photographic style idealizes the individual by mixing realism with the classicism of low angle shots and slow-motion movement shot in black and white. This isolates subjectivity from the existential conditions of time and place and reframes it as human essence. In *Nike*'s representations, signifiers of alienation plus signifiers of determination are defined as equaling transcendence. As long as one stays in the game, life has meaning. Image of philosophy and philosophy of image come together in measured *Nike* discourses such as this from a 1997 *Nike* Golf Tour ad.

I am not afraid to do what I want for a living. [Pause]
I am down to my last $100. [Pause]
I am without regrets. [Pause]
Just do it.

In *Nike*'s world, participation in the human community is defined by the will to act in accordance with our desires, and without regard to possible failure.

What happens when philosophy is reduced to a flow of images? Though simplistic and reductionist, it is democratic in the sense that an empowering philosophy becomes available to a huge number of people. When philosophy is turned into a capsule and linked to a totem-sign, it can make people feel good because they have aligned themselves with more than a run-of-the-mill product. But, of course, this makes empowerment conditional on access to disposable income as well as the relative stability of the sign and the consistency of belief embedded in it. There are various problems with this philosophy-in-a-logo approach, or what we might now refer to as ready-made praxis. First, while the consumer is now freed up to act, this philosophical system also abolishes the need for critical thought. Second, it tends to bury the relationship between biography and the socio-historical conditions within which people live. So while *Nike*'s advertising seems aimed at urging people to take responsibility for their own production of self, it cannot account for the great mass of human beings who live under conditions that deny them even this possibility. Most serious of all, the economy of signs is not stable.

OVERSWOOSHIFICATION

In a global cultural economy economic growth is contingent upon the growth of sign value. We have argued that physical labor is no longer the primary source of value in the consumer commodity. *Nike* has attached its sign to an expanding array of products and product lines in an expanding array of cultures. *Nike*'s growth seems unending. *Nike*'s sign value seemingly erupted beginning around 1986. And, in barely a decade's time, the *Nike swoosh* became a global icon.

Nike built the value of its *swoosh* by positioning itself as the company that puts athletics before commercialism. *Nike* separates itself from the pack of sporting-goods corporations by expressing this **calling of sport** in its slogans, advertisements, and public relations statements. Recall *Nike*'s sharp criticism of non-athletic product companies for overcommercializing the

Olympics: "If a cupcake maker put its logo on an athlete that's commercialism." Via *Wieden & Kennedy*, *Nike* has enjoyed success tweaking the media for transforming sport into an overcommercialized enterprise.

Of course, *Nike* has played a significant role in the commercialization of sport. In *Nike*'s early days when its star was long distance runner Steve Prefontaine, *Nike* aligned itself with the rights of runners to turn professional without losing their standing with the athletic governing bodies that controlled track and field competitions. Prefontaine, and *Nike* behind him, played the role of mavericks, declaring to the track world that there would be no more deals under the table, everything now would be above board. A quarter of a century later, *Nike* has evolved into a marketing giant because it has solved more efficiently than any other in the industry the task of moving its commodities through markets. In the 1990s, *Nike* has itself pressed the boundaries, and the stakes, of commercialization into hitherto uncharted territory. After all, it was Phil Knight who signed a controversial merchandising arrangement when he aligned *Nike* with Jerry Jones and the Dallas Cowboys, America's penultimate sports commodity machine. For the price of $2.5 million annually through 2001, this deal allowed "*Nike* to paint its trademark *swoosh* on the Cowboy's stadium, develop a theme park in the stadium, and outfit all Cowboys coaches and other sideline personnel in *Nike*-made attire."[9] On other fronts, *Nike* routinely seeks exclusive financial arrangements with elite college basketball and football teams, placing the *Nike swoosh* on virtually every top team's jerseys or shoes.[10] *Nike* has been known to engage in ambush marketing to associate itself with events sponsored by competitors. Against *Adidas* and *Reebok*, *Nike* competes intensely for the stars of tomorrow by showering the most talented kids with free gear, thus extending commercialization down to the high school level. *Nike* employees have, on occasion, visited an inner city high school campus driving a Hummer, distributing *swoosh*-marked paraphernalia, and shooting a few hoops with the kids. "That's our target consumer, the black, urban teen," said the *Nike* representative, after giving an impromptu lecture to the kids on the value of education. "It's the coolness factor – if they wear [*Nike* products], the others will follow."[11] All the activities that *Nike* decries in its ads – the bidding up of salaries, the turning of every surface into a commercial, the competition for kids' attention – *Nike* does. *Nike* is central to the commodification of sport, yet its symbol stands for the transcendent moment of sport for its own sake.

Nike has attempted to separate itself from the taint of commercialism by adopting self-reflexive, ironic, and winking attitudes towards the subject of advertising. *Nike* advertising stands out because its ads acknowledge the penetration of commercial relations into "everyday life in the modern world."[12] *Nike* acknowledges the presence of commodification in our culture by sharing jokes about the absurdities and excesses concocted in a culture driven by money. This advertising practice of sharing an aversion to the inauthenticity of commercial life has enabled *Nike* to position itself as an ally of viewers against corporate shills and hucksters. Listen to the language of Arkansas Red in a 1997 ad as he separates the essence of basketball from the commodification of sport. His "nobody owns us" speech paints the relationships of proprietary ownership as a limiting and controlling force in sport – but it is a source of unfreedom that is forgotten as soon as real players take the court to play basketball.

Nobody owns us, man.
When I say us, I mean ballplayers.
Nobody owns us, you understand.
And nobody can own basketball.
There's no one person that can own this game.
You can take away the NBA.
So what? Take it away.
You can take away endorsements
So what?
You can take away the logos on the shoes
So what, take em all.
But when you can take all that away,
That Zoe,
That Indiana boy,
And the Street boy,
You still gonna be butter! [but-ta]

Despite the fact that surely all would agree that *Nike* is the kingpin of basketball shoe logos, this *Nike* text scoffs at the commodity form (the *NBA*, the endorsements, the logos), adopts the vernacular aesthetic of those from below, and positions itself as an appreciator – par excellence – of the Truth of Sport, all without even mentioning the *Nike* name. The Truth of Sport, according to this *Nike* text, lies in the existential joy and pleasure afforded by playing. It doesn't matter what signs appear on the shoes, because all of that is just fluff that covers the essence of basketball. If this resonates with the viewer, then there is yet another investment of authenticity onto the *swoosh*.

This *swoosh* has paid off handsomely for *Nike* profits. Today, the *swoosh* is pervasive in public spaces devoted to sports – it appears across surfaces on caps, jerseys, walls, even defining backgrounds and snowboards. *Nike* currently dominates the sign marketplace with its "*swoosh*ification" of the world. Almost every camera shot during *ESPN*'s television coverage of the 1997 *X-Games* included a colorful orange *swoosh* naming the background – naming the place. *Swoosh*ification refers to this pervasiveness.

It is ironic then that at precisely this moment of cultural domination, *Nike* becomes vulnerable because of the *swoosh*. *Swoosh*ification hints at the possibility of an impending devaluation on the *Nike swoosh*. *Nike*'s success now requires that it take seriously the threat posed by massive overexposure to the value of the *swoosh* logo. At *Nike* headquarters there is talk of "over*swoosh*ification." A self-appointed watchdog group has formed at *Nike*'s Beaverton campus, calling themselves the "*Swoosh* Integrity Committee." Their concern? Attaching the "*swoosh*" to any surface it can find, trivializes it – coffee mugs, key rings, nasal strips – and cheapens the value of the *swoosh*.[13] Recognizing the potential dilution of the *swoosh*, this internal committee focuses on maintaining the integrity of the *swoosh* by keeping it off non-sports paraphernalia. This was, of course, the danger in developing into a branded apparel company. The move from footwear to apparel has geometrically boosted the *swoosh*'s visual saturation of social spaces. In the US, any day spent in public spaces sees the *swoosh* prominently displayed on shoes, shirts, pants, socks, caps, jackets, gloves and sunglasses, not to mention the wallpapering at sporting events, or in shopping malls. It is possible to experience a sense of oversaturation. When asked about this, Liz Dolan, *Nike*'s former brand manager, indicated a need for fewer *swoosh*es, not more. *Nike*'s goal, she said, is not that the *swoosh* be ubiquitous, but rather that it connotes "specialness."

The over*swoosh*ification watchdog committee will unlikely be able to solve, however, the basic dilemma that *Nike* (or any other firm in this industry) encounters in a maturing sign economy.[14] At best, it can be managed from moment to moment. Over*swoosh*ification is a metaphor for the loss of value due to oversaturation and overcommercialization. Those old capitalist demons of supply and demand have come back to haunt symbolic production in the age of mechanical reproduction.

CONTESTED DISCOURSES

Many of the meanings attached to the *Nike swoosh* are near and dear to us – ideals about competition and individual freedom, top performance, a universal code of morality and justice, and defiance of authority. This is what gives the *Nike* sign its value. But, the bigger *Nike* gets, the more it dominates its industry and the media, the more likely we hear of *Nike* practices that run counter to these values. The *Nike swoosh* has become a magnet for both praise and condemnation. Because *Nike* has sought to construct the appearance of a publicly spirited entity devoted to the social good, it has brought the issue of public morality front and center. How much does *Nike*'s imagery diverge from its practices? In some academic circles, this ratio between imagery and practice is the basis for what is called ideology critique. By any name, this kind of measuring stick has an important place in a democracy. However, when this type of critique is taken up in the mass media it becomes organized according to the logic of the spectacle. Thus the media have simplified the situation of shoe production in Southeast Asia to the same degree that *Nike* has abbreviated cultural issues related to authenticity, determination, social transcendence, and spiritual freedom and made them equivalent with the *Nike swoosh*. Opponents now compress all that they do not like about global capitalism and inscribe it on the *Nike swoosh*. With highly compacted and potent symbolizations comes a new form of symbolic politics.

Building sign value by positioning oneself as a moral presence necessitates that one's own practices be above reproach. But, *Nike* is a global corporation that competes in a world capitalist economic system where there are winners and losers: those who are paid highly and those who are paid poorly. The logic of capital demands that profit be squeezed from every part of the production/exchange process. As *Nike*'s sign value grows, the gap between *Nike*'s moral/commercial rhetoric and the world of real social relations becomes increasingly apparent because the media that carry, and cultivate, the system of signs, recognize that a celebrity sign – just as much as a celebrity figure – carries instant news value. Updating the folk adage of an earlier epoch, we now realize that **"those who live by the Sign also die by the Sign."**

Looking for contradictions, ironies, and moments of hypocrisy that can be turned into a story angle, the media lurks and pounces at every opportunity. *Nike* is now vulnerable precisely because the *swoosh* is so inflated with cultural value. Political action groups, mainstream TV programming such as *Prime Time* or *60 Minutes*, and sports writers now find a ready target in the *Nike swoosh*. And as the tides of spectacle politics turn, it has grown ever more fashionable to engage in *Nike* bashing. "The anti-*Nike* backlash is not just about the company's labor record. It's also a reaction to the global reach of the *Nike* brand, the wall-to-wall ubiquity of its corporate moniker."[15]

Oversupply leads to devaluation every time. In this climate, *Nike* has been challenged by those claiming a higher moral ground. And these moral attacks have come from almost every angle. It might be useful for a moment to revisit some of the public relations headaches that have surfaced in recent years as *Nike* evolved into a "ubiquitous" global presence.

In the late 1980s and early 1990s *Nike* found itself the subject of nagging criticism for culturally and economically exploiting the inner-city black community and not reinvesting in it. For instance, over the years there has surfaced and resurfaced what amounts to an urban folk legend about kids who kill other kids for overpriced sneakers. In the early 1990s, Jesse Jackson and Operation PUSH made headlines when they accused *Nike* of not providing sufficient employment opportunities for minority workers. And, when *Nike* ran a series of TV ads with Spike Lee addressing questions of racism, critics assailed the ads, arguing that they "smack[ed] of opportunism and hypocrisy."[16]

Starting with the embarrassing revelation that Pakistani child labor was stitching soccer balls, *Nike* was in the news week after week during 1996 and 1997. This was not the first time that *Nike*'s production practices in Asia had been rendered visible. In 1992, Nena Baker of *The Oregonian* wrote an exposé on "The Hidden Hands of *Nike*."[17] But there was not yet the necessary cultural atmosphere to give resonance to the story. *Nike*'s sign value was not yet pervasive enough. However when charges of poor wages and working conditions in Indonesia and Vietnam resurfaced in 1996, followed by rippling waves of media coverage of an incident involving Vietnamese assembly workers beaten with a shoe by a Korean floor manager in a *Nike*-affiliated factory, public attention stayed focused on *Nike*. To try to blunt the criticism, *Nike* hired Andrew Young, former UN Ambassador and mayor of Atlanta, in February 1997, to investigate its factories and evaluate its *Code of Conduct* for relations with third-world producers.

> As an advocate of human rights, I am involved because *Nike* has expressed its determination to be a leader for positive corporate change. Their commitment can result in growth and opportunity for the communities around the world where they operate.[18]

Still, the string of bad press continued as 10,000 Indonesian workers struck in a *Nike* factory "just days after *Nike* put its name to a groundbreaking anti-sweatshop pact between labor, human rights groups and apparelmakers."[19] Days later a violent rampage took place among these workers in Jakarta as protesters burned cars and ransacked offices, while 3000 workers in a Vietnam factory struck over wages.[20] As the public relations quagmire deepened, almost anything seemed to get thrown into the mix. Even in the realm of signification, *Nike* found itself under attack when the Council on American-Islamic Relations demanded a public apology from *Nike* for a shoe logo on the Air Bakin' model intended to signify a flame that instead resembled the word "Allah" in the Arabic script.[21]

To address the labor issues raised by its critics, *Nike* has engaged a series of studies and audits. After the Andrew Young report proved less persuasive with its critics than *Nike* might have hoped because of its methodology and because it did not address the wage issue, *Nike* contracted with an MBA team from Dartmouth's Tuck School to study wages and living conditions in Asia. The research reported by the Dartmouth group found that "*Nike* factory workers in Southeast Asia help support their families and have discretionary income" left over after meeting basic needs to both consume and save.[22] Just weeks later an activist group leaked an environmental safety audit that *Ernst & Young* had done on a Vietnamese factory that produces shoes for *Nike*. The leaked report indicated problems with noise and solvent pollution (toluene, a carcinogenic ingredient in the adhesive used). Critics saw the document as further evidence that *Nike* failed to take care of the well being of workers. *Nike*'s spokesperson replied by rhetorically asking how many others firms take the initiative to do internal environmental audits, and argued that the audit was yet another indicator that *Nike* was dedicated to responsibly locating and correcting problems. But the charges and countercharges continue as questions about the methodology of the *Nike* sponsored reports have been raised.[23]

These critiques of *Nike* take two general paths. One set of criticisms mentioned above addresses production practices and the contradictions of global capitalism, but without naming the latter. In behalf of poor youth on both sides of the planet, anti-*Nike* protests in November 1997 linked the price of athletic shoes in the inner city to wage rates in Asia as a matter of morality, not legality.

> Dozens of young people from 11 settlement houses around the city are planning to dump their old *Nike*s at the store to protest what they say is the shoe company's double exploitation of the poor. They are part of a growing movement that has criticized *Nike* for failing to pay workers in Asian factories a living wage – about $3 a day in Indonesia, for example – while charging style-setting urban teen-agers upwards of $100 for the shoes. "*Nike* is making billions of dollars in America off you guys," said Mike Gitelson, a social worker who helped start the protest. "Let's get this straight, *Nike* is doing nothing illegal. For us, it is a moral question. You can't make that much money off us and refuse to give your people enough money to live on."[24]

A second set of concerns usually pivot around cultural challenges to *Nike*'s legitimation advertising. Advertising strategies that had previously drawn public acclaim for *Nike*, began to elicit boos as well. Even *Nike*'s tribute to Jackie Robinson in an ad on the fiftieth anniversary of his breaking the 'color barrier' in professional baseball became a contested discourse. The *Nike* commercial crafted a sequence of shots of baseball players present and past, who each, in turn, thank Jackie Robinson for opening up major league baseball to black athletes. Sewn together as a visual poem voiced with sincere affect, *Nike*'s ad took on the reverential tone of a liturgical prayer:

for letting me be the player I always wanted to be
for letting me compete against the very best
for letting fathers and sons realize their dreams
for Reggie Jackson's 3 home runs
for Ernie Banks playing too
for Roberto Clemente throwing to third
for Hank Aaron's 715
for my 21 years in the major's
for the chance to play in October
for the joys of stealing home
for all us that never got to play
for enduring every taunt
and not lashing out in hate

for standing up with dignity
for standing up
for opening our eyes
for the power of an entire race.
Thanks, Jackie
Thanks, Jackie
Thank you
Thank you
Thank you Jackie Robinson
Thank you

The litany was signed with the *swoosh*. In conjunction with the campaign *Nike* donated $350,000 toward scholarships awarded by the Jackie Robinson Foundation. This drew praise from Robinson's widow and daughter. "You must understand, Phil Knight was the chairman of our dinner," said Sharon Robinson. "They had a connection to the Jackie Robinson Foundation that has been going on all year, even before that. We don't see it as exploitative at all. It's a beautiful commercial."[25]

But, sportswriters cried hypocrisy at *Nike* for running this commercial tribute to Jackie Robinson as a way of "insinuating" itself into great moments of sports history with which it had nothing to do. Suddenly, sports writers were playing the role of deconstructionists and ideology critics, challenging the way in which *Nike* advertisements seek to build the value of its image by investing it with authentic significance, in this case drawn from the memory of Jackie Robinson, a heroic American icon. The sportswriters didn't just deconstruct, they did so for the purpose of assigning an alternative sign value to *Nike*, that of a dark empire driven by the "greedy" Phil Knight.[26]

Consider a recent commercial featuring black baseball stars thanking Jackie Robinson for breaking the color line. It is a touching tribute, grainy film footage mixed with heartfelt messages. It looks like some philanthropic foundation put it together. But when the moment peaks, and your heart is open, what's the last thing you see? A *Nike swoosh*. Same way you see a *Nike swoosh* after those Tiger Woods commercials, in which the children of the world – all races, mind you – dream of being Tiger. You'll notice these ads do not try to sell you shoes or clothing – which are, after all, what *Nike* makes. But that should be your first warning. By its founder's admission, *Nike* is no longer in the shoe business; it's in the image business. It wants you to feel a certain way. It wants you and your kids to desire the *swoosh* subliminally, under the skin, without even knowing why. Call it planned addiction. First, *Nike* wants your mind. Then it takes your wallet.[27]

We might ordinarily expect to find stories about the global economy on the front pages, but we don't because news reporters have naturalized capitalism as the economy, not as one historical method of organizing an economy. And yet, we often find reports that question the morality of applying the logic of capital to the domain of sports. But why? Why has semiotic and moral critique become the bailiwick of sportswriters? To compete in the global cultural economy corporations must produce culture (signs) as well as commodities. One approach to investing commodities with cultural value has been to draw on the meaning of sports in people's lives. By investing commodities with moral purpose – and particularly with moral purpose that draws on the meaningfulness of sport – *Nike* has unintentionally made it incumbent on sportswriters to defend and protect their moral turf from profanation.

THE *SWOOSH* AND ITS CONTRADICTIONS

The story we have tried to tell treats *Nike*'s construction of the *swoosh* as the hub of a complex set of cultural contradictions. While *Nike* attempts to continually add value to its symbol by controlling its meaning and ensuring its pervasiveness, other participants have brought their own agenda to this negotiated space. When *Press for Change* or *Campaign for Labor Rights* bring unacceptable work place practices into the light of public discourse, the sign value of the *swoosh* may become tarnished. For them, the disparity between advertising images and production processes reflects the disparity between the lives of those in the core and those in the periphery. And when sportswriters condemn *Nike* for bringing the "image business" into the world of sports, corrupting youth by engaging them in "planned addiction," we see the contested terrain shift to *Nike*'s own image and its position in a system of cultural production.

One of the interesting sidelights to the media coverage of "the *Nike* controversy" as the press put it, has been how other companies disappear from view. Where are *Reebok*, *Adidas*, and *Fila* in these stories about production practices? Media criticism rarely identifies, and it certainly never inflates, the root logic of Capital, or the structure of the global economy. Instead, criticism on television and in the newspapers flows out of the gap between representation and practice. When *Nike* celebrates athletic activity as self-affirming, liberating, empowering, and transcendental, and by representational equivalence attaches itself to its own promotions in order to swell its sign value, *Nike* practices become a ready target because its advertising has made the *swoosh* so very visible, and so loaded it with significance. In other words, the very thing – the *swoosh* – that has made *Nike* successful in the world of consumption also acts like a magnet for negative publicity.

Strange as it may seem, an important institutional space for the public culture of a global system of capitalism has fallen to advertising. In this space, corporations construct motifs that depict globalization with imagery

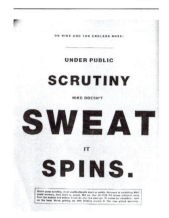

"Under public scrutiny Nike doesn't sweat it spins" reads this Adbusters anti-ad. Nike legitimation strategies have lost credibility in a cynical world. On another front, protesters picket a NIKETOWN store. The sign reads "Phil Knight makes $1526 a day. Indonesian Nike worker makes $2.50 a day."

of liberalism, multiculturalism, and universal humanism.[28] *Nike* speaks the language of universal rights, concern for children, transcendence over the categories of age, race, gender, disability or any social stereotype. As moral philosophy, its images speak out against racism, sexism, and ageism. *Nike*'s imagery celebrates sport, athletic activity, and play as universally rewarding categories. Playing makes for healthier, more productive citizens, and better self-actualized human beings. However, no matter what its imagery suggests, *Nike*, like any other capitalist firm, must operate within the relationships and constraints of competitive capitalist marketplaces. No matter how many P.L.A.Y. commercials *Nike* runs on TV, there will still be haunting images of production practices in Pakistan, Indonesia, and Vietnam. And as the world grows more unified, it becomes increasingly difficult to suppress entirely those gaps between image and practice, between humanism and capitalism, between moral philosophy and the bottom line of corporate profit growth.

When *Nike* engages issues of personal transcendence, race, gender and class in the public arena, it positions itself as a corporation with a sense of what is ethical, and not just what is expedient. But in a cynical commodity world, this kind of communication is automatically suspect. When idealism is expressed in commercial messages and transformed into a multi-billion dollar global industry, contradictions will surface. *Nike*'s engagement in public discourse comes at a price – the expectation that it make itself accountable to a higher standard than that ordinarily practiced in a capitalist world. This is a virtual impossibility since the capitalist firm must do its business in a capitalist world.[29] "Just do it" may be an empowering slogan but it is no match for the imperatives of capitalist institutions. And sure enough, in December 1997, *Nike* dumped its established "Just do it" slogan in favor of a supposedly more enabling slogan, "I can." Perhaps the shift was pursued to avoid the trap of letting one's public imagery get stale, perhaps it was a response to slower than expected sales, declining future orders, a buildup of inventory, a steadily slipping stock price, and the continuing stream of public criticism that leveraged familiarity with the "Just do it" slogan into anti-*Nike* campaign slogans.

In what we have called an economy of sign value, brand logos like the *swoosh* have become subject to an accelerated tempo of competition in image markets. When cultural meanings are turned into commodities that can be attached to other commodities for the purpose of making them stand out, all the old rules of currencies and commodities come into play. Symbols like the *swoosh* become vulnerable to oversaturation and an accelerated rate of value burnout. We have discussed in some detail how *Nike* has positioned itself as irreverent and rebellious to try to offset these tendencies by appearing to value authenticity over the manipulativeness of the marketplace. We have also seen how difficult it is to maintain this dual commitment to sincerity and irreverence when the material world keeps impinging. To do so demands that advertisers find ways to make their images relevant and to do so in an already saturated commercial environment requires taking risks – raising issues that commercials have previously avoided because they touch on the sphere of public debate. Compounding this, like any other firm that seeks to play in this global consumer economy, *Nike* must concern itself with how to balance over*swoosh*ification against the fear that other competitors will take over part of its sign space. *Nike* faces a self-contradictory image environment that is coming to haunt all firms that wish to play in this global system. Who would have ever dreamt that commercial slogans could give rise to something much larger?

NOTES AND REFERENCES

1. Jeff Jensen, "Marketer of the year: *Nike* honored: ubiquitous *swoosh* illustrates how brand represents not just shoes but all of sports," *Advertising Age,* December 16 1996, p. 1.
2. See Scott Lash and John Urry, *Economies of Signs and Space* (Sage, London, 1994).
3. Cited in Jensen, "Marketer of the year: *Nike* honored," p. 1.
4. See Robert Goldman and Stephen Papson, *Sign Wars* (Guilford, New York, 1996).
5. Tony Koenderman, "South Africa weighs on ambushing," *Advertising Age*, September 1997, p. 16.
6. Jennifer Steinhauer, "*Nike* is in a league of its own; with no big rival, it calls the shots in athletic shoes," *The New York Times,* June 7 1997, p. 21.
7. Dan Wieden, "A sense of cool: *Nike*'s theory of advertising." *Harvard Business Review*, July/August 1992, p. 97ff.
8. Max Horkeimer and Theodor W. Adorno, "The culture industry," *Dialectic of Enlightenment*, translated by John Cumming (Allen Lane, London, 1973), pp. 120–67.
9. Richard Sandomir, "Dollars and Dallas: league of their own?" *New York Times,* September 24 1995, pp. 1, 13.
10. Jeff Manning, "*Nike* Inc. *swoosh*es into deal at Ohio State," *The Oregonian,* December 30 1995, pp. B7, B8
11. Jeff Manning, "Guerrilla marketing: the other final four," *The Oregonian,* April 3 1995, p. A1.
12. The phrase is from Henri Lefebvre's, *Everyday Life in the Modern World* (Harper & Row, New York, 1971).
13. Putting the sign (the *swoosh*) on an object deemed to have little corresponding value, the value of the sign suffers.
14. See Goldman and Papson, *Sign Wars.*
15. Josh Feit, "Alas, poor *Nike*: the real reason *Nike* is the most reviled company in the galaxy," *The Willamette Week*, November 5 1997, pp. 20–24, 26, 28.
16. "When shove came to PUSH. (PUSH demands jobs for blacks at *Nike*)," *The Economist* 316 (September 22 1990), p. 28. Cyndee Miller, "Advertisers promote racial harmony; *Nike* criticized," *Marketing News*, July 6 1992, p. 1.
17. Nena Baker, "The hidden hands of *Nike*," *The Oregonian*, August 9 1992, pp. A1, A10–11.
18. "*Nike* hires Andrew Young's group to evaluate its code of conduct," *The Oregonian,* February 25 1997, p. C1.
19. Jeff Manning, "*Nike* strikers in Indonesia back on job," *The Oregonian*, April 24 1997, pp. E1, E2.

20. Jim Hill, "*Nike* plant shuts after worker protest," *The Oregonian*, April 27 1997, pp. B1, B12.

21. "Muslims demand apology for *Nike* logo," *San Antonio Express News*, April 10 1997, p. 2E. Samantha Levine, "Recall or no, *Nike* shoe still available," *The Oregonian*, June 27 1997, pp. C1, C7.

22. "Study: *Nike* pay more than adequate," *The Oregonian*, October 17 1997, pp. C1, C3.

23. Jeff Manning, "Audit: *Nike* factory workers at risk," *The Oregonian*, November 8 1997, p. B1. Dara O'Rourke, "Smoke from a hired gun: a critique of *Nike*'s labor and environmental auditing in Vietnam as performed by Ernst & Young," unpublished paper under the auspices of the Transnational Resource and Action Center (TRAC) San Francisco, California, www.corpwatch.org. November 10 1997.

24. David Gonzalez , "Youthful foes go toe to toe with *Nike*," *The New York Times*, September 27 1997.

25. Ken Rosenthal, "*Nike* ad may be self-serving, but end does justify means," *Baltimore Sun*, April 14 1997, p. 1C.

26. At the shrill end of these indictments was a piece by Joel D. Joseph, "Horrid business practices enrich *Nike*; Shoe company's fortunes come from exploitation of workers in Third World countries," *The Fresno Bee*, June 30 1996, p. B5. His condemnation began, "Phil Knight is the godfather of the *Nike* Mafia."

27. Mitch Albom, "Mind your money because *Nike* has designs on both," *Pittsburgh Post-Gazette*, June 14 1997, p. B3. See also, Tom Archdeacon, "For *NIKE*, it's about shoes," *Dayton Daily News*, April 6 1997, p. 1D.

28. Within this system of images, *Nike* stands for participation in the global community through sports, *Benetton* through political awareness, *Microsoft* through imagination synergized by its software, *IBM* through technological power, *Coca-Cola* through the celebration of harmony, the *Body Shop* through ecological and global concern. Corporate signs of global unification construct images of global citizenship, multicultural respect, and social and environmental concern. Such advertising encourages consumers to view themselves as citizens of the world, while the corporations appear as a unifying force in a world otherwise experienced as increasingly fragmented and conflictual.

29. For a recent account of the political-economic circumstances of producing shoes in the South Asian region of the global capitalist economy see Jeff Manning's series in *The Oregonian* in November 1997. Manning's "Tracks across the globe" consisted of three instalments: "Day 1: *Nike*'s Asian machine goes on trial," November 9, pp. A1, A14–15; "Day 2: poverty's legions flock to *Nike*," November 10, pp. A1, A6–A7; and "Day 3: *Nike* steps into political minefield," November 11, pp. A1, A6–A7. See also William Greider, *One World, Ready or Not: The Manic Logic of Global Capitalism* (Simon & Schuster, New York, 1997).

INDEX